# BECOMING A
# SCHOOL PRINCIPAL

# BECOMING A SCHOOL PRINCIPAL

*Learning to Lead,
Leading to Learn*

Sarah E. Fiarman

Library of Congress Control Number 2015936479

Paperback ISBN 978-1-61250-846-7
Library Edition ISBN 978-1-61250-847-4

Published by Harvard Education Press,
an imprint of the Harvard Education Publishing Group

Harvard Education Press
8 Story Street
Cambridge, MA 02138

Cover Design: Wilcox Design

The typefaces used in this book are Adobe Garamond Pro and Futura.

*This book is dedicated to my parents,*
*Sidney and Janell Fiarman,*
*my most important teachers*

*and to the staff, students, and families of*
*my school for helping me learn to lead*

# Contents

# Foreword

There is something you should know about Sarah Fiarman that you might not necessarily glean from this book: Sarah Fiarman is a *force of nature*; relentlessly upbeat, positive, and optimistic; energetic beyond the bounds of human possibility; possessed of a mind that can generate scores of ideas in a matter of minutes; acute in her capacity to sense and listen while at the same time acting; and, as if these dispositions weren't enough, a funny, kind, and self-effacing human being. Since I require considerable remedial support on most of these dimensions, I have always viewed Sarah with deep respect and, like an approaching hurricane, with a degree of caution and alarm.

How do I know these things about Sarah? Sarah and I worked together for a considerable period during her graduate studies at Harvard at a particularly yeasty time when we were developing and teaching practices of improvement for teachers and school leaders. I confess that when I heard Sarah was moving into a leadership position at "Douglass"—the school that is featured in this book—I felt a deep loss of her colleagueship and a degree of concern that the school and district in which she had chosen to work would not appreciate her special qualities as a leader, teacher, and human being. I confess that I have this feeling a lot these days, as my former students become colleagues and leaders in the field. I am less concerned about their preparation for the work than I am about whether the systems they are entering are capable of making use of their considerable talents.

As I might have expected, Sarah has crammed a career's worth of powerful insight and advice about leadership into a deceptively compact and accessible book. In the thirty-some years of this current period of education "reform," a massive industry has developed around the theory and practice of school leadership, generating huge economic rewards for publishers, consultants, providers of professional development, and, not least, for university graduate programs. I have watched this development with growing alarm, because, from the classroom level, I see very little, if any, impact in most of the schools I visit that the industry has had much impact on leadership practice. To be sure, the leadership industry—and its collaborators in the "reform" industry—has changed the language that we use to describe leadership practice in the education sector. Reformers have always been good at changing rhetoric. But the absence of a strong clinical component, focused on professional practice, in the education sector has meant the gap between rhetoric and practice is wide and seemingly unbridgeable.

The value of this book is that it steps courageously, but modestly, into this gap between theory and practice. It could only have been written by an exemplary, but self-effacing, practitioner of leadership. While it purports to focus on the novice school leader as its target audience, in my experience, it will be equally useful to people in the field who think they already know how to lead. The vision of leadership here is an ambitious one that stands apart from the practices I see in the vast majority of American schools I visit. "Instructional leadership" has become the dominant motif in graduate programs and professional development for school leaders, but, as with most ambitious reforms in the last century of American education, this theme is evident more in the language of professional reformers than it is in the practice of leaders.

The problem Sarah sets for the field is how to reconcile "the vastness of the job's landscape" with the fundamental imperative that the only real value leaders add to the organizations they lead is their ability to enable the improvement of instructional practice and student learning. A wise colleague of mine, Gabriel Camara, who has transformed learning in some nine thousand schools in Mexico, with the simplest of learning theories, has observed that educators invest enormous time and energy into "trying to make the crooked and complex into the straight and simple," while it is much more promising to start with the straight and simple and use it to displace the crooked and complex.

In their simplest form, the fundamentals of leadership practice that Sarah develops in this book are "learning" and "improvement." "Learning is learning," she argues, whether applied to adults or students; the fundamental task of leaders is to enable learning, full stop. Learning, she argues, in many different contexts, is a fundamentally developmental practice. Human beings *learn their way into* new understandings of the world they live and work in and into new practices for managing their own learning and the learning of others. Leadership practice and the organizations in which leaders operate succeed to the degree that they engage their members and clients in a continuous process of facing the uncertainty of *not* knowing the solution to the problems they face and, individually and collectively, discovering how to learn what they don't know. This perspective on leadership is refreshingly presented in rich, practical terms through the many lenses of the work that school leaders are expected to do. The tasks are complex; the underlying theory of the work is simple and direct.

Among the many useful themes Sarah explores, there are three that I think she sheds particularly powerful light upon. First, leadership-as-learning requires the capability to listen, empathize, and reflect back, even when what you are hearing and seeing threatens your identity as a leader. This view is a refreshing antidote to the prevailing view in some parts of the education sector that the work of leadership requires decisive use of command-and-control. Second, leadership-as-learning requires the cultivation of trust, which in turn requires the cultivation of predictable and safe learning environments in which it is permissible to make—and correct—mistakes. And third, while it may be true that leadership is often lonely work, leaders-as-learners have a responsibility to take care of themselves in order to provide the support they must give to others. Sarah had the guidance of a gifted and wise coach, whose job was to observe and counsel in much the same way she worked with teachers.

In the next decade or so, educators will have to decide how to construct careers in an environment in which the social activity called "learning" will no longer be under the monopoly control of the nineteenth century artifact called "school." A good place to start preparing for this future is to think deeply about what learning is and how it works in organized settings. This book helps us begin that conversation.

—Richard F. Elmore
*Gregory R. Anrig Research Professor of*
*Educational Leadership*
*Harvard Graduate School of Education*

# Introduction

We must not, in trying to think about how we can make a big difference, ignore the small daily differences we can make which, over time, add up to big differences that we often cannot foresee.

—Marian Wright Edelman

That last period of the school day started out sounding like any other afternoon—the purposeful hum of young voices talking in classrooms, a teacher's directions carrying down the hall, snippets of a conversation heard from two children walking to the nurse's office, staff members laughing as they checked mailboxes in the office or joked with the assistant principal as they took a piece of candy from his stash.

Suddenly, with the announcement of a few brief words over the PA system, all of this sound and activity changed. For the first few seconds, there was the immediate rush of response, hundreds of people moving into focused and swift action as doors closed, lights went out, everyone disappeared from view. Then a complete and eerie silence.

As a staff, we had planned carefully for this drill. Individual teachers had practiced the lockdown procedures with students earlier in the week, and our district security officer had shared the checklists principals were required to use to assess the three-minute long process. What hadn't been a part of the plan was the sudden rush of emotion that came over me as I stepped into the hall to monitor the drill.

My throat tightened as I pictured what was behind the closed doors. Students and staff crammed into dark bathrooms and classroom corners, pressed close together without any speaking in the unlit spaces. Were all doors locked? Lights out? Could anyone be seen or heard?

In those brief moments of unnatural silence, with my footsteps strangely loud in the halls, the concentrated weight of a principal's responsibility pressed down on me so hard it felt difficult to breathe. Was everyone safe? Had the students learned the skills, and were they able to implement them? Had we taught them what they needed for the unknown future? Would they have what it takes to survive?

As the school collectively held its breath, things suddenly came into sharp focus: the hard work of the staff, the trust of the students and families, the determination of every adult in that building to protect and care for the children, and the complex nature of the entire endeavor. Most of all, this moment brought home the magnitude of our responsibility. Parents deliver their children to school full of hope and trust. In receiving them, we enter a sacred commitment.

After checking the last classroom door, I turned around and, with relief, raced back to the office, forcing the lump in my throat to go away so that I could be calm enough to make the final announcement. "The lockdown drill is over. The lockdown drill is over." The school could breathe again.

Most minutes of the principalship aren't as dramatic as these. However, for most of us in education, when it comes to learning, the sense of urgency is the same. It's just usually spread over days and weeks rather than concentrated in three minutes. We know that for many students, what they learn in school and how well they can put it into practice will determine their future. In every case, the buck stops at the principal's door. The quality of instruction, the conditions for student and adult learning, what children leave school knowing and being able to do, the engagement of families—there's no one more responsible for these outcomes than the principal. Meeting this responsibility requires enormous passion, commitment, and endurance. And a willingness to be alone at times.

This book describes the vastness of this job's landscape and the journey of a new principal navigating the territory. Principals rarely get to talk with other principals about the work. How does it feel to be a principal?

What keeps us up at night? And what motivates us to engage in work that never ends—continual improvement for ourselves and our schools?

This book seeks to be that principal colleague. To provide a sense of camaraderie by saying, "That happened to me, too!" or "You'll never believe what someone just said." To share a wry laugh about the craziness of it all. To describe lessons learned in the hopes they can save colleagues some of the pain or exhaustion of learning from experience. And perhaps most importantly, I hope this book can encourage reflection—something all too rare in busy leaders' schedules.

The lessons and experiences included here are not intended to be a comprehensive list of the duties of a principal. Creating that list would take several more volumes. Rather, the book includes the key insights that in retrospect defined my first few years in the job. I hope practitioners, as a result of reading this book, will feel reassured and reinspired: Yes, the work is hard, but you are not alone in striving to do it with integrity and passion. The process is messy and bruising at times, but the results are powerful, long-lasting, and the rewards are great.

As with all of us in schools, my commitment to this work has roots in personal experiences and background as well as professional training and the examples of powerful mentors. To understand this leadership tale, readers should know some of the backstory.

Like many educators, I am in this field because of a desire for a more equitable society. Too many children today are denied opportunity because of the color of their skin or their family's income. Inequitable policies and poorly run institutions prevent these children from fully realizing their true potential—and because of this prevent our country from achieving its fullest potential as well. To work in education is to participate in the civil rights movement of today.

Coming from a mixed-race, mixed-religion family, I am familiar with conversations about equity and inclusion, which were common in our family. Lessons in unconscious bias came from direct experience. When I was in school, my mother had to advocate differently for my African American sister than she did for me, her White daughter. When my mother won victories, they were life lessons in the importance of taking a stand.

Growing up, I hadn't expected to become a teacher, but when it came time to choose, the career felt like a practical way to work on social issues. A teacher guides kids to resist and reject prejudice, to embrace and not fear diversity, to value their identities, and to excel academically so that doors open in the future. Discovering the utter delight and magic of working with kids was an unexpected bonus.

For close to ten years, I taught children in a public, urban, multicultural school and passionately loved the work. The school was in its infancy—born of the inspiration and sweat equity of parents and teachers who wanted an alternative to worksheets and one-size-fits-all education. In this small, start-up context, teachers were renegades, disregarding district policies when we didn't agree with them, enjoying enormous autonomy and influence as we created the traditions and culture at the school. The staff championed project-based learning, a multicultural curriculum, and an emphasis on community.

Most prized by teachers at this school, however, was the ability to succeed with the students who struggled the most. This was a mark of mastery. Teachers prided themselves on the growth they could elicit from a student and eagerly shared discoveries they had made about how to teach a complicated concept or how to turn around a recalcitrant learner.

Few of us had children of our own, and sometimes the hallways felt more like a college dorm. Teachers hung out well past dark debating constructivist versus direct teaching approaches (When should we teach the algorithm for long division? *Should* we teach the algorithm for long division? How can we *not* teach the algorithm?), discussing racial identity development (our own and students'), and framing and hanging student work with the seriousness of museum curators. Late nights were fueled by junk food and loud music and the thrill of feeling that we might actually make a difference.

Our principal indulged us, giving us keys to the building and reminding us—no, pleading with us—to tell her when we took kids out of the building for field trips. We took our freedoms and our lifestyles for granted. The school was our laboratory, and student learning was on the petri dish.

Because our students who came from varied economic and racial backgrounds consistently performed well on state tests, the central office didn't interfere with our efforts. Not one of my students ever failed the high-stakes state test. One year, my teaching teammates and I had the highest fourth grade math scores in the district. It was a heady time and a period of intense professional learning.

At workshops and conferences outside our school, we caught glimpses of the fact that our school was not typical and our principal a rare breed. We heard from teachers who felt constrained, unsupported, and certainly uninspired by their administrators. These workshops and conferences also provided a window into a national movement of school reform—an opportunity to expand influence and impact beyond the walls of a single classroom. I got hooked. After almost a decade of teaching, I went back to school to get a degree in administration.

During my first month of grad school, a professor asked how the workload compared to teaching. The hours of work were much the same—regularly twelve- to fourteen-hour days—but the pace was much slower. At grad school I actually had time to think and no one to be responsible for but myself. I had the privilege of working with generous faculty members who invited me into hands-on research opportunities. Together we tested theories in real schools and districts. We led staff development and wrote about educational leadership through large-scale improvement efforts such as the Data Wise approach to using student achievement data to improve instruction, the Instructional Rounds process of deep learning through collaborative learning walks, and the Peer Assistance and Review system of harnessing teacher leadership to improve the practice of peers.

All this work carried a familiar feeling. Our planning meetings involved intense inquiry, and once again, debates centered on how to get inside the heads of learners. Only this time, the learners were adults. While the context had changed, the goal remained constant: how to facilitate significant shifts in thinking, perceiving, acting. How could we shake up teachers' long-held beliefs about who can learn, what they can learn, and how best to teach? Should we explicitly teach Bloom's taxonomy? Should we have people inductively create their own taxonomies? But how can we *not* teach Bloom's taxonomy? This was comfortable and exciting territory. Being in grad school meant getting to do this kind of thinking and reflection all the time.

Two key lessons stood out in this work. First, learning is learning. Principles of teaching children apply equally well to adults. This includes the need for rigor, relevance, and relationships as well as the importance of snacks, fun, and breaks. (Some would say naps belong on this list, but time rarely allows.) This principle continues to be an important guide. When I am confronted with a dilemma in leading adults, I can almost always find a parallel with classroom teaching that leads to the right response.

Second (and related), adults may need to be pushed to take risks and learn just as kids do. When faced with unfamiliar tasks—challenges to their thinking or invitations to be vulnerable—adults often become uncomfortable and sometimes upset. For someone accustomed to positive responses, this lesson raised questions about how hard to push people. One of my professors recognized this need in me and offered advice.

"People learn when they're in disequilibrium, even though they might kick and scream when they're in it. These adults won't learn if we rescue them from that discomfort." This comment has stuck. When I find myself trying to keep everyone happy, that professor's comment comes to the surface. What do engagement and transformational learning look like for adults? How does a principal increase this learning? These questions are a central theme of the work and this book.

Out of these varied experiences and opportunities came a vision of school that revolves around deep learning. This isn't surprising; most schools have student learning at the center. But I wanted to lead a school where the whole organization—every child and every adult—is engaged in meaningful, rigorous learning all the time. My job as a leader, then, is to create the conditions for everyone to get better at what they do. For children and for adults, this effort means a commitment to examining learning and identifying problems, collaborating with peers to question and investigate, and learning more through this process than we would on our own. Learning like this can happen only in a context of trust created through conscious community building and sincere investment in each other's success.

Like many principals, I entered the role with a commitment to helping the school improve, a mission to use the school as a vehicle for community transformation, and an earnest naïveté about the challenges I would face. My first placement was as an interim principal at an extended-day public school. About 80 percent of students were African American and qualified for free or reduced lunch, and the school had just launched initiatives around project-based learning and community-building approaches to teaching.

The work was thrilling and terrifying. Finally, I had an opportunity to put into practice what professors had talked about in class. With characteristic workaholic tendencies, I completed all evaluations, put several people on professional improvement plans, and launched an instructional leadership team (only to find out later those activities weren't expected of interim principals).

It was hard to leave after I had formed relationships; invested in students, families, and teachers; and seen growth. One of the best good-byes came from the small group of Black grandmothers who gathered every morning in the lobby of the school watching to make sure their grandchildren (and neighbors' children and friends of neighbors' children) got off the bus and into class. After months of tight-lipped scrutiny, they declared they liked me and would recommend me to their friends across the city. Because I knew the extent of their network, this recommendation felt like the equivalent of the local newspaper's endorsement. Their blessing buoyed me on to the next school.

The demographic at Douglass, the school where I began my formal principalship, is quite different from the school where I was an interim administrator: about 50 percent are children of color, close to 40 percent of the students qualify for federal assistance for food, and a third of the school is enrolled in our Sheltered English Immersion program, which means they entered school speaking little or no English.[1] A significant number of students in our general education classes (varying from 20 to 60 percent across different grade levels) have a home language that is not

English. Parent engagement in terms of absolute numbers wasn't a challenge coming into this school, but parent engagement from an authentically representative cross-section of parents was.

In a time when people of different incomes and races increasingly live in separate worlds, this school provides a rare opportunity. The first day of school brings together families from over forty different language groups, from million-dollar homes to homeless shelters, from summer vacations of camps and ocean rentals to summers spent in front of a TV eating just one meal a day. All these families entrust their children to the school, and all expect their children to benefit from the experience.

Entering, I saw a school with enormous strengths and some devastating weaknesses. The school was founded on principles of project-based learning, which remained strong in many classrooms, but over the years, with retirements, this focus had lost a consistent level of rigor and purpose. The school had a history of some of the highest test scores for White students, but recent years had shown significant achievement gaps for students of color and high needs students, defined in my state as English language learners, low-income students, and students with special needs.

Teachers from the district high school routinely reported that they could recognize Douglass students right away: they all had facility with high-level analysis and critical thinking, and the kids of color couldn't spell or write a clear paragraph. When I entered, Douglass was one of the most chosen schools for White students but one of the least chosen schools among African American families.[2] These racial disparities were a source of concern to many on the staff and one that teachers and some parents asked me to address. Teachers wanted the school to be successful for all students, and many were open to discussing how to do that. They welcomed me graciously.

In many ways, our school represents many of the larger issues in education and our society. How do we design a system that meets the needs of such a large range of backgrounds, language proficiencies, and skill levels? How do we allocate resources (time, people, money) fairly, which means giving more to those who need more? In a context that continually tilts in favor of the dominant culture—in this case, affluent, well-educated,

White families—how do we rebalance the scales without making those in the dominant culture feel they're losing out? How do we create a community of people truly invested in good outcomes for all kids?

How does the story end? This book is not as much about reaching an end goal as it is about process. However, it's important to state up front that the steep learning curve described in subsequent chapters has produced good results. These results include quality student work from high needs students as well as the student body overall, above average and documented growth on results from state-collected survey data about the school and my leadership, high growth scores as well as absolute scores on standardized tests, and documentation of some incredible teacher collaboration. The school's waiting list now includes children of color and children who qualify for free or subsidized lunch. One year, the *Boston Globe* even rated Douglass the "#1 Dream School in Massachusetts."[3] These pieces of data along with others attest to important improvements in teaching and learning at Douglass. I'm proud of my good work, chagrined by the mistakes, and like all effective principals, remain focused on the ways the school still needs to improve.

## OVERVIEW OF THE BOOK

The book begins with the transition of moving into a new position of leadership. Despite the fact that schools had been my home for many years, this new role as principal was disorienting. Chapter 1 details this entry experience, which includes getting used to being in a position of authority and figuring out what exactly *is* the work of a leader. At the end of the day, a teacher can point to the work produced by her students as evidence of what she's accomplished. What does a principal point to?

Like many entering principals, I brought ideas of what would improve student learning. However, ideas don't roll out in a vacuum, and too often, reforms don't end up producing better outcomes. Chapter 2 describes the process of creating and nurturing the right conditions for improvement to take hold. To get better results, teachers need to expand their skill set. Establishing a culture of continuous learning accelerates this process.

This chapter also describes the challenge of introducing new collaborative structures for learning that bump up against the long-standing norm of autonomy in teaching and discusses the developmental nature of team building.

With an emphasis on learning and experimentation, what role does accountability play? Principals need to get the right balance of fostering learning and expecting results. Focus too exclusively on results at all costs and we diminish the potential for experimentation, innovation, learning, and significant improvement. Ignore results and risk becoming complacent about the status quo, lose the impetus for experimentation. Chapter 3 explores the work of finding the right balance, which is particularly tricky in the current context of punitive accountability systems.

Getting all the conditions right for learning is a critical step, but if the locus of control remains exclusively with principals, the scope of improvement is limited. Chapter 4 addresses the shift from a principal-centered improvement process to a teacher-driven one. This process requires both teachers and the administrator to change their practice and perspective. This chapter describes what a system of embedded teacher leadership looks like and how it galvanizes the staff and builds a collective sense of responsibility for improving learning. This system introduces a whole new layer of disorientation and disequilibrium for principals, along with some incredibly rewarding highs when the changes start to take root.

Changing structures and roles is not just disorienting for the leader. For a host of reasons, teachers may resist these changes. Adopting a whole-school outlook can feel unfamiliar and sometimes unappealing for teachers used to a classroom-based perspective. Adults don't always welcome the uncertainty that comes with learning new ways of working. This is especially true at a school like Douglass, which hadn't undertaken substantial schoolwide improvement efforts in decades. Chapter 5 describes how to interpret the resistance that leaders often encounter when undertaking improvement and how to hold steady in the midst of it.

All of this learning, disrupting, and changing requires what some researchers call *psychological safety*, or trust. Without trust, people may go through the motions of collaboration and learning, but the work will remain superficial. For teachers to try out new practices, they have to believe that their colleagues both have their back and will push them forward. Chapter 6 addresses how to move a school's culture to a place where people can be vulnerable and honest with each other and take the risks necessary to really improve. This work doesn't happen overnight, nor can it be mandated. It requires disciplined, ongoing effort and attention.

An important element of trust is communication. Beyond the polished words in newsletters and school handbooks, it's the day-to-day interactions among the members of a school community that build trust over time. Chapter 7 describes how leaders deliberately cultivate trusting relationships with staff and families through careful listening and speaking. Behind both forms of communication needs to be a sincere desire for understanding and an empathy for others. When we truly understand each other's point of view, we can work together toward shared goals.

These different points of view are shaped by personal experience and subtle (and not so subtle) societal messages. Chapter 8 specifically addresses the messages of racial bias that surround us all and influence our thinking and action. To counter this bias, we have to name it. This chapter describes my experience as a White principal working against bias and for equity in school relationships, my own thinking and acting, and everyday instruction in the classroom. The chapter is as much about mistakes as it is about good examples, and this is one of the takeaways. To get better at addressing racism, I have to get better at owning my own role in it.

Chapter 9 addresses issues of supervision and evaluation. What may appear to be a simple decision about whether a teacher is good or bad is actually much more complex. If there were a standardized way to make this determination, we would all be using it. No one arrives on the job with the full package of skills. No one. The job of the leader, then, is to ensure that new teachers acquire this skillset and that their more experienced colleagues continue to grow and develop as well. Figuring out how to do that well—and what happens when you throw in the towel and fire someone—is the substance of this chapter.

Amidst all of this work, how do we take care of ourselves as principals? Chapter 10 addresses self-care and the need to acknowledge that principals are learners, too. This lesson is especially important for those of us who are perfectionists. When we're hard on ourselves because of mistakes, we unintentionally slow our learning. "Embrace mistakes!" is my new mantra. Learn from them. They're a natural part of being a novice and a stepping stone to improvement.

Ten separate chapters suggests ten discrete areas of work to be tackled one by one. In fact, as with any complex effort, these topics are intertwined, overlapping, mutually dependent, and reinforcing. Effective supervision can't happen without trust. Trust doesn't occur without skillful listening. Teacher leadership both changes culture and requires culture change to come to fruition. Being alert to how bias limits perspective is going to help in every aspect of a principal's work. One of the challenges of school leadership is attending to each of the different threads and the whole web all at the same time.

Plenty of experts have written extensively about both threads and web. Their theories and practical suggestions about schools, leadership, and learning have been an important foundation of my work. A "Principal's Bookshelf" at the back of this book offers brief descriptions of some of the books I return to over and over again. It's by no means an exhaustive list, but my hope is that these resources can be as helpful to you as they have been to me in acclimating to this new work.

Writing this book has been an individual effort and in that way is truly *not* representative of the work. Very few tasks at school are completed by the principal alone. Various formal and informal coleaders in the school serve as crucial partners, ranging from an assistant principal and school secretary to coaches, interventionists, and strong teacher leaders across the grades. The staff members in these roles at my school are truly exceptional people and consummate learners. They've influenced my leadership—and our school's growth and success—in countless significant ways. Their advice and hard work have supported every effort I describe in the book.

While most of the stories take place at Douglass, some come from the first school where I was a principal. In addition, all names, grades, and other identifying characteristics of adults and students in these schools have been changed. This book isn't intended to be a tell-all about the people and events in a particular school. The goal is to highlight the challenges new principals commonly face and the learning that happens along the way.

Disclaimer for all those perfectionists out there: reading this book may not prevent a new principal from making mistakes. I hope, however, that it can help a new leader feel supported and encouraged. You have company on this journey. Let's walk it together.

CHAPTER 1

# Entering the Role

Everything's fine. I just close the door and curl up in the fetal position every now and then.

—New principal during his first month of school

The world of schools is like few other organizations. From the outside, people passing on the street see a modest-sized building, cheerful windows with pictures and posters taped to the glass; they may hear faint shouts from the playground. A seemingly peaceful and mild setting. Unless you have worked inside a school, you can never fully appreciate the complexity and sense of purpose that goes on within that unassuming scene.

Inside, hundreds of people engage in herculean tasks—usually in workspaces shared by dozens of people. The nature of the work is intellectually demanding: fundamentally transforming the ways individuals think and act. And the pace of the work is incredible. Few other workplaces measure their tasks in minutes. Six minutes in a school is expected to be enough for a complete meeting between two adults or individual writing conferences with two different students. It's also more than enough time for all hell to break loose in a class with a substitute teacher or in the cafeteria on a rainy day with no recess. And the work is relentless; students and teachers show up day after day with a full spectrum of needs that often require immediate attention. Outcomes are measured not just by test scores but by the actual unfolding of children's and adults' lives. Their futures depend very concretely on what goes on in that building. Leading this effort is daunting to say the least.

After deciding this would be my next career step, I shadowed a principal for a week. She included me in her daily routine and pointed out things along the way. One thing that stood out in those few days were the number of strategies she had for efficiency. *Never read feedback forms until all the responses are submitted. For interoffice mail, write the address on the back of the paper rather than put it in an envelope; this way, you save stuffing and sealing. When signing office paperwork, just sign, don't date—it takes half the time.* Watching and listening, I am sure my eyes grew wide. I wondered, "What kind of world am I entering where there isn't time to write the date?" Even after my shadowing experience, the job remained an enigma.

Connecting the dots between the principal's vision and the day-to-day actions of people in the school wasn't obvious to me. I wanted school to be a place where children's full selves were recognized, valued, and challenged. Where students grappled with meaningful and challenging tasks, loved learning, and showed pride in themselves and their work. In this vision, teachers own their responsibility for student learning, see themselves as problem solvers, continuous learners, tightly networked colleagues investing in each other's learning.

What specific actions would ensure this happened were less clear to me. So, on a Tuesday at 10:30 a.m., for example, what should a principal be doing to help make her vision a reality? What steps would decisively move the organization closer to the goal? What became evident was that the vision in my head was not going to happen through individual willpower or effort. It was entirely dependent on other people. The significance of that insight took awhile to sink in. This vision would become a reality only through the actions of people who are not me. And those people spend the vast majority of their days spread out, working in different rooms, rarely in one place. And then there was the issue that they related to their boss with an odd combination of deference and skepticism. The number of unfamiliar variables seemed to increase every day.

I'm sure I wasn't the only first-year principal who leaned in for a drink and felt as though someone had opened up a fire hydrant. Becoming a principal was overwhelming, confusing, embarrassing, and also incredibly rewarding. Despite the years I had worked in public schools, this new job—particularly in the first year—was like navigating an entirely new environment. It required getting comfortable being the boss, coming to terms with an unwieldy and impossibly large workload, and managing the emotional challenges of being the bearer and receiver of bad news on a regular basis. On top of these adjustments, and even after months into the job, two questions persisted. What exactly *was* the work? And what was my role in it?

## GET COMFORTABLE BEING BOTH HOTSHOT AND HUMBLE

During my first month as principal, a substitute teacher called the office for help. As I approached the classroom, a student inside yelled, "The principal is coming!" I turned around to see, wondering how the principal would respond. As I faced the empty hallway, the reality of my mistake sank in.

While other situations that year weren't as blatant (or as funny in retrospect), this was not the only time I found myself surprised to be the person in charge. On most days, a confident voice and warm smile masked the disorientation I was feeling. But the dissonance between others' and my own view of myself was striking. People viewed this person in professional clothes and a new title as a leader, but nothing inside me had shifted. Being in this role was like being on the other side of one-way glass. It appeared we were looking at each other, but whereas I could see them clearly, they couldn't see me at all.

I've learned that many peers also have felt this way. In fact, apparently it's not just principals who keep looking behind them. President William Howard Taft had essentially the same experience after he was elected. A week after being in office, he admitted that he hadn't gotten used to being in the role. "When I hear someone say Mr. President, I look around expecting to see Roosevelt, and when I read in the headlines of the morning papers that the President and Senator Aldrich and Speaker Cannon have had a conference, my first thought is, 'I wonder what they talked about.'"[1] So perhaps first-time principals can be forgiven for being slow to realize their new identity as leader.

## Stop Searching for the Secret Sauce

Like many new to leadership positions, I suffered from what's been described as *imposter syndrome*. It seemed only a matter of time before people would figure out that I didn't possess the expertise or leadership skill set others in the role possessed. As an organizational consultant once told me, "New leaders assume that everyone else has the secret sauce of leadership. They don't realize there is no such thing."

In my first year, I spent too much angst and energy trying to guess what a real leader would do. Surely, a "right answer" was out there, and if I were smarter, it would be evident. Compounding this was my work style. A natural tendency to consider things from multiple perspectives and encourage people to question my decisions and an instinct to associate certainty with arrogance led to second guessing my own judgment.

First years would be considerably easier if new leaders realized that there's no particular personality trait or leadership checklist or packaged set of moves that "real" leaders have. There isn't some golden set of steps that everyone else has figured out. If any secret does exist, it's to recognize the power of our personal values. If we trust those values to serve as our North Star, we'll have the confidence to learn what we need to do the job well.

At the same time, we must learn plenty of skills. Gradually, after settling into my new role, it became easier to trust my instincts, trust the learning process. But first I had to get comfortable being in a role of formal authority.

## Get Used to Being the Boss

I have conflicting feelings about authority. Because I am the product of a family of multiple generations of civil rights activists, unquestioned authority raises red flags for me. In addition, as a former teacher leader, I feel uncomfortable being at the top of any organization chart if it means that teachers are at the bottom. Reserved parking spaces for principals rub me the wrong way. Sure, it's hard to find parking in our city, but the consequences of a teacher being late are much more dire than if an administrator is still circling the block when the bell rings. As the office staff hear me say regularly, teachers are the surgeons in our building. Our job is to do everything possible to support them.

At the same time, like most people who have been elementary school teachers, I'm accustomed to a high degree of control in my work. Teachers are used to maintaining high, unshakable standards, making countless decisions about what learners should and shouldn't do, and facing resistance unflinchingly. As a result, relinquishing control is difficult. Yet my belief that teachers deserve to be treated as professionals and granted authority over important decisions requires sharing control. Navigating this tension has taken work. I care deeply about the outcomes, have strong opinions about them, and know that they will represent me as much as the school in our community. Turning decisions over to other people can feel risky.

Many sleepless nights during my first few years as principal stemmed from this tension with how to use authority. Working with a coach led me to look up from short-term goals and see the broader work and responsibility of the principal. I could still use the familiar reference point of teaching, but the learners now were adults. As with students, giving teachers greater responsibility results in greater investment. Greater responsibility also means attempting work that is unfamiliar. Mistakes are likely. They're what help people learn. Thus, yielding more authority was important—necessary—if teachers were going to feel ownership of the whole school's continuous learning process. But it also involved a tolerance for uncertainty that was challenging for me.

## Understand Other People's Relationship to Authority

As if it's not enough to have your own conflicting views, principals also face the full range of responses that staff members have to authority. Some people are comfortable deferring to a supervisor because that's what they have learned are the rules of work hierarchies and the way of showing respect. Some people expect a leader to claim authority unapologetically, to lead decisively, and to assume and receive privileges that come with the role, including the ability to make decisions that will not be questioned. Others view authority suspiciously, expect leaders to consult extensively with those they lead, believe that respect is not granted but earned, and interpret behaviors that set a leader apart as signs of aloofness or arrogance. Actions that are aligned with one view of authority often disappoint those who view authority differently. Added to the mix are different cultural expectations of and responses to authority.

As someone accustomed to meeting people's needs, I find it hard to know I'm not meeting everyone's expectations for a leader. However, being cognizant of these different perspectives—and the fact that my own view is not universal—helps explain the range of responses. For example, I'm more careful about sharing an opinion knowing that some people will take that as the final word. When the team leader nods at a meeting and then later shares her concern privately with me, she needs to know that I don't need her protection and in fact want her to share concerns publicly.

Some people may not feel comfortable disagreeing with a boss based on cultural, political, or social reasons. Knowing this, I learned to act deliberately to elicit feedback and differences of opinion, rather than assume that people will share when they disagree or are confused. This technique included asking people for specific suggestions for ways to improve various documents, policies, and approaches; sending an online survey about school administration; or just asking people at the end of a meeting to anonymously write ideas on sticky notes about how to make our meetings better. Even when specifically asked, some people were still uncomfortable telling a leader how to improve, so this required ongoing practice, reinforcement, and sometimes a firm push.

### Don't Confuse Yourself with Your Role (Other People Will Do That for You)

A principal is a figurehead, an ambassador, at times a team mascot. Fully understanding this role took me awhile. When people expected me to speak at school music concerts, for example, it felt odd. The music teacher had done all the work; why would the principal insert herself into the program? I've come to understand that a welcome from the principal serves in some ways as the letterhead on which the communication is set. Because I am not drawn to grabbing the spotlight, I found it helpful to remember that the principal speaks not as an individual but as a representative of the organization, and that's the way people will see it.

Understanding this position also helps in interpreting criticism. Smith College President Kathleen McCartney offers wise and compassionate counsel. Speaking of being a school administrator, she advised, "If you can hear criticism as love for an organization, you're all set."[2] Those angry _____ (parents, teachers, fill in the blank) are not e-mailing Sarah Fiarman; they're e-mailing the organization they care about and feel invested in. This perspective can prevent defensiveness. And what defuses tension the most is being able to muster true compassion for the upset party.

Over time, relationships of trust with the boss do develop, and this helps reduce people's stress and anxiety—and resulting angry e-mails—in an organization. New principals, however, don't have the benefit of this trust. At my first Back to School Night event, I (unintentionally) neglected to introduce Dorothy, a special education team member. Someone reported later that Dorothy had left the evening upset, assuming her work wasn't valued. An apology didn't dispel her distress. In contrast, a few years later, when Dorothy had gotten to know me better, she was less inclined to make assumptions about such mistakes. When I inadvertently left her off an e-mail for an upcoming meeting, I ran to her office to apologize. She interrupted me to say with a casual wave of the hand, "Oh, don't worry about it. I knew you would want me there."

This interaction was easy. No big deal. Dorothy was interacting with a person she knew and trusted. Years earlier, she had seen only the new boss whose actions had the power to change her work and worth. This power imbalance brings wariness, suspicion. Words don't change this feeling. People can read negative intent into any mistake. They rarely acknowledge that leaders mess up as they learn a new skill just like everyone else. Building a relationship that goes beyond the job title takes time.

One teacher said this outright. When I began the job and asked a subset of teachers for feedback on a professional development schedule, one teacher said what most were probably feeling, "The plan looks good, but I really can't give you feedback because I don't know you and I don't know if I can trust you yet." Would a colleague have received this level of wariness? Probably not. Bosses—no matter how warm, open, or inclusive—are a different category. Fortunately, time and experience break through this divide.

Being the figurehead also has significant perks. Students think I'm a rock star. Everyone wants to stop and say hi. Because I'm the captain of the ship, I get flowers and presents and cards that I'll save forever because of the handwritten messages inside. Delighted young birthday celebrants hand out cupcakes on an almost daily basis. One late afternoon when my car wouldn't start, families picking up their children from the afterschool program gathered on the sidewalk and wouldn't leave until AAA came. They couldn't leave the principal.

## Help! I'm Stuck in the Role and Can't Get Out

Being a figurehead means that even with the best assistant principal, wonderful coaches, and a supportive and thoughtful administrative team, the role still feels lonely. In fact, being the figurehead exacerbates the isolation of the role—no one else in the building has the same role, *and* many people hold you at a distance because they don't see you; they just see the role. Often, just digging into the isolation is easier than trying to buck it.

When someone asks, "How are you?" for example, the answer isn't always straightforward. In the split second before responding, there's a lot to consider. Hmmm . . . should I just be frank and say, "Well, I am struggling with a decision about whether to fire your colleague, I just had a hard conversation with another one of your colleagues about her lack of planning, I'm questioning my judgment pretty regularly, and I haven't been able to get through all of my e-mail messages—some of which are from you." I usually default to, "I'm doing fine; how are you?" For some people, this response is all they're looking for.

However, too much distance is not healthy. We all need allies, someone who knows and understands the personal challenges in the work. During my first year, when people were trying to figure out the new principal, I didn't have many solid relationships to lean on. During this time, a particularly wise and warm teacher would sometimes look intently at me and ask, "How are you?" It was clear she always saw me as Sarah—not as the principal. Many times, tears sprang to my eyes as I realized it was the first time all day that I'd felt like a person rather than a boss. Leaders need relationships like these. It's worth the effort—and sometimes the risk—to cultivate them.

Time helps. As the staff and I have cultivated real relationships, I feel more comfortable letting down my guard with most people. It's also become easier to identify when people are reacting to the role and when they're reacting to me. Friends and family know what to say: it's not all about you. It's not all about you. It's not all about you. Sometimes I remember.

## THERE'S TOO MUCH TO DO— SO DO SOMETHING ABOUT IT!

One year an administrative intern joined me at the beginning of November when school was in full swing. That first day consisted of back-to-back meetings with coaches, teachers, parents, teams, and students. The next morning, I suggested she read my e-mail from the previous day to get a sense of what came before and after the school day she'd witnessed. Then she shared her first impressions.

The intern said she'd gone home from the first day at 4 p.m. "bone-tired" and ready to put her head on her pillow. She learned that the students loved to see me, that some teachers didn't, that parent concerns were complicated, and that she needed to pack a portable lunch that she could eat on the run. She also noted that my first e-mail was at 5:36 a.m. and the last one was at 9:47 p.m.

Granted, that day had been unusually busy, but it's probably not uncommon for a principal's schedule. And it's also too much. The solution to having too much to do can't be to just work longer hours. That's neither realistic nor sustainable. You end up feeling like Bilbo in *The Lord of the Rings* when he said he felt "like butter scraped over too much bread." There needs to be another strategy.

From talking with principal colleagues, I have learned work triage is the most common and also necessary strategy. We don't—because we can't—attend to everything that needs attention. Math team membership is dwindling; the bathroom stalls are too small; first grade phonics skills are poor; report cards need to be redone; lunch times aren't working as well as they should; we need to revise the hiring process for our specialist teachers. . . . Unfortunately, the list goes on. Like many principals, I've harbored guilt about those items that remain on the list month after month.

Recently, a principal friend helped me feel more in control of the fact that I don't get to all the work. Kevin views triage as a deliberate, conscious decision, rather than an unintentional outcome. He writes down the most important issues that require focus. He names the other issues—issues that require work but that go lower on the priority list. They won't get his attention at this time. Then he sets a date at which time he'll take out the list and reconsider the prioritization. Can he check off some tasks? Do any of the secondary items need to be moved to the top priority list? Using this approach, he doesn't question himself or look at that staff member or that issue and feel guilty that he's not attending to the problem. He's attending to it. It's on his list. It just isn't an issue he's able to work on right now.

Members of the school community don't necessarily adhere to the pre-made priority list, however. People bring their problems to the leader, and everything seems to be a three-alarm fire! As Jerome Murphy observed in an article about school administration, "Honking and hissing like geese, faculty and staff members will cruise into the boss' office, ruffle their feathers, poop on the rug, and leave."[3] As the pile grows, being able to identify the real priorities is important. What issues really do require attention and which are (a) someone having a bad day and needing to vent; (b) seasonal—it's November or March when staff reach the end of their rope and small sparks cause large explosions; or (c) something that feels like a crisis at the time but will actually fade in a few short weeks? My first year I often bounced back and forth from one issue to another like a pinball. Experience has helped me discern when and how to be involved and to be less flustered, offer support, redirect the person to self-sufficiency, and not worry so much at night that things are about to implode.

And then there's just the day-to-day reality of schools—when things do implode. The best-laid plans will be completely disrupted at times because of circumstances beyond a principal's control. An assistant teacher reports that a substitute is making inappropriate sexual comments about a student. A student runs out of the building and down the street, and we need to call the cops. All of the milk in the cafeteria seems to be bad, and some kids are throwing up. A new student who speaks no English is screaming in the school courtyard, and no one can figure out what's wrong. Looking back, I remember how startling it felt to have so little control over my time and schedule. Now, I expect it and have come to embrace unpredictability and variation as unique features of working in a school. Somehow that realization makes the work even more compelling.

## Understand the Invisible Work of Meetings

Compounding the confusion about the leader's work is the fact that it's less tangible than a lot of other work. During my first few months, getting any work done felt hard because I had so many meetings. The only concrete thing to point to at the end of most meetings was a longer to-do list. Not a thrilling prospect. Soon, however, it became clear that (most) meetings *were* the work: developing expectations for curriculum maps, prioritizing the work of coaches, reviewing student data, planning for staff meetings, analyzing and revising the school's response to students in crisis. Meetings done well are the substance of improvement. Part of the learning curve was figuring out how to capitalize on this tool of collaboration, time, and focus.

## DIFFICULT CONVERSATIONS ARE A CENTRAL PART OF THE JOB

My office has a wall of windows. When a visitor commented on them, I acknowledged that having all these windows was a challenge when so many people cry in my office. The visitor looked startled and said, "I assume you mean children?" I shook my head. The majority of people who cry are adults. Some of the hardest parts of the work involve the quantity of difficult news that goes through the office.

As the head of a school with a large community of staff, students, families, and volunteers, the principal is going to be privy to many people's life challenges. Staff members or students and their families experience serious illnesses, marital problems, domestic violence, drug and alcohol addictions, restraining orders, and just hard days. Every day brings something. Sometimes it's just a teacher coming to share about a difficult interaction with a student. Other times it's a parent sharing that she feared for her children's safety when her ex-husband had custody. This isn't just a new principal phenomenon. At any point in a principal's career, these challenges will feel heavy.

Thankfully, early in my first year, I read an interview with a principal who specifically described how he navigates emotional challenges like these. He started by doing the math. He works and interacts with two to three times more people than there are days in a school year. Most of those people have a challenging experience or at least a very hard day at least once a year. In his role, he's likely to hear about a large number of these. Judging just by the numbers, then, he'll hear about *at least* one piece of very hard news every day. Since that's the nature of the job, it doesn't take him by surprise any more. His job is to help people weather these challenges with strength and perseverance.

Hearing this peer's calculus helped. Instead of letting people's burdens take me by surprise and weigh me down, I can do two things: see if anything will make the burden feel lighter for the person involved and, more often, simply listen with compassion and hope.

## Build a Muscle for Giving Hard News

As difficult as it is to receive hard news, giving it can feel worse. As leadership gurus Ronald Heifitz and Marty Linsky write, "If leadership were about giving people good news, the job would be easy."[4] Building a muscle for giving hard news is an important part of the principal's job.

Principals regularly have to tell people things they don't want to hear. The principal calls a family to explain that a child will not be allowed to go on a special field trip because of his pattern of unsafe behavior, lets a teacher know that she is not meeting professional standards or will not be rehired, tells someone the school can't pursue what sounds like a rewarding project because it just can't take on one more initiative. Other people may not find this to be a challenging part of the job. I do.

Many of the difficult conversations in the course of a typical day could simply be avoided. No one would complain. After all, few administrators are closely supervised. Oh, how much more comfortable it would be to just let these things slide. As a colleague once said about the work that we do every day, "Every day I have a choice: I can have a pleasant day or I can do my job." Like building a muscle, regularly doing the heavy lifting makes it easier over time—not pleasant, but easier to take a deep breath and lift. Seeing the connection to improved student learning helps build the personal conviction that those hard conversations must be tackled.

I once commiserated with a principal friend about days like these. He had just had a conversation with a teacher he was probably going to have to fire in mid-October because the teacher's classroom management was so poor. My friend is a no-nonsense principal, so I was surprised to hear him share some of my discomfort. We were in a park throwing a Frisbee and his assertive, sharp tosses accentuated the list, "I hate meeting with the guy to give him negative feedback. I hate giving him an ultimatum to change. I hate seeing things out of control in his classroom and kids missing out on learning. I hate that I have to document every conversation now so carefully and follow up with every detail so minutely. I hate that I have to use valuable resources to fix the problem. I hate that I'll probably have to fire the guy and he'll be without a job in the middle of the year. And I hate that the kids have to get a new teacher and lose out on so much learning."

My colleague wasn't saying that he was avoiding the tasks. He was going to do a series of things he hated to do—every day. That's a remarkable job to sign up for. It's all part of the complex package that is a principal's job. The really uncomfortable work. The incredible rewards. The moral sense of purpose impelling us forward because we believe that the work we do will make a difference in students' lives.

## SO, WHAT IS THE WORK?

Several things make it hard to recognize what the real work is. There's too much of it and it all seems urgent. Much of it is hard. Little of it is tangible. Results take a long time.

In my first weeks as principal, it seemed a marvel that the entire school hummed along even though I had no idea what people were doing. Hundreds of children and adults moved smoothly from place to place and activity to activity without my involvement whatsoever. I found myself thinking, "I could walk out of the building right now and no one would notice. What value do I bring to this organization? What exactly is my job?"

Figuring out the answers to these questions has taken a surprisingly long time. Even with my training in district-level reform and an understanding of concepts like building capacity and self-efficacy at the classroom and school level, the answers didn't come easily. Somehow, in the messiness of the day-to-day, the way forward wasn't clear. As I confessed to a coach, "Writing a book about this is much simpler than actually doing it."

This uncertainty was not shared by Douglass kindergarteners who succinctly defined my work during their unit on community jobs. After listing mail carrier, baker, police officer, and doctor, their teacher included principal on the list and asked the class to describe my work. She later reported that many children waved their hands eagerly with the answer.

"She opens the door for us in the morning!" was their chorus of confident responses. Presumably at 8:25 a.m. after completing this important work, I return to the office to wait for buses to arrive the next morning.

While I appreciated the kindergarteners' conviction, there had to be more to the job than door duty (although it is my favorite part of each day). People ascribe all sorts of power to the principal, and yet as a new leader, the feeling I experienced the most was powerlessness. When, as principal, I saw the first grade reader who seemed stuck, the angry fourth grader who manipulated her way out of assignments, and the lonely child who needed help making connections, I wanted to do something. Now. In those few classrooms, where the teaching wasn't solid, I wanted to fix the problem personally and immediately.

The problem, which I came to understand only slowly over the course of my first year, is that the principal *can't* provide daily reading instruction or mediate weekly between a fuming child and her teacher. That's not a viable solution. The principal's job isn't direct intervention. The principal's work—providing tight supervision, developing excellent professional development, hiring the right people, deploying resources strategically, creating the conditions for leadership and learning—is certainly vital to improving student learning and is just as certainly more than one layer removed when you peel the onion of student learning. Whereas teachers may see the effect of their actions right away on student learning, not so with principals. A principal's actions must first influence others before they have a chance of filtering through to students.

Transitioning to this role, to less direct control over the outcomes, was a critical shift for me. I resisted it for a long time. What if settling into a one-step-removed role leads to feeling complacent? Shouldn't a principal *feel* a sense of indignation when a child is not well served? Shouldn't that situation *feel* deeply troubling?

Absolutely. However, while feelings of indignation and moral righteousness can help a leader fire people, they are not the approach most likely to help a teacher or team of teachers improve. The sense of urgency I felt didn't match the timeline and framework needed to lead staff learning. Like engine gears rotating at different speeds, these different time frames couldn't engage. I had to adopt a new scope of responsibility. Instead of working to help an individual child learn, my job now was to help the organization learn.

Being a principal means maintaining a long-term view of improvement. Making this mental shift from a teacher of students to a teacher of adults seems obvious now but felt like abandoning ship at the beginning. A mental shift is required to see that methodical, systematic investments in adult learning over time will pay off. When teachers acquire new skills or deepen existing ones, we'll see the results in student learning. That struggling first grader's experience will improve by the end of the year—as will the experience of students in that teacher's future classes.

CHAPTER 2

# Getting Traction with Improvement

*If you want to go fast, go alone. If you want to go far, go together.*

—African proverb

We're used to thinking of a school as a unified organization—"That's a good school. That one isn't so good." In fact, research shows that there tends to be more variation within a single school than across different schools.[1] So a principal's job isn't to take a bad school and make it good. Rather, the challenge is to make a school *more consistently effective* across all classrooms. To create a school that is not a collection of separate teaching units but an internally coherent organization unified by a set of best practices.

How does a school become unified in this way? Different principals have different approaches. The vision guiding me has at its core teacher collaboration and continuous learning. Teachers build a shared vision of teaching and learning through ongoing examination of the nitty-gritty specifics of instruction. Piece by piece, they learn about and collectively define what effective instruction looks like for content areas, thinking skills, and character development. They continually seek out areas for growth and address them collaboratively.

Having a clear vision isn't the same as knowing how to get there, however. In fact, this vision seemed in direct opposition to the expectations of many teachers at Douglass. Like teachers in most schools, Douglass teachers had a long tradition of working independently and a firm belief in their professional right to autonomy. Becoming an administrator brought me face to face with this tug of war in leadership decisions. Should teachers have autonomy over their teaching practice, or should they be required to conform to schoolwide expectations about common effective practices? Should I manage tightly around results and give teachers the freedom to figure out how to get there? Or is the better route to invest in teacher learning to produce those results? And, then there's a question my maverick teacher self never thought I'd ponder: how much should a school leader mandate about teacher practice?

The truth is, there is no simple answer. Throwing weight on either side of the tug of war will not be sufficient. It's not a single decision between the two. As Harvard Professor Kay Merseth has said, some challenges in education aren't problems to be solved but rather dilemmas to be managed.[2]

Being a principal requires a constant negotiation of trying to get the right balance of autonomy and coherence—a sense of unified purpose and action—while operating within the powerful influence of the traditional norms of teaching. The same thing goes for mandates: some things must be mandated; other things are dead in the water with a top-down requirement. Achieving the right balance—different for every staff—determines the success of school improvement.

## VISION MEETS REALITY

I entered Douglass ready to lead toward this vision of coherence, collaboration, and continuous learning, but I quickly got a healthy reality check. In my first weeks at the school, I found that while Douglass had a track record of many successes, most teachers pursued individual growth and goals in isolation. The school had no shared expectations, let alone a culture of collective learning. The overall culture was definitely friendly but not collaborative.

Most importantly (and some would say, as a result), Douglass was not serving all students equally well. This truth was evident in the data but also in whispered conversations at school. One day after people had dispersed at the end of a meeting, a highly respected teacher lingered. Stephanie lowered her voice and didn't use names, but she wanted me to know. At bus dismissal, a former student had stopped by on his way out of the building to tell Stephanie that in his current class, the teacher didn't think he was smart. "He doesn't make me do my work over when it's messy. He doesn't push me the way you did." Stephanie didn't want to finger a particular colleague, but she wanted me to know two things: beneath the shiny exterior, the school was not as cohesive as it might seem; and her former student was African American. Even Douglass fell into the all-too-familiar pattern of schools across the country. Teachers didn't share a common vision of how to teach, didn't have uniformly high standards, and it was hurting some of our students, particularly Black and Brown students.

As teachers like Stephanie and her student knew, teacher quality was not consistent across the school, and even within a classroom, teachers were not consistently effective with all students. Many individual teachers excelled at reaching all learners, pushing kids to perform in ways that amazed their families and the students themselves. However, right next door were teachers whose standards were loose and whose students' achievement and behavior varied widely. Some teachers prided themselves on working closely with special educators to accommodate students' special needs. Yet a few of their colleagues openly said they were more effective when kids with special needs were removed from their classroom.

Except for whispered comments like Stephanie's, teachers didn't talk about instructional differences across the school. In fact, the halls still echoed with stories of a recent, mostly unsuccessful attempt by district and school administration to address the school's unequal outcomes through a coherent literacy curriculum. Teachers were expected to replace existing curriculum with the designated materials, change their schedules, and follow specific teaching structures as well as new systems of assessment. Some teachers studied and embraced the new curriculum, finding it provided needed structure and useful resources. For others, it was an unnecessary district intrusion, and they quietly continued with their previous teaching practices. The school's most effective teachers were fairly evenly divided between the two camps.

After two years of intensive, school-based professional development, staff had widely divergent views of what the curriculum entailed. One teacher said he rejected it because it lacked systems for ongoing assessment. Another complained that the new approach required teachers to assess students too frequently. Similar contradictory opinions circulated about the role of phonics and explicit instruction. And during a visit before I became principal, I witnessed teachers spend most of a professional development meeting arguing about whether the district had the right to determine when they assess students and whether they should have to input the scores online.

The new curriculum had revealed differences in teacher practice and beliefs. Special educators worried that children of color were overidentified as learning disabled when, in their view, the real problem was inadequate reading instruction. One teacher even wrote to the superintendent to complain that English language learners were not getting the literacy instruction they needed from our staff. To say there was no shared practice was an understatement.

Thus the problem was not just the variability; it was the fact that all of that time and effort didn't help reduce it. Despite a significant (two years!) whole-school improvement effort, some students were still getting much less effective instruction than their peers next door. Douglass lacked not only a common view of effective teaching but also a shared set of expectations of how the adults work together to improve outcomes. Without any internal coherence at the school, the new initiative broke down at the classroom level, where it was interpreted and implemented according to varying individual beliefs, priorities, and understanding.

As I got to know teachers, I listened intently to their varied perspectives on the literacy reform, trying to understand why so much time and effort hadn't produced more consistent results across the school (and in fact had produced increased division among the staff). What could I learn from this rollout, and how could I be sure that initiatives I championed wouldn't end up with the same tattered results?

## The Case for Coherence and Autonomy

At Douglass, it was clear that variation in practice meant that our most vulnerable students swung from one approach to another from year to year (and sometimes even day to day when special educators had different approaches from classroom teachers). If we wanted to serve these students better—to create a truly student-centered approach—we needed to decrease variability in expectations, systems, and approaches and increase coherence at the school.

At the same time, as a former teacher who prized her independence, I was leery of mandating specific practices. Teachers' professional judgment needs to be respected. We rely on teachers to exercise this judgment each day in hundreds of interactions and decisions. Good teaching requires the authority to make professional judgments about what students need and the flexibility to adjust when they're not seeing results. In addition, like other professionals, teachers require a sense of control over their work to feel satisfied.

As a new principal, I often found myself waffling between views. I'm sympathetic to the notion that we should hold teachers tightly accountable for student learning results while granting complete independence in how teachers produce those results. I'd like to support this view. It would certainly go over easier with the staff. This is why, when a teacher eloquently and passionately made the case that there were many paths up the mountain and each individual should be allowed to take her own path, I was initially stumped. I didn't know how to counter this argument because it sounded right to me.

That is, I didn't know how to counter this argument until I thought about our current results. The facts showed that at Douglass (as at other schools), these different paths haven't resulted in high achievement for all. Far too many kids are below grade level for us to be satisfied with the status quo. This is the point where the many paths theory breaks down, and I told the teacher this. We can't claim success with this approach when we're not all getting to the summit. And furthermore, in this highly atomized context, when we try to get better—with teacher practice all over the map—it's hard to focus our collective expertise and energy in any single direction.

Another reason I was committed to greater coherence across the grades is that it leverages a key advantage of most schools: students are with us for multiple years. If we view all of those years as a single experience rather than chopped up by grades, we have the potential to deepen and extend our impact on learning. When we treat each year separately, we provide the student with a disjointed experience and weaken our impact. Consequently, I needed to help teachers recognize and value their collective power to design eight years of learning for students. Teachers' definition of autonomy needed to expand so that it was not only about individual decisions and actions but also decisions made and actions taken in collaboration with colleagues. With this understanding, collective decision making as a grade level or whole staff can provide the sense of satisfaction and professionalism that comes from exercising individual autonomy.

When there's greater internal coherence at a school, improvement can get traction. I got a lesson in this in my third year by observing two different teams respond to a new (and mostly useful) improvement initiative. The district English Language Arts (ELA) department required all teachers to use a few new writing units, which could be adapted to some extent to fit existing projects. I told teachers they shouldn't throw out meaningful curriculum they were already using. Rather, they should analyze the new curriculum and their own and draw from both to create the best possible approach. The fifth grade teachers had already established a rhythm of effective collaboration. They had common curriculum, rubrics, and assessments and were regularly in and out of each other's classrooms so they knew their shared expectations and practice well. With concerted, collective effort (and lots of snacks), this group of colleagues analyzed both sets of units, found the gaps the new unit filled, and used these results to roll out a new and improved curriculum. Although reluctant at first to rework their existing plans, they said in the end that the changes made for better teaching. Improvements in student writing bore this out.

The process was completely different for the third grade group. One teacher at the grade was recently transferred from another school with a more rote approach to teaching than Douglass teachers were used to. Another was a long-term veteran used to accolades for creative curriculum but not used to the compromises needed when designing units and timelines with others. At the beginning of the school year, the full team had not yet hashed out their different expectations for student work. Overwhelmed with all of the differences in style and expectation, they each implemented the new units their own way without any collaboration. Later in the year, our ELA coach had to do work with each individual teacher on the team to backfill skills that were missing or had been implemented haphazardly. Instructional improvement varied on this team. Student writing didn't show the same growth as on the fifth grade team.

## The String and the Shopping Cart

Two metaphors to describe coherence have stuck with me over the years. Perhaps they've stuck because each provides such a simple visual for a concept that gets complicated once it hits the ground. Or perhaps I regularly think of these metaphors because actual examples in the public school world are harder to find. For whatever reason, I regularly think of a string and a shopping cart when I picture the work we're doing at Douglass.

Education leader and Harvard professor Richard Elmore has often said that trying to effect change in a school (or on a team) without internal coherence is like pushing a string. Picture it for a moment. The place where you push moves forward while the rest of the string lies limp. Then you methodically and laboriously move on down the string. It's an inefficient and tedious process.

In contrast, when teachers work closely together, develop shared expectations, and take collective responsibility for the work, as the fifth grade team did, they create internal coherence. They can adopt, adapt, design— *learn*—nimbly and productively. And even better, when connections across the entire organization are tightly woven, the whole school can respond to a new idea as a cohesive unit. Teachers engage with, improve on, and implement new ideas collectively. Learning and improvement accelerate—and stick.

Another metaphor conjures up that creaky shopping cart that we've all used at one time or another. When the wheels each orient in a slightly different direction, valuable energy goes toward tugging and pulling and pushing the cart to go forward. This is the parallel to the third grade group whose progress was disjointed and slow. When the wheels are aligned, the cart rolls forward smoothly, freed to focus on where we're going.

The benefit—and simultaneously the problem—with these metaphors, of course, is they make coherence seem like a simple concept. Just align the wheels and glide onward. Make that string more like a straw and roll forward. In schools, those wheels and that string are people—often smart, caring people who have their own opinions and maybe a different vision. Getting them all together can get messy.

### Barriers to Coherence

Schools aren't set up to favor coherence. At Douglass, as at most schools, teachers are spread out in individual classrooms with little, if any, overlap with colleagues. Even though some teams had common planning time when I started, the purpose and use of that time varied. Some teams talked about use of shared spaces like the playground, others planned field trips, some addressed individual student needs, few planned curriculum together.

This situation signaled another challenge. In addition to the logistical barriers of space and time, a long-standing cultural barrier existed. Most teachers at Douglass expected to operate autonomously. Research confirms that this thinking isn't unique to our school. Even as new generations enter the profession, researchers continue to find this norm of autonomy influencing how educators respond to reforms.[3]

At Douglass, as at other schools, there were exceptions to the norm of autonomy—teachers who were new together and started collaborating from day one or a younger grade teacher who partnered up with an older grade class because the teachers were personal friends. These examples notwithstanding, it's rare for colleagues to talk about the specifics of instruction, let alone push each other to get better.

Talking about specifics is rare because it's hard and scary and takes time (probably in reverse order of priority). It takes time to meet with peers (time—the most scarce commodity in schools). It's scary to share student work (*What if people think it's stupid? What if my standards are lower than others'?*) and to plan lessons together (*What if people notice that I don't really know the causes for Westward Expansion?*). It's hard to know what to say when a colleague demonstrates low expectations (*She works next door, and I don't want things to be uncomfortable between us. Who am I to judge her work?*). And did I mention the part about it taking time? Who has extra time in schools?

I had studied the teaching norm of autonomy in graduate school but hadn't understood how difficult challenging it would be. I also didn't fully grasp what the norm would look like up close, in day-to-day behaviors. In addition, Douglass seemed different. After all, staff members were caring, reflective, dedicated, and always willing to help a colleague. It seemed only natural that these same people would want to collaborate and learn together, too.

And yet, with the exception of a few pockets of intense and meaningful partnership, teachers at Douglass operated in complete isolation from each other. Even report cards looked different from one classroom to another. When asked to share a good idea with a colleague, a particularly strong teacher said she was uncomfortable and declined for fear of being seen as a know-it-all. Isolation of practice was as strong in this warm, supportive school as at any other typical school.

## Find the Balance of Loose and Firm Leadership

Increasing collaboration and coherence required disrupting the existing culture at Douglass. People don't easily abandon familiar norms of interaction. As a consequence, initially, I spent a great deal of time trying to convince people of the value of this vision.

When teachers whose practice I respected pushed back, I often felt myself backing down from my tentative first efforts at coherence. Everything was up for negotiation. Should classrooms at each grade include the same units, or should teachers go their separate ways? Should all teachers work with a coach? Should we use protocols at meetings, how much will everyone collaborate, how much time will people spend in meetings?

People always have a good reason for why they shouldn't go along with a new proposal. My desire to be respectful of people's professional expertise led me to believe that everyone needed to consent before we implemented any new initiative. Gender stereotypes informed my cautious approach as well. Without realizing it, I had internalized the stereotype that women who are assertive are bossy and arrogant, characteristics I definitely wanted to avoid. Instead of taking decisive steps toward my vision, I was bogged down in seeking people's approval. This all led a trusted outside observer to remark, "It sounds like the teachers are running that school, Sarah, and not you."

This comment—and implied concern—threw me for a loop. I didn't want to be an autocratic principal "running" that school. I wanted teachers to feel empowered, respected for their expertise, authorized to make day-to-day decisions about their work with children. Wouldn't that look like teachers in charge? And yet, the observer's critique caught my attention because I had been feeling ineffective. People were as isolated as ever, and improvement efforts took hold in pockets rather than consistently across the school. What was I doing wrong?

These early efforts to intrude as little as possible on effective teachers signaled that—despite the lofty vision of coherence—I prioritized professional independence over students' learning. In addition, I was putting more effort into not ruffling feathers than into addressing student learning. This may be how schools have traditionally operated, but it's not the way large-scale improvement happens.

Through repeated experience and reflection, I have come to realize that hands-off leadership is not the opposite of autocratic leadership. It's lack of leadership. What the school needed was someone who had a clear vision for whole-school improvement and who could set up the nonnegotiables necessary to get us there. Firm, decisive leadership from the person at the top doesn't have to be oppressive; it can be empowering.

## IF THERE'S A TEAM, THERE'S A PLACE TO LAUNCH THE WORK

One of my first steps at Douglass was to set up a network of teams. If we were going to work on learning and building coherence across the school, we needed a place to do it. While teams in and of themselves don't change culture, they help the complex work of culture change happen.

Some teams at Douglass are schoolwide so that they focus on alignment across the grades. The instructional leadership team (ILT) addresses all academic questions, the A-team addresses everything nonacademic, and math and literacy teams dig into their content areas and are conduits for coaches to share information from district departments. Various other teams have been set up as needs arise, such as to lead whole-school assemblies, design our data use system, and plan for the transition at the time we went through a district restructuring. At first I thought my job was to enlist team participation to advise me in leading the school. Over time, I learned that these teams need to be set up so *we* can lead the school.

Whole-school coherence seemed a faraway goal, however, when teachers were still not aware of what was going on next door. To address this problem, I required same-grade teachers to plan common curriculum and engage in team-based professional development together. Teachers needed a way to examine teaching and learning together to build more coherence in their beliefs, approach, and outcomes. And this approach also needed to help people move from a culture of autonomy to one of collaboration. We needed a skill-building and culture-building system for collaborative learning.

### Engage Teachers in Collaborative Learning

I'm under no illusions that simply telling people they need to learn together will produce results. We've all endured meetings about instructional improvement that improve nothing more than our stamina for sitting still. We've probably also all heard a directive from the boss that we allowed ourselves to ignore. But when the learning feels compelling, when teachers drive the learning, they engage deeply and improve their practice. Everyone wants to feel more effective.

For these reasons, I introduced a data-based improvement cycle as the format for team collaborative learning. The steps are common to many improvement processes: teachers examine student data; identify an area of weakness; diagnose the corresponding problem in instruction; come up with an action plan and a way to assess it; and act, assess, and return to the beginning of the cycle.[4] I referred to the meetings as *inquiry cycles* since at that time, *data* was a bad word at Douglass. (However, as teams have gotten practice choosing the data to dig into and choosing the data they'll use to measure progress, the term-that-must-not-be-named has become more acceptable.)

One of the key features of the inquiry process is the professional authority—autonomy even—that teachers feel in determining the direction of the improvement work. Teachers look at their own students' learning (data from student work, assessments, and observations) and identify problems they really want to solve. Here are some examples from Douglass:

- *Students don't know how to write a paragraph using evidence from the text.*
- *Our kids' writing is flat; they don't demonstrate good word choice.*
- *Kids get lost in solving word problems in math and don't get the right answer.*
- *Kids don't want to read.*

When the inquiry cycle is working well, teachers bring posters, checklists, rubrics, and sample lesson plans to meetings. Sometimes they're responding to an assignment they've given themselves; other times the response is spontaneous because people are excited about what they're learning and want to share. Teachers arrive in the meeting room with rolls of colorful charts, copies of checklists to share, and stories of how their kids responded to the new strategies.

- "Anthony walked right up to the poster to find another word for *went* and then he used it in his writing."
- "Yesterday Ruth asked if the class could share adjectives from their writing and some kids cheered!"
- "Most kids use the rubric, but the kids with organizational issues are still having problems. Can we come up with some sort of visual to help them?"

The work feels real and important. Teachers are motivated to improve their practice, energized by working with colleagues, accountable to their team for the goals they set themselves, and kids' learning improves.

This is the end goal, but inquiry cycles didn't start out this way. By the end of the first year, some people had a glimpse of what the process might be but knew they weren't there yet. In written feedback on the inquiry cycles that first year, teachers described some of the challenges. Here are two teachers' thoughtful and honest reflections:

> I think many teams are stuck and are being very "safe" around what they are looking at—[in my team] it's not really a "problem of practice" and we are certainly nowhere near the idea of looking at practices that influence the teaching of spelling.

> Imagine if we developed a way of being able to honestly look at our practice, each other's and talk amongst ourselves to this end, non-judgmentally. While we are best-intentioned, honest and hard-working people, getting at our specifics is not something that comes easily.

Building a culture of continuous learning and internal coherence in schools requires swimming upstream. It demands continuous, deliberate effort. Each year teachers got better at engaging, and I got better at understanding how to support them.

## TEAM LEARNING IS DEVELOPMENTAL

Some people say that this messy and complicated approach of ongoing adult learning won't work with every staff. They might even read the preceding teacher comments and conclude that because some teams were struggling, the process should be discontinued. No one can afford to waste time in schools. Rather than continue, it might be better to cut bait and try a more top-down approach.

It's true that teacher capacity varies and that not all teams are ready to lead their own learning. However, I've come to see this variation as the starting point rather than the end point. Teachers' lack of skills in collaboration or reflective practice isn't a reason to abandon the approach of collaborative learning. It just means that some teams need more skill building and support.

## The Math Meeting

One fall, I joined the third grade team while they looked at the results of a recent math assessment that most of the students had failed. While the students were at specialist classes, the teachers pushed a few desks together, pulled up chairs, and looked at the student tests. After flipping through the results, they launched into an age-old conversation about student deficits. Their engagement was high. Speaking over each other, they lamented the students' problems. Kids were careless (*Shantel knows her multiplication tables. How did she come up with 3 × 8 = 36?*), or they couldn't break apart multistep problems and got lost in the middle of a single problem (*Look—I can see where Jordan gave up. The pencil just trails off the page.*).

What the teachers didn't talk about were their questions—things they were less certain about. One teacher had worked specifically with Sophia, a funny, vocal leader among her peers who could enter a room singing the latest hit song but seemed to completely shut down in math class. Because of Sophia's anxiety around math, the teacher had taught her tricks for recognizing what operation to use in different word problems. When they tried sample word problems, Sophia had seemed to get it—and was delighted. Yet her score was one of the lowest in the class. Why hadn't the tricks worked here? The special educator had given Justin graph paper to line up his numbers, and while this approach seemed to increase his accuracy, it wasn't enough. What else did he need? And one teacher waited until after the meeting to privately ask the math coach why there were so many questions about putting fractions on a number line. The teacher didn't understand the value of this format but was too embarrassed to ask in the meeting.

I listened to what the teachers were saying (and not saying) for what felt like a long time, disheartened by the overall response of the team, concerned about the tone it was setting for some new staff members in the group, and wondering how to change the direction of the conversation. I finally asked, "So what can you do to help them break apart the problems carefully?" The group paused for a moment, and then one teacher returned to explaining that the students were careless and got lost while solving a single problem. I redirected them to my question even though it felt pushy and intrusive.

The previously animated group got quiet, and the silence felt awkward. Like the air coming out of a balloon, they deflated before my eyes. At the same time, the purpose of this meeting needed to be clear: to take responsibility for improving results and come up with new teaching strategies. The change in energy of the meeting was noticeable, and it took effort to resist the impulse to make things more comfortable.

One of the teachers finally suggested that they could give the kids a series of problems that would get progressively more complicated—adding a single layer each time. They talked for a bit about different teaching resources where they could find these problems. The conversation seemed to hover here for longer than needed; it was safe. They all chimed in about different resources they used.

I asked the teachers to get more specific. "How would you introduce the problems? How would you ensure kids were learning something new and not just repeating past mistakes?" Someone said it would be good to tell the kids the purpose of all this concerted effort so the kids could become more aware of their problem-solving process. They decided on a process they would use to teach how to break down the problems. They agreed to solve a problem as a whole class each morning in the different classrooms and then give a post-assessment to the whole grade in six weeks.

The tone remained somewhat strained and uncomfortable. I guessed that later they would probably complain among themselves about my heavy-handed involvement in their team meeting. While I felt glad that they had left the meeting with action steps they had built together, I felt discouraged that they had needed so much redirection. In retrospect, I realized this collaborative learning was a big cultural shift. It was unfair to expect them to intuitively know how to put themselves on the line, to violate generally understood norms of autonomy, without any experience to tell them it was worthwhile or any precedent to show what effective team learning looks like.

Like their students who learned to solve multistep problems in math that year, these teachers are adopting a new approach to solving problems. Their discomfort is a necessary growing pain of learning a new skill—talking about practice in great detail with colleagues. They needed to be pushed to work in a new way, but they also needed support. I learned to better support them by providing more direct facilitation of their work instead of assuming they could lead this new work on their own. This and specific protocols for analyzing data and more deliberate trust building prompted some breakthroughs.

This meeting also revealed gaps in my skills. In the meeting, my concerns, motivation, and thinking were all private. I pressed teachers to act in certain ways—talk in specifics, make a joint plan, collectively own the student weaknesses—but never shared why. As with the students' math learning, I could have engaged the teachers in understanding their work at a higher level. Why were they doing what they were doing? What were the goals of these meetings? How could their contributions push their collective learning?

While the concrete supports like protocols and a facilitator were definitely a part of their progress, ultimately, this group made the most progress when they took more ownership of their own learning. When they came to realize that pushing through the discomfort was worthwhile in the long run, they didn't need external pressure from me.

At another team meeting toward the end of the year, one of these same teachers asked one of her colleagues to share the strategy she used for teaching a particularly complicated math concept. The two colleagues debated back and forth about the merits of a particular visual representation and ultimately collaborated to build an improved method of showing the principle. This team had come a long way, but it was not without effort and certainly didn't happen overnight.

### Remember That Teams Aren't Birthed Fully Formed

At first, this third grade team from the math meeting was a real thorn in my side. They were stuck and expressed no interest in getting unstuck. Their work together was superficial. They didn't admit when they struggled, and they refused to commit to real changes in practice. Other teams were making progress, digging into their practice, designing specific action plans, discussing how well those plans worked, and getting results. I spent a lot of time feeling frustrated with the errant team and their lack of progress. Their students deserved better.

It finally dawned on me how closely my frustrations with the team mirrored the stereotypical teachers' lounge pastime of blaming students for not learning. (In fact, it wasn't that far from the blame game the teachers had been engaged in about their students' math performance.) This was a classic example of *external attribution*—abdicating responsibility because the problem is perceived to be due to factors outside our control. Responsible educators don't subscribe to external attribution. Yet here I was complaining about a team not making progress and not taking any responsibility for it. Rather than blame the teachers, I needed to accept responsibility to help them learn.

For a variety of reasons, building a process of collaborative learning is bound to be rough at first. One reason is that it goes against those long-standing norms of teaching. One colleague described a first data inquiry meeting when the presenting teacher unconsciously—or perhaps self-consciously?—clasped her folder of student work close to her chest for the whole beginning of the meeting. Showing the details from student learning can feel like standing naked in front of colleagues. Examining student work, asking questions, making suggestions—this all demands a different relationship with peers. It's unreasonable and unrealistic to expect teachers to make this shift without considerable support.

As a result, during the first round of inquiry cycles, while some teams really pushed each other about complicated areas of practice, such as how they would teach analytic writing, some teams chose very safe topics such as coming up with a common spelling list. Although this latter goal was progress in terms of coherent curriculum, it required little conversation about the specifics of instruction. The low-risk goal also reflected the loose framing I had provided the first time around.

## Take Responsibility for Teaching the Skills of Collaboration

Another reason the work didn't take off right away was that I didn't un-pack all the skills needed to engage in teamwork. In retrospect, it's only a slight exaggeration to say that I threw people into the structures, gave them some protocols, and said "Go!" I assumed that people had a lot of skills that it wasn't fair to assume they had. Facilitating a group is hard. People don't automatically know how to write an agenda, help a group come to a decision, or delegate responsibility. The learning curve is steep. In retrospect, it's astonishing how far the Douglass staff went without significant training.

Feedback after each cycle helped improve the process. When teams spent too much time on analysis and ran out of time for action planning, we learned to require teams to backward plan their timeline at the get-go. When some teams struggled to get past their initial discomfort, coaches and I helped facilitate some team meetings so that the process could get off the ground. When teams reported that they lost momentum when the meetings were scheduled too far apart, we adjusted the dates. Sharing action plans across teams raised the level of work of more hesitant partici-pants and allowed teams to get ideas from each other. (The kindergarten team was not playing around. They had the tightest, most ambitious plan in the school, and they were proud of it!)

During the first year, without much support, teams exhibited an enor-mous amount of variability in their work. Much like the level of variabil-ity we were trying to combat across individual teachers, little coherence was evident in how different teams carried out the inquiry work. In fact, teams were operating completely independently of each other, re-creating on the team level the very silos that we were trying to combat at the classroom level. To combat this, we've learned to take some staff meeting time for teams to share their work. In addition, representatives report on team work at ILT and A-team meetings. Without attention, however, the pull of the individual classroom or team is greater than the pull of the larger group. Building coherence requires constantly disrupting the tendency to retreat back to silos.

### Protect the Learning

Principals not only need to support teachers' learning but at times also need to protect it. Leaders do this by establishing and maintaining clear expectations about adult behavior. Sometimes a team needs an explicit intervention, as the math discussion example shows. Other times an individual needs a clear redirection. This latter was the case with Gina, a veteran sixth grade teacher.

Gina has effective classroom skills but an abrasive personality; she routinely refused to participate in the work of her team. One day, I pulled Gina aside to say her confrontational attitude with peers had to stop. With the district's teacher evaluation documents on the table in front of us, I showed her the standards she was not demonstrating in the professionalism category. She stopped fighting her team and resigned herself to engage. Gina isn't a cheerful team member, but she no longer derails each meeting.

In a highly evolved team, the teachers in this group would have addressed Gina's behavior themselves. My hope is that they will build the skills to be able to do that. However, at that point in this team's development, they needed support.

When teams struggle, I no longer throw up my hands. (Okay, sometimes . . . but only as occasional venting with a trusted colleague.) People aren't instantly going to know how to push each other's practice. Their struggle signals they may need to develop a skill or build more trust. Occasionally, they need firm reminders of clear expectations.

Supporting adult learning requires deliberately supporting the learning of teams.

## PLAN FOR LEARNING

Understanding the developmental nature of team learning was an important lesson. So what are the implications going forward? Principals need to do more than just embrace the fact that team learning is developmental. We need to plan for it.

### First Pancake Mentality and Piloting

Expect that learning will be messy. Whatever you planned for professional development will have to be revised as soon as you start learning together. At Douglass, when we began digging into language development, we discovered it wasn't just a matter of vocabulary lists. We found we also needed to strengthen our project-based curriculum to develop meaningful contexts for learning and practicing vocabulary. This changed our PD mid-year. Any plan you create is at best a rough draft.

At one of my first staff meetings, I acknowledged that our venture into a process of teacher-led inquiry cycles would be the equivalent of a first pancake. In a batch of pancakes, a lot of variables have to align. The heat, batter, and pan all have to be right. It's a well-known fact that the first pancake is never the best. The color isn't right, it cooks unevenly, and it's never as fluffy as the next batch. But the thing is, you have to make the first pancake to be able to get to the second one, which is inevitably better.

This thinking has become a mantra of sorts among staff members: it's the first pancake, so let's allow ourselves to learn from this experience. It was clear it had become part of our school's jargon when the school librarian reflected on a lesson I had observed and casually said, "Yeah, it's great to see the kids writing such creative book awards. But you know, it's just the first pancake. Next year's awards will be even better."

An extension of this thinking is to embrace not just messy first tries, but failure. In the business world, people frequently tout failure as a learning strategy. Arianna Huffington calls failure "a stepping stone to success as opposed to the opposite of success."[5] Still, it feels different to experiment with something as valuable as the education of children. How can we afford to get first grade wrong for a child?

When I raised this issue with a business professor in graduate school, he cautioned that an important recommendation from his research was to prevent failures on a large scale. To prevent high-stakes failures, organizations should pilot new ideas—innovations—so that they contain failures on a scale that the organization can withstand. The idea of failing with kids still felt unsettling, but the piloting idea stayed with me.

We started to approach change more gradually—trying to pilot whenever possible. A few teachers tried out a staggered schedule for providing one-on-one interventions with students. Another teacher tried a new assessment system. However, even knowing the value of piloting, I'm surprised how often I feel the urge to roll out new ideas schoolwide. If an idea is good, why shouldn't everyone do it?

The answer is that no matter how good our intentions, when we're trying something new, we just won't get it right the first time. We've got to plan to learn from that effort. It is almost always worth slowing down to pilot the effort with a smaller group or on a smaller scale, to figure out how to learn from the effort, to attend to the ways that different staff members will need different support, and to prevent the entire staff from slogging through the first round of mistakes. Let the majority of the group have the second pancake.

The key to both pancakes and piloting is planning ahead for the learning. John Dewey states that "we do not learn from experience . . . we learn from reflecting on experience."[6] Just because things are messy and imperfect doesn't mean we'll learn from them. If we don't reserve time to reflect on the messiness, we're going to miss important lessons.

With our most recent improvement effort at Douglass, we finally built this part of the process into our plan. The ILT set up a system for revision from the beginning. Instead of reflecting and modifying on the fly, we have three established meeting times throughout the year when the leadership team will reflect on our process. We know we'll make revisions, and now there's time carved out to do this. Such changes won't take us by surprise or be an afterthought. If we're truly a learning organization, we should plan to learn.

## Meetings as Places of Learning

A meeting to plan a meeting—it sounds like a joke about the redundancy of office life. And it's true that ILT members have sometimes rolled their eyes when we schedule a subgroup meeting to plan the next meeting. Despite the ribbing people give, these meetings signal that we're serious about learning, and so we take the time to plan for it. As facilitation gurus Kathryn Boudett and Elizabeth City write in their book on the subject, there's a direct link between more effective meetings and increased student learning.[7]

Not every meeting requires collaborative planning. If we're deciding on a number of technical items such as the date to send out progress reports, whether we should include third graders in the primary grade music concert, or how many kids we can accept into our afterschool program, we probably just need a list of topics. But at many meetings, the issues are more complicated.

Teachers should leave an ILT meeting with new insights, feeling they have helped build an idea or plan. The same thing should apply to coaching or grade-level meetings. Teachers should feel they are addressing substantive and important questions when they meet with their colleagues. Our Ethiopian students don't ask questions in class; could there be a cultural expectation about school that we should learn about? Why do we see a drop in Black boys' reading after second grade, and what can we do to reverse this? What should get more time in our meetings next year—addressing our low reading scores or implementation of our new math curriculum?

These kinds of meetings require planning. And with complex topics, they may require planning with multiple people. Like a teacher planning for a lesson, a leader (or subgroup) needs to think about objectives. What are the goals? How will this meeting build on the knowledge already in the room—and increase it? How can this meeting tap teachers' expertise to improve our collective work?

## PUTTING IT ALL TOGETHER: LEARNING NEW STRATEGIES FOR TEACHING READING

After years of working through the cycle, talking about specifics even when uncomfortable, and building trust, teams learn and instruction improves. A meeting from our fourth year of implementation revealed some of the hard-earned progress.

Inside the Douglass all-purpose meeting room, second grade teachers booted up laptops, took handfuls from the bowls of nuts and chocolate, and gave a collective sigh as they slowed down for the first time that day. Having just dropped their students off at recess, they swapped the latest story about the snow castle on the playground that miraculously survived fifth grade recess the previous day and the student who brought in her pet mouse that morning. "And where is the mouse now?" one teacher asked nervously. The group laughed and joked as they pulled up spreadsheets of student reading levels and passed around copies of the team agenda.

Teachers took turns going down the list to review students who fell below benchmark. As one young teacher went down the list, she sighed with disappointment at the low rate of growth for some of her neediest students, most of whom were nonnative speakers, low income, and children of color. "I haven't figured out a way to read with each of them each day. I don't know how to do it. They read with me Monday, Wednesday, Friday. The other days they read on their own and do phonics work on the iPads or sometimes they go out with Marie [special educator]." She then raised her hand as if to stop the response before it happened, "And I know, I know, they're supposed to get a double dose from me on those days, but I have to read with all the other kids at some point and I can't fit it all in. I'm not reading with my top readers more than twice a week at this point."

The veteran teacher sitting next to her listened quietly and nodded sympathetically. These two teachers had the largest classes in the school and at least ten different home languages in each class. "Yeah, it's more challenging for me, too, this year." Another teacher at the table said, "Sometimes I think we try to do too much in a reading lesson. Maybe they don't have to be twenty to thirty minutes long. Maybe ten minutes each day is enough."

Her colleagues considered this with interest. What would that look like? What would you leave out? The group talked about this approach for a few minutes and raised as many questions as answers. How would you select your teaching point for the lesson? What would the follow-up practice be? How would you group the students? What would the rotation look like if kids had shorter teacher-led reading instruction but on a daily basis? "This should be the focus of our inquiry cycle," the first teacher said emphatically.

Despite the disappointing scores for some of our students, this meeting was a victory in many important ways. Teachers spoke frankly about their struggles; no one got defensive about the data. Teachers had a shared sense of urgency as they looked to each other to identify specific strategies to improve student learning. Anyone witnessing the meeting that day and at subsequent meetings would have seen a group of professionals talking in fine-grained detail about how to improve their collective practice and get better results.

A few weeks after the initial meeting about reading levels, with the support of the literacy coach, the teachers on this team launched their inquiry cycle into the way they teach reading. They began with a research article about reading instruction and over the next few weeks broke apart the steps they had been using and attempted to assemble a more efficient and effective structure. In class, their reading lessons ran differently. Hesitant at first, sometimes rushed and sometimes too slow and running out of time, the teachers worked to find the right rhythm.

During this time and after the inquiry cycle concluded, the learning continued outside the meetings. Before school or in the late afternoon as they finished setting up for the next day, different combinations of these teachers could be found in a classroom huddled around an iPad, leaning in to watch a few minutes of teaching captured in video. They would analyze the pacing, prompts, and student responses. It was an ongoing inquiry—the question that could not wait to be answered.

This team met its overall goal for reading that year. A few students remained below grade level, but at our end-of-year meeting to check on progress, teachers had detailed diagnostic information to share about what they had tried, how the child had responded, and where to go next. These teachers said they were improving their reading instruction in ways they hadn't anticipated at the beginning of the year. The team developed common patterns of asking questions and more practice giving each other feedback, opening up their practice, and increasing trust within the team.

Teachers learned together. They built a set of shared practices. And students became better readers as a result.

# CHAPTER 3

# Pointing to the Data

Extremes are easy. Strive for balance.

—Colin Wright

*Data* was initially a bad word at Douglass. Teachers have good reasons to feel this way. Too often data have been used as a weapon, causing more harm than good. In addition, many responsible teachers worry about spending too much valuable classroom time administering formal, externally created assessments. Instead, they would rather use embedded, ongoing formative assessments that connect directly to their teaching and give real-time data they can use the next day. In too many cases, data use in schools has gotten out of balance. Some educators have lamented that if we spend all our time weighing the cow, we don't have time to feed it. At the same time, the accountability movement has brought needed attention to the lack of effective teaching for our most underserved students. When used responsibly, data can help educators accomplish the goals they all want to achieve.

An experience in my first year as principal brought home the value of looking at data. After an evening school council meeting in the fall while parents and teachers were gathering their coats and bags, a father of a second grader came over to ask me a question. He pulled out a recent data report and turned to a graph of one grade's results at our school. He had been looking at the report, he said, and saw impressive results in many ways, but he had noticed the extremely low performance of our African American students in that grade. Pointing to the graph, he asked what I thought.

This statistic was concerning to me as well, which I told him while also mentioning our unusual cohort that year. While it's true that we needed to improve, in a small cohort, a few kids can skew a graph. . . . During my response, this parent kept looking at the graph, and his finger continued to point to the percent passing rate. It remained there as I launched into context and explanation. The father's strategy was effective. I had to keep looking at the low passing rate.

As we spoke and the parent continued to point, my explanation felt weak. These were excuses for an inexcusably low passing rate. My commitment to following up with those teachers grew. We couldn't have a similar number to point to the following year. After a few minutes, this parent graciously thanked me and said good-bye. As the door closed behind him, I made a silent commitment that the data would change for those students.

The problem was that this team didn't see a need to change. Like other teachers across the school, this team was resistant to that same district-mandated literacy curriculum mentioned earlier. In the years before I began at Douglass, these teachers scorned the approach and administered the new district-required assessments half-heartedly, paying little attention to the results. The integrated curriculum that they used was inspired and highly praised. Many students produced high-quality work and demonstrated well-developed critical thinking skills. As a result, teachers didn't feel an urgency to do anything differently.

At a meeting with the team, I shared the data about their mostly low-performing African American students. "They're mostly second language learners," the teachers responded. "The majority live in poverty, and the unconnected, restrictive writing prompt doesn't measure the higher-order thinking that we teach."

I asked one of the teachers what she thought these students lost by being grouped with higher-performing students. (Too often, in our district, the question is only asked the other way around.) She thought for a minute. She was taking the question seriously and doing some soul searching. With reluctance, she admitted, "Basic skills in reading and writing."

This acknowledgment marked a turning point for the team. For perhaps the first time, these teachers understood one urgent reason for them to improve literacy instruction. They understood why the work was important. Courageously and humbly, the team asked for professional development around reading instruction and determined their next inquiry cycle would focus on concrete skills for organizing paragraphs.

This team of teachers went on to incorporate specific and significant improvements in their literacy curriculum. They revised curriculum units and rubrics, and included much more explicit teaching of content students previously were assumed to know. As a result, at the end of the year, their student results were some of the best in the city—including and especially the academic growth of their African American students.

Keeping a finger on the data helped the team own a problem in their instruction. They couldn't ignore the skills covered in these assessments and gained a sense of urgency for the work. The data provided them a clear purpose for their own learning. As a result, they invested more than in the previous years of rolling out the literacy initiative. However, the data provided just the starting point, not the solution. A critical part of the success story is how the team bravely left their established methods and curriculum and plunged in to learn new strategies. It was the combination of accountability and support that propelled them forward.

Paying attention to results certainly plays a role in improvement. In particular, at a school like Douglass (and so many others around the country) where there can seem to be lots of success, data can help us zero in on the growth of a subgroup that's not being equally well taught. Tracking this data keeps us focused on increasing equity.

It's important, however, not to let the balance tip too far in measuring results. Leading researchers in business as well as the education world caution about this. Business professors Ronald Heifitz and Donald Laurie compare the balance of accountability and support to a pressure cooker.

A leader needs to get the right amount of pressure so that things cook but not so much that the lid blows off.[1] In their book, *Restoring Opportunity*, Professors Greg Duncan and Richard Murnane state simply (and wisely) that in order for schools to improve student learning, leaders need to provide a combination of "strong school supports" and "sensible accountability."[2] The process of establishing balance and achieving the right definition of "sensible" needs to be ongoing.

## MAKE SURE DATA USE IS HEALTHY AND NOT HURTFUL

Many educators feel bruised and beaten by the public sharing of student test data. When simply published or displayed, without any context, these numbers tell part but not all of the story. Using data without context may ultimately inhibit growth rather than spur an individual or organization to improve. Context is needed not to make excuses but to more meaningfully understand what we should learn from the numbers. Without this, data have the potential to increase resentment rather than urgency.

At some district meetings, my school's public data looked poor, when in fact we were starting to turn a corner through slow improvements happening on the ground. And in other years, our school's data have been hailed as exemplary when a closer look would have revealed a cohort of kids in a younger, untested grade that we weren't serving well. In both situations, simply displaying the data didn't capture the most meaningful issues for us at the school. Both situations felt like a waste of time and focus. Replicating this problem in the way we use data at the school level isn't going to help us improve.

Leadership professor Amy Edmondson says the risk in overemphasizing results is more than resentment. It prevents an organization from making needed improvements. She finds that organizations in the knowledge business (like schools, hospitals, the technology industry) have to prioritize and organize strategically for *learning*, not just results. She cautions leaders against exclusively results-oriented practices that lead to people unthinkingly following directions instead of problem seeking, and where fear and intimidation are seen as motivators for performance.[3] Even though it may be messier and take more time, an approach that supports ongoing learning is going to produce the greatest benefit for an organization that has not yet figured out how to fully achieve its mission.

After regular data analysis meetings over the years, most if not all Douglass teachers have internalized the finger on the data point mentality. They know that student learning is the most important measure of our effectiveness. The question is, Are they so fixated on results that they don't feel they can take the risks necessary in learning new skills? Should we ignore results as we adopt a new approach to one topic or another? And what is my role in how teachers relate to the data? As principals, we need to be aware of the messages we send both explicitly and implicitly and the influence they have on teachers.

At a fifth grade team meeting one November, the math coach led a discussion of what we saw in the latest assessments measuring performance on standards covered that fall. As teachers shared and discussed, I used a yellow marker to highlight areas of concern in the spreadsheet in front of me. The number of students in yellow was unusually high. Out of the corner of my eye, I noticed Maria, an experienced teacher new to her grade, following the path of my highlighter carefully.

A few weeks later, Maria came to my office and broke down saying that it was impossible to meet my expectations, which were unreasonably high anyway. In that moment, I remembered how carefully she had watched the highlighting. In the absence of any other signals, she assumed that those fall math scores were the measure I used—that she should use—to assess her professional worth.

Maria needed to be able to hold two competing views in mind simultaneously: the scores are important *and* she's a learner along with her students. Improving student learning is always the goal, *and* there isn't always a direct route to getting there. Learning requires experimentation, which means a range of both dips and bumps in the results along the way. Conveying this concept to teachers is complicated, to say the least. It comes back to Amy Edmondson's urging to pay attention to results but to support and foster a culture of learning even more.

As a result of meeting with Maria, I went out of my way to encourage her to experiment and learn. She tried new ways of teaching, and her students made progress, including in math. However, the data meetings shook her confidence, and she wasn't the only teacher who felt so downtrodden by the data. How can looking at data feel more like a temperature check rather than a jury verdict?

### Send a Clear Message—Again and Again

Establishing a culture of looking at data takes time. Because this practice is new, it's already stressful. On top of that, add the current political context that claims assessment data provide the final word on teacher effectiveness, and the pressure ratchets up higher. It's only recently that I've realized how powerful these two forces are on a teacher's psyche. Even while I strive to be balanced, the prevailing expectations around data use are so strong that people assume I approach these data meetings with judgment. They assume that I view assessment data as the only information that matters. If we don't deliberately put weight on the learning side of the scale, it will always skew toward results.

Words aren't enough to change the climate. Actions need to send the message that adult learning is a priority and a value. We continue to seek ways to signal this message at Douglass. We share and celebrate learning and progress at staff meetings and designate time to do the same at data meetings. While many teachers have become accustomed to viewing the data as a tool, some still find it incredibly stressful. I can't—and shouldn't—eliminate *all* the stress. Being responsible for children is a significant charge. But it's worth the ongoing effort to get the balance right for everyone.

A principal colleague has been doing these quarterly data meetings a year longer than I have. She's a progressive educator who values experimentation and creative ways to assess social and academic learning for the whole child. Every year, when these data meetings come up, she makes homemade coffee cakes for each team to emphasize her support and care for teachers during the review of data. The staff know her views, feel her support, and yet, for the first few years of data meetings, someone cried at almost every one. She told me she felt at a loss for what to do to change the tone.

I empathized with this leader's dismay. Blame isn't the goal of data meetings. When we talked again this year, she said she was beginning to see a difference at the meetings. Teachers trust that she has a balanced view of the data and are themselves beginning to see data as a tool rather than a judgment. "They're not crying," she said hopefully. She may not have to bake coffee cakes much longer.

## Get Close to the Action

In addition to allowing people time to adjust to this new tool—especially one so public and loaded—we also need to balance test data with other concrete sources of information. Regarding data analysis meetings, educator Paul Bambrick-Santoyo states that looking exclusively at the test data spreadsheet is like looking only at the scoreboard after a game has finished. Of course, the scoreboard tells us important information, but to be able to talk about improvement with any credibility, we need to have watched the game.[4] Watching the game means knowing a teacher's practice well. Only this is going to provide the specific information needed to help a teacher improve. However, there's another reason observation is important.

Reflecting on Maria's breakdown in my office, I realized I had observed in her classroom only a few times that fall. Even though she was tackling new material, she was a strong teacher, and that year several struggling teachers required—and got—a great deal of my supervision and time. But in retrospect, paying less attention to her classroom was a mistake. In her first year at a new grade, she felt vulnerable. Knowing that her boss had a good picture of her practice might have made it easier to look at the data together.

Classroom observations help any teacher (new to a grade or otherwise) feel that the principal has been there as she's been sprinting up and down the field, sweating, showing persistence, diving for the ball with her whole heart in the game. This teacher was working her hardest, but the scores didn't (yet) show it. She felt that that was all I knew of her practice that year and worried that she was being judged negatively. More frequent and ongoing observations would have reassured Maria that I had a more complete picture.

## Seek Out Evidence of Growth

When students perform below grade level, saying "Don't worry about it; Jimmy will be fine" would be insincere because we know that Jimmy's future depends on success in school. His family is counting on his teachers and his school; he won't get another chance at education. Just saying to the teacher "You've got a really challenging group" is also not helpful because where does that leave the teacher (or Jimmy)? What helps is noticing evidence of growth. Any evidence that the teacher's actions are making a difference goes a long way toward reinforcing the teacher's sense of efficacy and fuels a desire to persist.

This evidence, however, might not show up on formal assessments. It includes interconnections between subjects, the character traits teachers work so hard to instill, the grit and persistence that allow a child to grow even when he is years below grade level. As principals, we have to find ways to collect these and other forms of progress that are not captured by some of the blunt assessment measures.

Teachers have reported that it's encouraging to hear me recognize growth. When a student repeatedly fails grade-level benchmarks, teachers can feel demoralized, which can foster self-doubt (or worse—blame for the child). Focusing on growth combats this discouragement. One of the benefits of a small school is being able to watch individual children move through the grades and learn over time. This allowed me to tell one teacher, for example, "Crystal's writing has really improved! You must be working well with her."

Crystal's writing the previous year had been a struggle. Her simple, painstakingly written sentences included few words and little detail. Now here she was writing with voice and confidence. The teacher e-mailed to say how much she appreciated that I understood the specifics of the situation. While Crystal wasn't yet at grade level, she was making clear and important progress. That improvement needed to be honored and valued.

We institutionalized the importance of growth at Douglass when we created "data walls" to track students' reading progress at each grade. On these simple trifold posterboard displays, students were represented on individual sticky notes sorted into columns indicating reading levels. The boards came out at staff and team meetings throughout the year when it was time to check on progress. We purposefully set aside time at meetings for teachers to move the stickies up the number of levels a child had progressed.

One teacher joked with colleagues that she had become obsessed with the data walls and the growth they measured. When she was reading with a student in class one day and noticed growth, her first thought was, "I get to move her sticky!" Recently, we've moved to a spreadsheet model with color-coding and easier storage and tracking over the years. This tool still sends a clear message that growth is important, but some staff members miss the visceral satisfaction of moving stickies across the board. Teaching is hard work. Concrete evidence that you're making a difference provides valuable encouragement.

And what if growth isn't evident? This issue continues to be one of the most valuable data points to raise with teachers. When Sofiane, a student from Haiti with significant learning disabilities showed little or no growth in multiple subjects, I met with her teacher to look at the data. Mike was a teacher about whom I had concerns, and his first comments about Sofiane's poor attitude and work habits weren't reassuring.

It's true Sofiane was often loud and brash; her insecurities meant she was usually criticizing the person across the room to distract from her own confusion with the work in front of her. But beneath all that bluster, she was desperate for affirmation and sincerely wanted to be successful in school. What about growth for Sofiane? Any evidence of growth?

Mike couldn't point to any. Unfortunately, I can't report a teacher turnaround. It's no coincidence Mike no longer works at Douglass. However, pointing to the growth data got Mike's attention more than any other feedback had. After our meeting, Mike sought out advice from colleagues about what to do with Sofiane. Knowing I would be asking about growth in our next conversation, he was finally willing to try a new approach.

Mike's example also clarifies that while it's important to honor our learning process as a staff, this doesn't mean we ignore results altogether. Even if we haven't arrived at our goal, we should have ample evidence that we are moving. Some teachers need to hear this more than others.

Knowing teachers' practice gives us important information along these lines. Do we see the commitment to continual growth and improvement? Does the teacher continually reflect on student learning to assess her practice and use this information to revise her practice and further her learning? The vast majority of teachers want to be more effective and work hard toward that goal. That said, in the balance of accountability and learning, a few teachers benefit from increased attention to the accountability side.

### Internal Accountability Will Get You Further than External Accountability

Another healthy way to use data is peer to peer. One of the outcomes of increasing coherence is that teachers feel a growing sense of accountability to peers. Teachers align curriculum, practice, *and effectiveness* to increase the quality of student learning. They feel accountable to their peers for improving student achievement, and this *internal accountability* provides a less punitive and more meaningful sense of urgency than do many external accountability systems from the state or district.

For example, for years, Jonathan, a veteran teacher, was unconvinced of the research-based finding that children need to read books at their level every day to be able to promote optimal reading growth. He disagreed, saying he built self-esteem by having all students read the same books even if they were higher than some students' reading levels. Reading scores didn't provide definitive proof either way. His kids always made progress. I felt they could make much more (particularly those who remained below grade level).

At a team meeting, while reviewing all students' reading progress, Jonathan's colleagues asked him about book levels. A special educator at the meeting who worked closely with Jonathan shared specific data about how this approach had helped another student make clear progress. Jonathan was one of the most opinionated members of the staff but also one of the most dedicated, and he listened carefully to his colleague. Another teammate shared that she had changed her practice to better diagnose students' reading levels and had seen good results.

The momentum of the group's thinking grew, and Jonathan was carried along with it. He probably also knew they would have the same conversation the next quarter when they met and he wanted to have better progress to show. The shift didn't happen overnight, but after the meeting, this strong-willed teacher asked the special educator for help finding the right level books. He began to differentiate his reading instruction and had results to share at the next data meeting. Pressure from me—external accountability—was not enough to push this independent-minded teacher. However, the internal accountability created from feeling he had to answer to his peers produced the right amount of urgency for this teacher to learn a new skill and apply it with his students.

Internal accountability doesn't spontaneously occur. Rather, it's an outgrowth of teachers' increased collaboration and collective learning. Its absence is an indication that the collaboration isn't deep or meaningful enough. The lowest-performing teacher at my school is a clear measure of that team's and the school's level of internal accountability.

When new teachers join Douglass—some by choice and others by district transfer—the strength of each team becomes clear. One year, a new teacher displayed low-quality student work right across the hall from a colleague's display of much higher-quality work. Students' hastily written and illustrated math word problems were clear evidence that teachers on this team weren't talking about work when they planned. The looseness of this team slowed this new teacher's learning. It was also an indication that the team lacked internal accountability and needed more help.

By comparison, teams with higher degrees of internal accountability at Douglass have quickly raised the standards of new teachers, including how they plan (using clear learning targets, creating rubrics) and how they teach (clearer directions, using word walls). One new teacher was impressed by the level of work her colleagues expected of each other and said, "I didn't think schools were actually like this."

### Increase Accountability to Parents

The implicit contract between parents and teachers is a strong one: each day, parents trust us to teach their children well. Most educators appreciate the significance of this relationship. We feel accountable to parents and don't want to let them down. Harnessing this sense of accountability to parents helps get the amount of urgency right.

For this reason, I told the school council (made up of elected parents and teachers) it was their job to *ask* to see our achievement data at multiple points throughout the year. An incredibly supportive group, they hadn't wanted to put the teachers and me in the hotseat until they heard that's what we wanted. And, to be truthful, part of me didn't want that. It's never appealing to be in the hotseat. But parents are a constituency teachers value. Reporting to them keeps us honest about getting the results/learning balance right.

Similarly, when one particular cohort of students did poorly on state tests for two years in a row, I took a deep breath and invited the parents to a meeting. I had no obvious plan at the time I sent out the invitation, but it was clear that facing all of those parents together in a room was going to make this issue inescapable. That was the goal. Increasing parent attention would help us keep a finger on the data. Making promises, out loud, in the school library to that concerned group of parents provided a high degree of focus. None of us could be distracted from the need to turn things around for this group of kids.

That year, the teachers and coaches deeply examined student work and made changes in their curriculum and practice. Parents appreciated knowing how we were working on the areas of weakness and probably helped kids focus on them at home as well. Students in that previously struggling cohort showed our school's highest level of growth by the end of that year.

Building in concrete accountability systems with parents also occurs in other ways. Teachers at Douglass have long had a tradition of inviting parents into school to look at evidence of their children's learning. On top of this, students are increasingly leading conferences with their parents to explain and give evidence of the standards they've mastered and those they have yet to achieve. These deserve to be seen as the high-stakes assessments they are. When the third-grade teacher knows that Charlene's mother will be in class by the end of the month, the teacher can't avoid it; she's got to help Charlene have a breakthrough in writing.

## Find the Right Balance

When it's working, using data is the springboard for meaningful reflection, planning, and action. At Douglass, we have more to do to develop our culture around data, but it's clear that we've come a long way since we couldn't even use the word. A recent, brief interaction demonstrated the good progress we've made over five years. This example features Jodie, the vocal sixth grade team leader, who was one of the staunchest opponents of using team time to examine achievement data during my first year.

One day, a few years after we had begun looking at data together, Jodie burst into the coaches' office to ask for the item analysis of the state test before her upcoming team meeting. It was January; the test was from the previous March. With just a few minutes before her kids returned from lunch, Jodie hurriedly explained, "I just thought that if I had some data it would help our planning. I want to show them the section the kids didn't do well in last year because we have to figure out a new way to teach it."

Later that day, one of the coaches came by my office and excitedly remarked on the interaction. "Did you notice that Jodie wanted data? Could you believe that?" The grade level's poor test results weren't the end of the team's conversation but the beginning. Jodie believed she could use those results to point her team in the right direction and help them do better.

Finding the right balance between accountability and support requires continually reminding ourselves of the only goal: improving teaching so our students learn more. If data help us meet this goal, they're useful. If they don't, we're wasting precious time, energy, and morale. Getting the balance right requires staying close to teachers and teaching so we know when data are helpful and we can adjust when they're not. When teachers like Jodie come to see data as a tool rather than a weapon, and when they're empowered to lead the school's use of data, we're most likely to get the balance right.

CHAPTER 4

# Developing Teacher Leadership

A leader is best when people barely know he exists, when his work is done, his aim fulfilled, they will say: we did it ourselves.

—Lao Tzu

Principals invest considerable effort to develop meaningful teacher collaboration, build internal coherence, and establish a healthy balance of accountability and learning. As leaders, we might be tempted to feel satisfied once we've established these conditions in our schools. After all, these are not easy steps to take, and they clearly set up the school to improve in important ways. However, if we want to maximize the improvement, another key ingredient remains: teacher leadership.

My understanding of how to develop teacher leadership—my very definition of teacher leadership—shifted dramatically the year I worked with leadership coach Elliot Stern. As part of a fellowship, I had the opportunity to select someone to coach me for a full school year. Elliot was a familiar figure among local educators. After working as a highly respected principal in Boston for almost twenty years, Elliot served in the city as a district deputy superintendent where he earned a reputation for being tough, relentlessly focused on instructional improvement, and, in his own passionate way, demanding that principals take greater ownership of their own learning. From all I heard, he sounded intimidating but also like someone who would make me better at my job. I signed up to get his help.

Elliot arrived for his first observation at the end of August. He sat at the back of the school library during the first staff meeting of the year taking notes, watching closely, and getting up to listen in when people talked in small groups. After the meeting ended, he followed me down to my office to review the work. The day had been too busy for lunch, so I gulped down a sandwich as we spoke. Eager for feedback, I figured we would talk about the way I had responded to different teacher questions and the various structures I had introduced (the new coaching structure, the new formative assessment structure). I wasn't prepared for the feedback Elliot gave.

First, he empathized, "You work incredibly hard. You must be really tired . . . and lonely." Yes, I thought. He understands. And then came the coaching. "You are at the center of too much, Sarah. You shouldn't be leading this meeting—teams of teachers should be planning and leading it. Instead of just focusing on what you need to cover at the meeting, think about what leadership skills teachers need in order to help the school improve. How will this meeting develop those skills as well? And what's the message you want new teachers to learn about the culture and expectations around leadership at this school? You're losing valuable time. You've got to develop more leadership among your teachers."

Elliot wasn't talking about what we conventionally think of as teacher leadership—roles outside the classroom or formally granted authority. These opportunities are important, but an even broader, more potent approach to engaging teachers in improvement exists. This approach doesn't require special positions and doesn't take teachers out of classrooms. Through Elliot's coaching, I've come to think of teacher leadership less as a specific role and more as a mindset.

When staff members look beyond their classroom and join with colleagues to solve gradewide or whole-school problems, they are acting from a leadership mindset. They feel responsible for all students, not just the kids in their own classroom or case load. Teachers with a leadership mindset consider their colleagues' learning needs as well as their own because their sense of success is wrapped up in the success of the whole school. In schools where each teacher maintains a whole-school perspective, you feel the difference.

A few individuals will always step up to do this kind of work on their own. For example, at Douglass, one teacher noticed things were chaotic on the playground in the mornings, and so devised a better system for bringing kids into school. Other teachers recognized an opportunity when they saw kids sitting in the cafeteria before school and designed a structured, morning tutoring program. Teachers like these make a difference in the school community.

Gradually, greater numbers of Douglass teachers are adopting this viewpoint. We're not there yet, but the evidence is growing that we're getting closer. A few teachers told their colleagues that we needed an articulated set of schoolwide values and then created them with the whole staff. A subset of second and third grade teachers set up joint meetings with their respective teams to address the big drop in writing proficiency from second to third grade. Teachers said we need a task force to specifically discuss and make recommendations about issues of race at our school. Increasingly, teachers and teams are getting more assertive in directing the learning of the whole school.

This mindset isn't created by adding specific positions or titles. Developing this form of teacher leadership requires shifts in school culture. Teachers who adopt a whole-school mindset are disrupting a deep-rooted cultural norm. As a consequence, they'll face predictable challenges and require support. Cultivating teacher leadership also demands a particular mindset from the leader—an ability to trust teachers enough to give back meaningful work, to anticipate and provide necessary support, and then to get out of the way.

## GET OUT OF THE WAY

Surprisingly, even for the busiest leaders, being able to delegate and relinquish control is often quite hard. Even though the meeting Elliot observed included plenty of small group work and sharing, I was still the one in front of the room; I was the one who set the agenda. It was my meeting, not ours.

As leaders, we are often our own worst enemies when it comes to sharing leadership. We're usually hired for an administrator position because we have demonstrated that we confront problems head-on, work hard, and apply ourselves until we find a solution. We're good at—and take satisfaction from—showing initiative, contributing, fixing.

With improvement work, effective leadership is not measured by the solutions the principal brings but by the amount of problem solving and innovation generated by the staff. When the urgency for improvement is fueled by teachers' questions and collective problem solving, we've generated the most powerful tool for increasing student learning. In contrast, if teachers always have to wait for the principal's direction, we're creating a bottleneck in the process, slowing down innovation and causing people to retreat to old ways of acting. To increase solutions and support a culture that seeks them, principals need to get out of the way.

The need to step behind the scene has required a shift in my practice. As a teacher, I was a mover and a shaker in meetings. In my new understanding of the role of principal, I participate far less and ask questions more. It's been humbling to discover that when I hold back and listen before sharing my thoughts, someone in the group inevitably shares a similar idea or insight. It has become far more satisfying to see teachers engaged in and owning the work than to be the one with the clever solution.

While student learning (as evidenced in a wide variety of ways) continues to be the most important measure of a leader's success, it's no longer the only yardstick. I now look for other important indicators to assess whether we're on the right path toward developing this whole-school leadership perspective across the grades. Do conversations about improvement continue when the principal is no longer there? Does the scope of collaborative work extend beyond what the principal has named? Do teachers ask each other questions about student work instead of waiting for the leader to do so? Learning to ask these questions is shifting my role. When we get the results right, it also shifts student learning.

## What Can Happen When We Do Get Out of the Way

After a year of my working with Elliot and considerable effort invested in developing this form of teacher leadership, the get-out-of-the-way approach was put to a serious test. I invited teachers to join a team that would revise the school's system for monitoring student progress throughout the year. As long as the plan met the goal of improved teaching and learning, the team had full authority to write the plan with the understanding that I would grant final approval.

Sixteen teachers representing all grades, programs, and experience levels of our staff said they wanted to be on the team. After some arm-twisting, two agreed to facilitate the end-of-year, all-day meeting to develop the plan.

As it turned out, quite a few challenges popped up when the day of the meeting came. One of our invited experts was late, the technology wasn't smooth, and conversations went longer than planned. As we got further away from the carefully allocated times on the agenda and still nothing had been decided, it looked as though the group would run out of time. Summer vacation for these teachers was starting the following day.

Over the course of about an hour, from the back of the room, I engaged in a silent, urgent internal debate about whether or not to intervene. With great self-control, I recognized that the team needed to truly own the process and it was up to them to figure out what to do if we ran out of time. Despite everything in me wanting to, I didn't intervene.

In the afternoon, after breaking into small groups to tackle different parts of the design, the teacher facilitators called everyone back together to share ideas. The first to go in front of the group was a usually quiet second-year teacher holding a piece of chart paper marked up with dates and responsibilities. In a confident, strong voice, she explained her group's plan and took questions. Other groups stood to share ideas, directing their voices to each other, talking about how to get whole-staff buy-in, what support their colleagues would need, and what would be necessary to thoughtfully document student interventions and progress.

People began to talk about next steps for the group, despite the fact that I had never mentioned any commitments beyond this meeting. "We need to figure that out before we present this to everyone in August" and "We have to be sure to explain that clearly when we present this" and "Can we use that PowerPoint for our overview?" Then someone said, "We need to meet again," and everyone agreed. Fourteen of the sixteen people said they could come back to finish the process. At this point, they needed to know there wasn't money budgeted to pay people for another day. Even after they heard this, the hands stayed up.

Members of this group ended up meeting on another of their summer vacation days and again just before school started to flesh out the full plan and coordinate their presentation to colleagues. As they stood in front of sixty colleagues gathered in the school library, these teacher leaders presented with authority and a good dose of humor (by way of a game-show format led by that shy, young teacher). Staff members laughed at the right moments, discussed the serious questions, voted on some dates and logistics, and genuinely thanked the group members for their hard work.

This meeting revealed the power of Elliot's definition of teacher leadership. The fact that one of our newest teachers felt able to step up in this way demonstrated that this had become part of our school culture. The plan that the team came up with was different from what I would have designed; it was, in fact, an improvement. One reason is that they included a piloting period to help us learn before expanding.

One of the most striking aspects of this experience was the fact that the staff accepted the plan without any pushback at all. Energy at the staff meeting and afterward wasn't spent debating whether to use this process but rather how to implement it well. In the revisions that we've continued to make, this is still the case. These teacher leaders galvanized the rest of the school to engage with each other in this improvement process. But it took time to get to this point. Time and support.

## PROVIDE SUPPORT FOR TEACHERS
## TO LEAD IMPROVEMENT

Over time, I've learned specific strategies to develop this leadership perspective within the staff. Perhaps most important has been the realization that, like countless initiatives in education, it's not an easy win. Teachers don't automatically embrace opportunities to think outside their classroom or to take the lead. Half-hearted delegating can feel insulting rather than empowering, and staff members—including the principal—need specific skills so that collaborative problem solving is more than window dressing and actually leads to improved student learning.

### Recognize the Challenges Teacher Leaders Face

Early on, I required all grade-level teams to create curriculum maps documenting their units of study and aligning these units with student learning standards. In preparation for this task, I asked the instructional leadership team to determine the scope and content of the maps: what guiding questions should be included, how they should be designed so that we could easily share and compare the information across grades, what the appropriate scope was to ensure alignment but not overwhelm us with too much information. The staff knew about the expectations and the ILT's decision-making role in the process.

Over several weeks, ILT members discussed these questions, solicited input from their teams, and revised several versions of the curriculum map. After reaching agreement, they sent out the final template to teams to use during assigned release time. Shortly after that, I was with one of the grade-level teams when teachers expressed questions and concern about the process and format for the curriculum maps. Some of their questions were for me, "Why do we have to do this?" but some were related to the ILT's work. "Where did this template come from? We don't understand what it's asking. What are we supposed to write for 'guiding questions'? This feels like busywork to us." Their team leader had not shared any of these questions or concerns at the ILT's multiple meetings about the topic.

Turning to the team leader—their representative on the ILT—I suggested they ask her since she had been part of the design process. She looked uncomfortable and had clearly not done her job of leading her team—informing the team of the process and getting their input. Or maybe, out of fear that her colleagues would push back, she had distanced herself from the work of the ILT, saying things like "They want us to use this template." Maybe she'd shrugged dismissively when sharing the ILT's template—communicating clearly to her team that it wasn't anything she was responsible for. Or maybe it was just a matter of the ILT being a new process at our school and her assumption that discussions at meetings were just that—discussions—and she had no more responsibility to report on them than so many other topics talked about around the school (quality of the cafeteria food, rumors about the new superintendent, etc.).

Witnessing this brief interaction provided useful, albeit disappointing, data. I had made too many assumptions about the level of leadership teachers were prepared to take on. Sure, teachers needed more facilitation skills, but more importantly, it was clear I had underestimated the challenge of being a leader among peers.

As the preceding example demonstrates, there's a cost to leading your peers. Making decisions on behalf of the whole school inevitably means compromise, which means disappointing some people some of the time. When teachers on the ILT or literacy team or A-team (the everything-but-academics complement to the ILT) come to agreements and need to advocate for proposed changes with their colleagues, they may face skepticism or resentment. "Who are you to be telling me what I need to change?" "Since when do you get to decide what I'm going to prioritize or when or how I'm going to teach it?" or perhaps the most likely response, "I don't have time to think about anything outside my classroom."

Team leaders need to have the confidence and conviction to speak up for the change and explain why it's good for students. With leadership comes responsibility, and sometimes people just don't want it. There's solidarity in being "just" a member of the staff, and leading improvement efforts may mean losing that sense of solidarity. Peers may view you as pushy or self-righteous. You may not experience the same kind of camaraderie you're used to.

In addition, as a teacher leader, you are no longer a passive observer. You can't complain and shake your head. Now that you're carrying part of the problem on your shoulders, others may shake their head at *you*. In this context, stepping up involves potential risk. If a principal wants more people to take the lead, the surrounding culture also has to change.

Culture change happens when a teacher's sense of responsibility shifts from just the students in her classroom to all the students at her grade level. When staff members feel more loyalty to the whole school than to their team. Instead of asking themselves, "Will my team be mad about this? Will my team feel comfortable with this plan?" teacher leaders develop a mindset of asking, "What will benefit the whole school?"

Then the scale tips and, while it may still feel risky to take leadership, it also feels unavoidable. It's a compelling, critical responsibility. The culture shifts so teachers can't just shrug their shoulders and turn away. This is the evidence I've learned to look for in assessing my work—teachers sharing students, investing more in collaborative planning, speaking up about concerns, and advocating for specific improvements. Momentum builds and more teachers engage in building our "collective intelligence" and generating schoolwide solutions.

## Prepare People for Pushback

After the curriculum mapping experience, ILT meetings included time to anticipate potential team concerns and how to respond to them. We took time for people to share strategies for presenting an initiative to be able to develop this leadership skill set. Knowing that you'll be reporting back to your ILT colleagues also helps bolster people in their advocacy role. It may feel easier to lead a difficult conversation with your team when you know others are doing the same and you feel a sense of accountability to them.

When one team planned to introduce a new structure for data use to the staff, we first conducted a "premortem" protocol to anticipate what might cause the plan to fail, including all the ways that colleagues might respond.[1] At the time, I wondered if it was a good use of time. Later, when members of this team presented to the staff, I recognized the value of the protocol. These teacher leaders fielded questions and addressed anxieties from their colleagues with patience and poise. Because of the preparation, their colleagues' doubts and worries were familiar to this team—they'd worked through them already. In addition, doing the premortem had solidified the group's collective commitment to the new structure; they didn't want it to die.

## Give People Tools

Facilitation can be hard even for small grade-level teams—perhaps especially for these teams. When the team is just four to five people, getting together for a team meeting can feel casual, no different from when teachers gather for conversation over lunch. This casual nature poses a challenge for the designated team leader who has to get through a busy agenda of items, including sometimes eliciting a team decision. Some astute staff members helped me realize we needed to provide more concrete support for these leaders.

Our literacy coach championed the idea of explicitly building skills for teamwork. Through a collaborative process, we created an "effective teams checklist" for teams to use to set up and monitor their teams. The list includes things like creating norms and agendas, staying on task, sharing air time, and having clear goals. This list means that facilitating an effective meeting is no longer up to an individual; it's a set of expectations that everyone agrees to.

In addition, the ILT has been very deliberate about using protocols and modeling effective team structures as a way for team leaders to experience these tools as a participant before using them as a leader. We practice giving "warm" and "cool" feedback on documents that people prepare. We use the affinity protocol and the 5-whys protocol to identify possible root causes of a problem.[2] In addition, we use detailed agendas and rotate facilitation, note taking, and the role of timekeeper with the expectation that team leaders will take these practices back to their teams.

A funny thing happens when you expect and model certain structures for group learning. People start to use them. One team leader very honestly confessed, "At first I thought the whole agenda thing was infantile and insulting. But I have to admit, it's useful. Now we use them more at our team meetings and it's actually helping." One team started taking notes online so everyone could follow along during the meeting. "We love it!" one of the team members boasted, "It keeps us on track with our team decisions." Now others also have adopted the practice.

Another effective way to foster a whole-group perspective is through a formal debriefing process at the end of meetings. This is not a novel idea. Many people do it, and I had been meaning to do it for years. However, we always seemed to run out of time. With our renewed focus on effective teams, those final minutes are now sacred. It's amazing how much difference those brief three to five minutes have made in improving our process and fostering a big picture perspective among more people.

While it sometimes elicits friendly groans as the clock nears the end time (or occasionally runs slightly over), we now end every meeting with a few minutes for the plus/delta protocol. The protocol consists of two questions: "What helped your learning?" (plus) and "What could help your learning more next time?" (delta). Or, alternatively, "What made this meeting productive? What could make it more productive next time?" It's important to note the forward-looking nature of the questions. Rather than "What didn't go well at this meeting?" people are asked to think about improvements for the future. The questions are usually answered in a whole-group discussion, but sometimes people respond anonymously in writing.

During the plus/delta process, people make suggestions not only about the agenda or the facilitator's decisions, but also about group behavior. "We started late and we could have gotten more done if we'd started on time. Next time we should all try to get here a minute ahead of time." "We disagreed with each other and that helped push our thinking." "We got off-topic and so we didn't get through the agenda. Next time we need to stay on-task more." Through this process—used at whole staff meetings as well as committee meetings—everyone adopts a leader perspective in thinking about how to improve the next meeting.

Our note-taking process has gotten crisper and more helpful as a result of suggestions made during these plus/delta debriefs. From "We need to include our meeting goal clearly on the meeting notes" to "We need to include times next to each agenda item so we can all monitor our talking time" to "The plus/delta from the last meeting should be on the notes to remind us what we want to improve upon" and "Can we include our process goals on the sheet to remind us what we're working on in our group behavior?"

### Use Documentation to Cultivate a Whole-School Perspective

Surprisingly, for something so mundane, documentation plays an important role in developing a sense of collective responsibility. At first, I didn't require that people document their commitments. It felt like micromanagement. Now we carefully document team and schoolwide action plans, curriculum, and policies. Documents that set forth shared teaching expectations shape culture. They affirm a coherent approach to specific aspects of practice and counter the typical egg-crate model of expectations varying from classroom to classroom. Even adding just a few paragraphs is enough to send the message "We collectively believe this as a [grade or school], and we are committed to carrying it out."

Shared curriculum maps and report cards now guide teams' planning. The first/second grade team designed and committed to using a five-step process for teaching and solving word problems that has now been passed on to the third/fourth grade team. The literacy team's "handwriting policy"—more like a passionate manifesto born out of heated debate—establishes a consistent set of practices that build from grade to grade. No longer will children end up with doctor's handwriting in third grade. We have a schoolwide commitment.

Make no mistake, there's still variation across the school—there's a whole lot that goes on in an elementary classroom, and it doesn't all have to be aligned. While in one class students take home "Friday Folders" stuffed with their latest work to share with family, down the hall students post weekly reports to the classroom blog including updates on the caterpillars about to burst out of their cocoons. One teacher's husband helps her students prepare "You Were There" videos to show what they've learned in history. And another teacher takes the teaching of root words to new heights with hallway displays, illustrated guessing games, and Scrabble tournaments. But in some areas, teachers share their expertise to build common goals—and the plans and strategies to get there.

The documents' power is not in giving the final word. On the contrary, these documents generally go through frequent and ongoing revisions. The power is that they belong to all of us, or rather, we all belong to them. They represent an agreement to follow through with specific practices. The documents take improvement efforts away from the individual and assert them as collective endeavors.

The documents also hold us accountable. When a staff member explained the importance of getting the school improvement plan right, she said she wanted a document she could post on the wall and refer to all year. It would remind her of timelines, practices, and benchmarks that she had agreed to follow.

In this way, shared documents can help teachers who may shy away from exercising leadership with their peers, especially when asking people to talk about their own teaching practice. A document is impersonal.

Documents helped the staff adopt new ways of talking to each other. During the first inquiry cycle, some teams had a hard time moving from the learner-centered problem to the related problem of practice that teachers needed to own. One team in particular kept talking about how students struggled with reading responses and never moved to examining their teaching to find related gaps. It was hard for peers to push each other.

As a consequence, teams got templates with space and prompts for teachers to work through each step of the inquiry cycle. "What can we change in our own practice that will have an impact on student learning related this area?" For some teachers, reading this prompt from a sheet is easier than feeling as though it's coming from themselves. *This is a question the whole school is working on; I'm not trying to be personally pushy with my teammates.* Documents—an external source of authority—remove the pressure from the peer leader and make it easier for the group to view improvement as collaborative work. Eventually, we want teachers to exercise leadership without a crutch, but at the beginning, people need support to make this shift.

## GIVE BACK MEANINGFUL WORK

Increasingly, teams of teachers lead staff meetings. Standing in front of fifty to sixty peers quite literally provides a whole-school perspective: the presenters *see* the whole school at once. When you have to share a point of view, convince colleagues of the value of something, or give an update on work accomplished, you wonder what the listeners are thinking. You have to *think* from the mindset of colleagues across the school as well. Experiences like these—real work that demands considering the needs of all students—develop a leadership perspective. To achieve this, principals need to give teacher teams meaningful work, trust them to do it, allow them to experience both positive and negative repercussions of the work, and let people fail as they learn to succeed.

### Trust People; Don't Micromanage

When teams are untested, turning over substantive work can feel particularly risky. What if they don't do a good job? What if I don't set the parameters right and they go in the wrong direction? It can be tempting to turn over inconsequential decisions. What should our school mascot be? Should the dance assembly be in the fall or the spring? These tasks are safe since their decisions won't affect anything of real substance. Of course, that's also the problem. If we want people to look beyond their classrooms and invest in the work of teams, they need to feel that their work matters—that their considerable time and effort will make a difference and that we trust them.

Ultimately, a principal has to trust people to do good work. With whatever the work is—curriculum mapping, setting team improvement goals, creating whole-school assemblies, designing the before-school tutoring program. This requires setting clear parameters ahead of time. Rescinding decision-making authority later on can lead to feelings of resentment and disengagement as people feel micromanaged by the leader. After setting clear expectations, a principal needs to step out of the way and let people do the problem solving.

Turning over control hasn't been easy. I often have a preformed idea, and I have to confess, it usually feels like a good one. I have to hold my tongue and remind myself another, overarching leadership goal is in place here. The goal is not to see my idea play out, as satisfying as that would feel. It's to engage teachers in owning the problem, designing and implementing a solution, and gaining the sense of satisfaction that comes from making improvement happen. Now that I've seen this cycle occur and witnessed the pride teachers have in their team and in their work, it's easier for me to give up personal ownership.

An important lesson about trusting people came early on. One fall, teams examined student writing data to determine a focus for their inquiry cycle work. After careful analysis and discussion, teams created and submitted goals and plans. As I read the fourth grade team's goals, their focus on narrative writing seemed misguided. Improving expository writing would have more applications across content areas and, it seemed to me, would provide more benefit than what they'd chosen. I told them my concern.

The fourth grade team was one of the more hard-working teams in the school; they assured me they were covering all the genres and could show me the evidence. After another cautionary e-mail from me and a few hallway conversations, one of the teachers asked to meet. We had a strong relationship, and she spoke frankly and helpfully. "It feels bad that you keep questioning our decision, Sarah. It feels like you don't trust us."

This wise—and brave—teacher was right, and I'm so grateful to her for speaking up. Most teachers would have kept this opinion to themselves, perhaps resentfully, and wouldn't have given me a chance to learn from the situation and repair the trust. There had always been two goals in this process: improve student learning and establish and strengthen a process for adult learning. Balancing the need for both is a critical leadership move.

Yes, the choice of an action plan focus is important. It needs to be based on careful examination of demonstrated student learning. However, there is rarely only a single area that needs improvement. When there's more than one area to choose from, the difference of which genre to improve pales compared to the difference teachers feel when they fully own the process.

Sometimes it's less important to be right in the short term and more important to support a teacher-led process that will generate more right decisions in the long term. The teachers learned new teaching techniques and applied them with good results. Students' writing improved significantly, and as an unexpected benefit, their reading of fiction did as well.

In other situations, trusting a teacher or a team has meant allowing them to miss the mark. Because parameters have been set ahead of time, these aren't large-scale failures by any means. But sharing leadership means increasing messiness. The first time a teacher leads a staff meeting, it's likely that we'll get off track with time and we won't get to everything on our agenda. No doubt I underestimated timing as a new facilitator, so why would the situation be any different for someone else? After the meeting, when there's time to reflect, this developing teacher leader will get useful insights into group dynamics, her own reactions, and what to do differently next time.

## Resist the Temptation to Make the Work Easier

Meaningful improvement efforts are often, frankly, a lot of work. They can feel complicated, time intensive, and sometimes stressful. Teachers already work hard. It's tempting to try to do them a favor by completing some of the work for them. Again, this is a case of short-term gain, long-term loss. Teachers won't protest when the leader reduces the load, but they won't gain as much from the task either. Taking responsibility for the outcomes of a whole grade or for the success of the school does entail more heavy lifting. As a result, however, teachers also experience the satisfaction and increasing sense of effectiveness that comes when their work produces results.

One year, there was a lot of excitement about improving our work with English language learners, the focus of our school improvement plan. Staff members had read a book over the summer about language development, and at a whole-staff meeting, small groups brainstormed key takeaways and specific practices we should implement. At the next ILT meeting, we worked to summarize these practices in a document to share with staff. There was lively discussion and a sense that we were articulating something important.

As we neared the end of the meeting and weren't yet finished, the facilitator asked what the next steps should be. Someone suggested condensing the practices into a shorter document with a few overarching categories so it could guide our work across classrooms. Nods around the table showed everyone's agreement.

Here was a group of teachers who had agreed to meet for an additional ninety minutes after completing a long day of teaching. It wasn't a secret how much work these grade-level representatives had on their plates. Out of respect and admiration, my impulse was to volunteer to do this job—to be a team player and carry this weight for the team. Instead, mindful of lessons about developing teacher leadership, I steeled myself and asked, "Is there someone who would be willing to create that document before the next ILT meeting?"

There was a long silence and during that wait, I wondered if I was asking too much—if this would turn the tide from engagement to resentment. Finally, one teacher hesitantly offered, "I can do it if someone does it with me." Another teacher quickly agreed to do it with the first. A third teacher also offered her help saying, "I don't think it will be too hard." Someone else made a suggestion about formatting, and suddenly the conversation took off again.

A few minutes later, when the meeting ended, most people remained in the conference room as conversations continued. The three volunteers huddled at one end of the table looking at calendars and figuring out a time to meet. There was lots of nodding and brainstorming as they talked about what they thought they would do with the list. The next meeting's facilitator and the just-finished facilitator planned when they would draft the agenda for the next ILT meeting. The room was filled with a sense of purposeful work—and collective responsibility.

The document this group generated ended up being a crucial reference point for our learning that year. We pulled it out at almost every ILT meeting and used it to guide grade-level action plans. At times throughout the year, we would return to it and ask, "What did we mean by _____?" and members of that original group of three would answer. On occasions like this, I was grateful that I hadn't offered to condense the list and that the document that served as our touchstone was created by teacher leaders. Witnessing the payoffs from this experience has made it easier to resist my helping instinct that limits the influence of teachers' leadership.

The impulse to help teams also comes in other manifestations. Sometimes we may be tempted to intervene when colleagues resist the leadership of teacher teams. However, if teams are truly going to take the lead, we also have to let them take the heat for their decisions. This realization was brought home to me in an experience with the A-team.

Over the course of four months, the A-team had collected input from teams and staff meetings to be able to engage the whole school in the design of a shared approach to discipline. At that spring morning's meeting, however, the whole process seemed ready to fall apart when the sixth grade team suddenly reported they didn't want to have to follow a whole-school plan. The sixth grade representative avoided her colleagues' eyes as she shared this information, which reached the listeners like a punch in the stomach. A-team members sagged in their chairs. From the beginning, they had known they faced a challenge proposing a single approach that everyone could agree to and abide by in their classrooms. Yet support from many colleagues had encouraged the A-team during the long and involved effort. With this latest news, however, what little energy they had left was quickly disappearing.

My jaw tightened at the representative's report. In my view this was nothing more than a last-minute tantrum from the sixth grade teachers. The A-team members looked so defeated; it wasn't clear they would be able to recover their sense of schoolwide authority. Everything in me wanted to march down the hall to give that sixth grade team a stern talking-to. However, I could easily picture how that approach would backfire: the boss comes and demands that you follow your peers' recommendations. It would undermine the A-team's authority and call into question the concept of teacher leadership. People could easily think it was all just a ruse for me to get my way in the guise of team leadership.

In the end, the A-team's teacher chair met with the sixth grade team and hashed out misunderstandings, concerns, and confusions. Having this teacher leader meet with the team felt like sending her into the firing range, but she came out unscathed and even more confident. After their conversation, the sixth grade teachers came to a better understanding of the process and their role in it. They supported the new plan. Over the years, their participation has grown from half-hearted at the beginning to more full participation now, and the A-team's plan has become a backbone of our school.

## Turn Over Leadership Before People Are Ready to Lead

As Richard Elmore frequently reminds people, "You learn to do the work by doing the work." What makes this hard with leadership is that when people first lead, they aren't very good at it. And that's exactly the right time to turn over the reins. There's the paradox.

Placed in a formal leadership role (such as facilitator, presenter, or team leader), teachers learn to think from a new perspective. Out of necessity, they assume the big picture view of how to move a team, committee, or whole school forward. Doing so builds ownership, greater investment, and more expert ideas of how to address learning problems. Over time, the experience also builds concrete leadership skills.

The truth is, no one is ever fully ready because you only fully learn to lead by leading. This makes it harder to turn over this task but also easier to know when: earlier than you think. So I need to feel comfortable giving the work to teachers and committees before I think they're capable of doing the perfect job. I need to embrace it as a leadership development strategy.

At my coach's prompting, I allow teachers to facilitate and take notes at all ILT meetings. At first, these roles were hard to turn over. Were people really ready for that level of group leadership? Facilitating these meetings was no easy job. The agendas were always too full, people got off-track, decisions weren't easy, and bringing issues to closure was challenging. Turning over those responsibilities seemed premature. And yet, how would people learn to carry out these responsibilities except by leading?

Based on a model that Elliot shared, we now have rotating roles, including note-taker, facilitator, timekeeper, and—how did we survive without it?—snack provider. Before facilitating an ILT meeting, next week's facilitator meets with the coaches, the previous meeting's facilitator, and me to write an agenda and develop a plan for the meeting. This process is time consuming but results in well-planned meetings and, hopefully, increased leadership capacity.

The difference at meetings is appreciable—more people speak, more people offer dissenting opinions, there are fewer questions about the agenda and more suggestions of how to improve our work together. When a visitor remarked that our ILT meetings are loud affairs, I took it as a compliment. People care passionately, speak forcefully, and rarely have to be cajoled into sharing their opinion.

A few months into this practice, previous members of the ILT joined our group for a planning meeting about the following year's professional development cycle. As the ILT facilitator moved us efficiently through the agenda, summarized people's thinking, and identified decisions that needed to be made, the former members exchanged glances. "This is really different from when I was on ILT!" one person said. The others agreed. With admiration, one of them said, "You are working at a totally different level."

Not every meeting is like this. Maintaining this momentum takes ongoing practice from all of us. I'm constantly drawn to direct the meeting. It's useful to remind myself that when teachers carry the responsibilities of facilitator, they're building muscles that help the whole school. After practicing this way for a while, a norm develops across the school that teachers take the lead in running meetings.

This year, assistant teachers asked for a time to meet as a team as well. Two assistants agreed to share the role of team leader. Right away they met to plan the agenda, sent it out to their colleagues, took notes at the meeting, e-mailed the notes to team members, and followed up with me to get resources (videos, a protocol, and an article) to use in leading the next meeting. With input from their colleagues, they planned and led meetings about effective classroom management strategies, recognizing learning disabilities, and working with autistic students. I smiled when I saw that their agenda template included time reserved for the plus/delta protocol.

## Make Teacher Leadership Visible

The default culture is strong. People are used to working in isolated silos. They need reminders that the norms are shifting. Their peers now take a broader perspective and they should, too. To normalize this changing perspective among teachers, naming it helps. "Something Shirley said at the math team made me think of this." "Have you checked with the A-team? I know they're still revising the homework policy." "Yes, the third grade art project is great. That team started planning it a few months ago." And at almost every mention of the school values, I remind people of the collaborative, team-based process we went through to create them. People need to know that teams are meeting, what they're doing, and how we're benefitting from their work.

When the physical education teacher asked about devoting a school day to fitness, I directed him to ask the A-team. It would have been very easy to approve this request or to send a question in the staff e-mail—or even to ask the A-team myself. However, for people to internalize the authority of teams, a leader needs to continually cultivate staff members' sense of accountability to each other. When the Sheltered English Immersion team leader brought her team's concerns about new assessment procedures directly to the ILT, it was clear people were getting the hang of internal accountability and teacher leaders' authority.

## ADOPT TWO-TRACK THINKING

Supporting teacher leadership requires a mental shift in what a leader pays attention to. In past meetings, my attention was exclusively focused on the topic of discussion. What will we focus on for our school improvement plan? How should we involve parents in the new school values? What should be included in the new staff handbook? What should be the plan for our next two staff meetings? Once I recognized my responsibility to cultivate leadership, meetings became more complicated. Instead of one focus, I now have two. One goal is the stated outcome of the meeting—a plan for whatever it is we are deciding—and the other is to build leadership around that issue.

Thinking on these two different tracks at the same time requires being in the conversation and simultaneously stepping back from it and observing. How can I help people think about the problem from a schoolwide perspective? How do I help more people feel responsible for this work? When we're stuck in disagreement, how can I engage the group in figuring out how to get our momentum back again? Someone is blaming parents. Rather than stepping in to address this issue myself, how can I engage the group in responding to it? We're doing a plus/delta exercise in a meeting, and no one mentions that some team leaders didn't do their assignment. What would get the teachers to talk to each other about this rather than have it come from me?

Two-track thinking goes by a variety of names. Ronald Heifitz and Donald Laurie call this "getting on the balcony."[3] In their research, they find that successful leaders spend time on the dance floor to know the details of what's going on, but they also get on the balcony to have a view of the whole organization. To understand what's needed from a big-picture perspective. Similarly, an award-winning symphony conductor described her job as thinking about three things simultaneously: what the symphony just played (so she can make adjustments), what they are currently playing (so she can actively conduct), and what they're about to play (so she can anticipate what they'll need from her).[4] Both of these metaphors help explain this complicated leadership task, but only practice helps develop the skill.

When teachers disagree about whether the action plan has too many goals, in the past I would have made a difficult decision about how to proceed. After learning to do two-track thinking, I now force myself to pause and think of how to enlist the group in solving the process dilemma: "How should we decide what direction to go in? How will we decide?" Teachers shouldn't feel they're arguing before a judge. At these meetings, they're engaging with each other. They should own the process as well.

Sometimes, getting off the dance floor and onto the balcony is particularly hard. When a teacher facilitator is leading a protocol and doesn't hold people to the steps. Or the facilitator lets a discussion go on too long and people are antsy. In the context of school, where time is so precious, it feels hard to lose time or engagement at meetings. If too many meetings are slow and inefficient, people may turn off. My instinct is to quickly correct the situation and get us back on track. At the same time, as leaders, we have to be aware that when we insert ourselves in such situations, we risk diminishing others' authority and slowing their learning. That also would be a substantial loss.

At the end of the day, knowing when to intervene and when not to do so is a judgment call. Perhaps there's a way to intervene that still affirms the teacher leader's authority. More often, the misstep in question is not actually that bad and ignoring it not so consequential. And always, it's about choosing what to prioritize; this requires a fluid ability to go back and forth between the balcony and the dance floor. To listen to the music the group is currently making and to anticipate what complicated pieces they'll have to play in the future. What does the group need right now? What does this teacher need in her growth as a leader? What will propel our learning the most? All the while, the meeting continues as we learn to make these decisions in real time.

# CHAPTER 5

# Resistance and Work Avoidance

Most of us spend too much time on what is urgent and not enough time on what is important.

—Steven Covey

Why is it so hard to improve what we do? This is not an idle question. For our students with the greatest needs, improvement can't be delayed. The third grade immigrant student who is a beginning reader and starting to fall behind in other subjects. The low-income kindergartener who entered school behind his peers and appears to have an uphill climb ahead of him. The sixth grader with a learning disability who mystifies her teacher with her nonsensical responses in math. Students need school to work for them. For many students, it does. For too many of our most vulnerable students, however, it doesn't. These students' success depends on all of us improving the system soon enough so that it will make a difference for their learning.

Improvement efforts falter in schools for a variety of reasons. Poor leadership explains a lot of the problem. Frustrated and tired staff members who are initiative-weary may be another reason. But some initiatives fail to gain traction even when everyone shares intentions, goals, and commitment. Even in those situations, teachers and leaders don't follow through with plans, or the follow-through is half-hearted and gradually morphs back into what practice used to look like. Or a steady stream of very reasonable questions and concerns about the plan distracts a leader from launching it. Why is this, and how can a leader speed up the growth we all—students, teachers, administrators—need?

Most leaders aren't surprised when they experience resistance to new ideas. Realistically, it would be more surprising if everyone leapt up and clapped—as if they had been wanting to make a change and just hadn't had a leader tell them to do it. Entering Douglass, I knew that introducing collaborative problem solving and increased coherence involved changing the culture of the school, which would mean holding people in discomfort over a long period of time. Few people do that willingly, so I knew there would be pushback.

I hadn't anticipated what the pushback would look or feel like, however. In fact, for a long time, I didn't recognize it as resistance. And therefore, I took people's comments and concerns at face value. "Sarah, you're taking away all of our autonomy!" "You're micromanaging our time." "You're asking too much!" "Professionals should get to choose whether they want to work with a coach." Tossed about by the rough waves of reactions like these, I frequently questioned my decisions. Should I lessen what I'm asking people to do? Is this the straw that will break everyone's back? I struggled to know how to read the situation.

As experienced leaders know, these forms of pushback are the predictable resistance that comes with improvement. Learning this lesson proved to be an important first step. I had to first recognize what resistance looks like and then understand the reasons behind it. Once the roots of the response are diagnosed, they can be addressed. Importantly, leaders also need to recognize how they themselves may unconsciously be part of the problem. No one is immune to resisting this work. If we don't face up to our own resistance, we may slow the very growth we seek for our schools.

## RECOGNIZE RESISTANCE

Sometimes resistance is direct. "I don't want to share my class reading data with the team." In this form, a leader can address the disagreement directly. Other times, it's less obvious. A grade-level team repeatedly cancels and reschedules the release time designated for the teachers to create their curriculum map. A teacher keeps running out of time to implement the newly designed intervention. A leadership team fills the agenda with other topics so the clock runs out before having to tackle the dreaded item. The principal adds more detail to the budget presentation instead of observing in classrooms. These forms of resistance are harder to address because people may seem agreeable to the concept, but the work just doesn't get done. Leadership experts Ronald Heifitz and Donald Laurie identify this as "work avoidance."[1]

As a classroom teacher, I could spot work avoidance a mile away. The child who sharpened his pencil nine times during writers' workshop or who always had to go to the bathroom during math class. The endless questions from the child who was scared to initiate unfamiliar tasks. Or the classic case of the child kicking his neighbor under the table because the assignment felt too hard. These students all had worries or fears about the work at hand and chose ways to avoid having to face the difficult task head-on.

Much to my surprise, as a principal, I discovered that adults engage in very similar patterns of work avoidance. Even kicking a neighbor has its adult equivalent in snide remarks in the staff room. However, it took a long time for me to recognize all the adult versions of work avoidance—in my own habits as well as those of others.

## What Work Avoidance Looks Like

When a leader is trying to turn the ship in a new direction, small behaviors can derail improvement simply by diverting attention and energy. This became clear while I was working with the math team one year. When it was time to engage in detailed conversations about instruction, a highly skilled veteran teacher became uncomfortable. She was used to more casual conversations with colleagues and a hands-off approach from administrators.

Slowly a pattern developed. When the conversation turned to practice, this teacher would launch into a critique about how mandates from the central office inhibited good practice. She always made good points, and, along with others at the meeting, I would find myself caught up in discussing the merits of various central office moves. The meeting would end, and we would have avoided talking about instruction . . . again.

Eventually, it became clear that these conversations were diversion tactics. Not conscious ones. Rather, when this teacher got uncomfortable with the conversation, she would instinctively move away from it. Because this behavior wasn't obvious as work avoidance, I joined in, enabling the distraction further. This prevented her—and the team—from moving to a higher level of reflection and practice.

After eventually identifying what was going on, I realized I needed to hold steady with the work at hand, no matter how uncomfortable. If I had been more skilled in developing teacher leadership at the time, I would have named the problem as I saw it and asked the group how they wanted to solve it. In this case, I shared my observations and suggested an approach going forward. When issues out of our control came up in the meeting, anyone around the table could flag this situation for the group. We would then stop to assess whether there was an action step we should take to address the concern. If there wasn't, then we would end the divergent conversation.

To her credit, this teacher later thanked me and acknowledged that she had been taking up meeting time talking about things we couldn't change. As she did more listening, she heard colleagues share and has been able to open up very slowly to talking about her instruction. She's still not comfortable with the process, but she's no longer working so hard to avoid it. And I've learned the benefit of holding firm.

We all do things instinctively to make ourselves feel more at ease. It's the leader's job to recognize this behavior and hold steady, even when people unconsciously avoid the hard work.

## Name It to Address It

When an outside observer first suggested that staff members at my school were exhibiting work avoidance, I pushed back hard. My staff members work incredibly hard. They are far from slackers. What's deceptive, however, is that adult work avoidance *often looks like hard work*. The issue is

less about avoiding work in general and more about avoiding the particular work that is on our plate at the time—work that may feel hard,
unfamiliar, or uncomfortable.

An adult may not go to the bathroom every time she needs to tackle a
new and unfamiliar task. Instead, she may spend hours researching grade-
appropriate books for an upcoming unit and thus run out of time to address the important and complicated work of differentiating the lesson
for the lowest-performing students. Similarly, I find myself putting off
difficult conversations in favor of writing up an observation or doing just a
bit more planning for an important meeting. There's always an abundance
of work to do in schools, so without much effort, the stuff we don't want
to do simply sinks to the bottom of the priority list. Even though there's
no deliberate resistance, the work just doesn't get done. Naming these behaviors as work avoidance helps us recognize the need to address it.

## IDENTIFY REASONS FOR AVOIDING THE WORK

People avoid the work for a variety of reasons. They may not know how to
do it or it's unpleasant or other issues feel more important or some combination of reasons. Unfortunately, leaders can't expect people to know or
share their reasons directly. (It would be easier if they did: "I don't want to
plan this lesson together because it exposes my fear of math to my peers"
or "I am scared to try this new thing because I'm worried I might fail in
front of people I respect.") Whether it's outright resistance or more subtle
work avoidance, leaders need to first recognize it as such and then diagnose the root cause to be able to figure out how to address it.

Misdiagnosis—or lack of diagnosis—wastes valuable time. This point
became clear one year while I was working with a veteran teacher who
was vocal in her pronouncements that a particular set of formative reading assessments were not useful with her students. Coaches, colleagues,
and administrators took turns explaining the relevance and usefulness of
these tools, and still she resisted doing them or did them quickly with no
meaning.

Then the real reason for this teacher's resistance surfaced. In the middle of a whole-staff review of the assessment tool, she was overheard to mutter quietly, "Just one more thing I don't know how to do." The coaches and I had misdiagnosed her resistance. Rather than learn the merits of the tool, she needed to learn how to implement it. What came out as frustration was in fact a need for more training. When we understood the need, we were able to intervene. It was a delicate process—she was clearly uncomfortable with her lack of expertise—but with more training, she learned to use the assessment in ways that she acknowledged were useful. I only wished we had diagnosed her need earlier.

As leaders, we have to listen past the words to try to identify the real problem. Someone nods in agreement but doesn't change her behavior. What could be behind that? How is this person thinking about the problem? When people say "too hard" or "not worth it," it's a signal that they may need more skill building. Importantly, knowing the signals requires knowing the learners—in this case, teachers—really well.

## There's Not Enough Trust

For the third grade team that struggled to plan a math lesson together, the main barrier was a lack of trust. Later that year, the team went on a day-long retreat to design a unit that they would all teach together. They began with personal sharing about each other's families and interests. They had time to hash out their hopes and worries about the unit. After the retreat, one of the teachers came back to me and almost by way of apology for that earlier meeting said, "You know, Sarah, we just didn't know each other. After we shared, we got so much more done."

People have to trust each other to take risks with each other, to give and get honest feedback, to ask for help or say they don't understand. Lack of trust is a frequent source of people's resistance. When there's trust, it's much easier for people to tackle the unknown.

## We Don't Know How to Do It

As in the reading assessment example, often the reason people avoid doing a task is that they don't know how to do it. This is one of the more straightforward concerns to address but one of the most difficult to diagnose because people don't want to admit it. The lack of understanding often comes out in some form of blaming.

In a talk on school improvement, Professor Janice Jackson once reflected on her experience working with an underperforming school where the students were mostly poor and mostly children of color. Teachers repeatedly told her, "My kids can't _____ [fill in the blank: learn to analyze, solve multistep problems, read complex text]." Listening to the story, I expected Professor Jackson, who herself is African American, to express indignation. Of course, these students can complete these tasks! How could teachers display such low expectations of their students?

Instead, this wise professor showed compassion. She had come to understand that when teachers say "My kids can't do that" they really mean "*I don't know how* to teach my students to do that." Professor Jackson's insightful diagnosis of this root cause was likely the reason for her success helping schools. She didn't spend time trying to convince teachers that their children could in fact master the skills. Instead, she invested in skill building and got results.

## It's Uncomfortable

Sometimes the work is just plain hard or unpleasant, and it's easier not to do it. We've all done this. This type of avoidance is easier to recognize in others than it is to see in ourselves.

It's time to meet with a teacher to share negative feedback or to tell the team that their work isn't rigorous enough or to write a letter to the community about a complicated issue. These examples are tasks that at some point or another I've put off, continuing to copy them from one week's to-do list to the next. I always had a legitimate reason to put off the task or not get it done. "I need more observational data before meeting with that teacher." Or "It's been a really tough day. I think I should wait until I'm fresh before talking to that team leader about the poor quality of the team's curriculum maps." Or "Maybe I'll get more information about the situation tomorrow. I'll wait before writing the letter."

These mental responses are often accompanied by a vague, nagging sense of unease. The reasoning feels shady. (Guilt is a good red flag here.) Learning to name this behavior as work avoidance helps me be more honest. For whatever reason, the task feels uncomfortable. That's not going to change. There will be more disagreeable tasks tomorrow. The only thing to do is grit my teeth and do it. Mark Twain's sage advice applies: "Eat a live frog first thing in the morning and nothing worse will happen to you the rest of the day." Do the thing we dread first.

## We're Perfectionists (And We Don't Like to Delegate)

As the saying goes, sometimes the perfect is the enemy of the good. For many hard-working educators, our identity is wrapped up in doing things well. The problem is that learning a new skill involves being a beginner. Learning is bound to be messy, and that unformed messiness is bound to make perfectionists queasy. Naming this feeling helps. Perfectionists need to be pushed to have the courage to be mediocre.

Alysha is a teacher who falls into this category. Ever diligent and hard-working, Alysha wanted to schedule specific time during the day for reading and math interventions with students. She designed an admirable but overly complex plan. It was to be highly individualized, varying each day for each child. It sounded wonderful but was just too complicated for her to pull off at that time. So she kept putting it off until she would have time to implement it to her standards. Meanwhile, some kids needed targeted help and weren't getting it. She needed to adopt a less complicated, possibly less "perfect" system so that something got off the ground. After hearing this feedback, she scaled back, began implementing, and interventions began taking place. First, though, she had to be pried loose from the need to get it perfect the first time she tried it. She had to be reminded of the need for first pancakes.

Teachers aren't the only ones whose perfectionism and tight control of the outcomes mean that nothing gets done. Too often I have found myself carrying a load that seemed to only get higher and higher, blocking my view, and yet I wouldn't let any of it go. In fact, all I had to do was stop clutching those items—and my vision of how they'd be carried out—so tightly and share them with others.

In my first year, for example, two Sheltered English Immersion teachers said they thought whole-school assemblies would help all students feel part of the same community. It was a great idea but organizationally challenging to coordinate. I said I would consider how we could do it. Not surprisingly, as a first-year principal, I saw plenty of other issues that felt important. Despite assemblies feeling useful, they didn't happen that year. Or, regrettably, the next.

Looking back on this situation, I find it hard to understand why I didn't do the obvious. I should have told the two teachers, "Great idea—make a plan and let's do it!" As a new principal, I felt every new idea was up to me to implement. Every problem was mine to solve. In addition, with ideas I cared about—such as an assembly that might include a large audience of parents—my perfectionism kicked in, and I wanted to make sure the event would be perfect. Knowing how much effort this would take meant the idea moved even further down the to-do list. When leaders carry this bloated feeling of responsibility, it's no wonder a lot of work gets left undone. It's exhausting to think about.

Finally, the logical step became clear. I released my need to control the assemblies and asked if teachers were interested in planning them. A group of five people signed up and began meeting before and after school. What happened shouldn't have surprised me, but it did. The resulting routines that they designed for Douglass assemblies were beyond anything I could have imagined or planned myself. The teachers created a whole-school, student-narrated video about our values, an original Douglass school song, a routine of affirming different languages spoken by our students, dancing, student presentations, poetry, and more. It was a powerful lesson: as an administrator, I need to give up the notion that for things to be right, I have to plan them. Share the work to get it done.

## We Don't Prioritize What's Important

In the midst of a steady, relentless drumbeat of demands for all of us in schools, prioritizing the right things takes vigilance. In *Rethinking Teacher Supervision and Evaluation*, former principal Kim Marshall quotes author Robert McKain, who wrote, "The reason most major goals are not achieved is that we spend our time doing second things first."[2] For the hard work of improvement to happen, our daily actions have to align with our priorities. Easier said than done.

This need to prioritize correctly is particularly true when a school leader falls victim to what Marshall calls "Hyperactive Superficial Principal Syndrome."[3] We race from one task to another, speeding around the building solving problems, tackling whatever falls in our path, flitting quickly from one task to the next without ever pausing to consider whether we're doing the right work.

For example, consider the principal whose mentor told her to take a minute to write the top three work priorities for the year in big print and post it over her desk. "Look at them often so you stay focused on the right things," said the mentor. Great idea, thought the principal, who never got to the task because . . . she was too busy.

Thinking about what might be the underlying cause of this busy-ness syndrome is useful. Adult development experts Robert Kegan and Lisa Lahey call it a "competing commitment."[4] We're committed to tackling the priority items—the long-term planning, the time for reflection, the careful planning for each meeting. And yet we have a competing commitment—often hidden from our conscious thought—that is trumping the first.

For example, teachers' deeply held commitment to teacher autonomy may trump their very strong commitment to supporting students who would benefit from increased alignment from one grade to another. For a principal, an overriding pull might be to feel needed and to be an active, visible helper and problem solver, accessible at all times. As long as we feel the need to meet that commitment, we won't meet other commitments such as developing teacher leadership. We won't be willing to step back from the action and devote less time to attention seeking and more of our focus to high-priority work.

For me, the work that often gets left undone is the future-looking strategic thinking. For a year, I had a repeating note in my calendar to review the professional development needs of each teacher and make a plan to address them. Like so many other strategic items, this issue deserved careful attention and time. The problem was that it didn't have the urgency of the child who just ran out of the building or the teacher who is at her wit's end with a parent's complaints or the conflict that is brewing on one of the grade-level teams or the fact that the lunch line is still so slow that some kids have only five minutes to eat. So it just kept moving ahead to the next week until the year came to an end. I needed a strategy to save me from my own behaviors that were preventing me from doing what needed to be done—a way to prioritize what's important.

## CONTENDING WITH WORK AVOIDANCE

What can a leader do to make sure improvement takes hold—both for herself and others? Diagnosing the resistance is the first crucial step. Which of the root causes described previously is behind this particular case of resistance? With diagnosis in hand, a principal is better equipped to address resistance however it might appear. Another critical step is to create an environment where people are more able to tackle the hard stuff. Two ways to do that are by making it safe to fail and urgent to improve.

### Make It Safe to Fail: Model and Reinforce a Learner's Stance

Fear plays a significant role in why people don't follow through with improvement efforts. Fear of making mistakes, fear of peers' judgment, fear of failing, fear of being unsettled for an extended period of time during a learning process. Learning will always involve some sense of risk, but feelings of psychological safety can reduce it. Leaders lubricate the improvement process by increasing trust and normalizing learning.

Leaders' attitude toward learning provides a model for others, so it's important to be thoughtful about how we approach the work. Whenever I ask for feedback about my leadership (in a survey or plus/delta session), I share the comments publicly—both positive and negative. For example, after feedback from my leadership coach Elliot Stern, the staff heard that I was working to develop teacher leadership and reduce principal air time. When we host guest speakers or when a team or teacher presents information to the staff, we have an opportunity to model a learner's stance.

Saying "I'm a learner—I don't know how to do this" is a strength, not a weakness.

Taking a learner's stance also means I have to be careful not to beat myself up when mistakes happen. Teachers watch carefully. If I'm visibly crushed that my facilitation of a meeting went poorly, the message is clear: if you're going to facilitate a meeting at Douglass, it has to be perfect. I can wax on about first pancakes until the cows come home, but my actions will carry the most potent message. Leaders have to model how to mess up as part of modeling how to succeed.

When respected peers set the tone of being learners, they also pave the way for others. Drawing attention to these actions helps people see their impact. *Did you see how the tone changed at that meeting after you shared your confusion? What helped you feel able to do that? How could we get more people to do that?* Hopefully, they'll feel encouraged to continue to act in this way—to show courage in order to help others do the same.

In fact, the very teacher who muttered "another thing I don't know" eventually came to fill this role. She sincerely desires to support newer colleagues, and so this was a logical way to enlist her backing. In a few one-on-one conversations, we talked about the leadership she could provide to her team by sharing when she didn't understand something. The message started to sink in. When her team began learning a new strategy, she asserted clearly at the outset, "I don't think I use word walls very well. I'd like to learn how to use them more effectively with my students." This veteran teacher set the tone for the rest of her team to be learners. Her increasing comfort with not having all the answers helped her team tackle an unfamiliar task.

Particularly in our current climate when the focus is so often exclusively on results, we need reminders to celebrate and reinforce our collective learning process. It comes back to that process-results balance. Increasing adult learning is what will lead to improved results over the long term. We need to put the spotlight on this learning and reinforce our identity as a problem-seeking (not problem-avoiding) organization.

A moment that brought this thinking home happened at the end of my second year as principal. We had completed the first full inquiry cycle focused on improving writing at each grade level and had come together as a staff to hear each team's learning. Teachers sat in mixed-grade groups so that a representative from each team could explain the team's process. Animated exchanges among teachers in the different groups filled the library with a productive buzz. Colleagues leaned forward to read the student work a teacher was explaining. Teachers peppered each other with questions about student responses, how they measured growth, what they thought they should do next, how they solved the problems they encountered.

Teachers showed rubrics and templates and laughed sheepishly when describing how many versions they had gone through to get everyone on the team to agree. They also talked about wishing for more time to collect another source of data or to try another strategy. Colleagues asked, "What was hardest?" "Were kids able to transfer the vocabulary to other subject areas?" "Would you do it the same way another time?" Teachers were talking about problems but in a way that exuded confidence. They didn't ignore the magnitude of the challenges, but they didn't feel overcome by them either. They had a sense of their own power to enact change, a greater sense of agency and effectiveness.

Teachers who embrace learning in this way demonstrate what psychologist Carol Dweck calls a "growth mindset."[5] Learners who advance the most are not intimidated by enormous challenges. They view these challenges as opportunities to learn. This is a critical mental approach. When people grapple with a hard problem, try out new practices, and see results, they discover that the challenges of trying something new pay off. This practice reinforces the cycle of learning and helps people feel increasingly effective—and therefore more likely to engage in the cycle again. People with a growth mindset are less likely to avoid the work.

## Increase Urgency with the Right Kind of Accountability

Earnestly committing to our priorities usually isn't enough. As most of us know from our personal piles of unfulfilled New Year's resolutions, good intentions alone won't get us to follow through. We need to be strategic. If we could make the important things seem more urgent, they would be harder to avoid.

Keeping a finger on student learning data can increase urgency. The key is to make sure the process feels meaningful. When teachers themselves decide what kind of accountability to use in our school improvement plan, their inquiry cycles, or their own evaluations, it's more likely to motivate follow-through with goals.

Another way to increase urgency is to establish public accountability for important work. I publicly promise to report on various projects to relevant parent, teacher, or leadership committees because I know doing so will force me to actually complete these tasks (or at a minimum, initiate them so there's something to report). Similarly, we increase the likelihood of something getting done when team leaders have to give an update to the instructional leadership team, teams have to share their plans with the rest of the school, or teachers have to present their work to colleagues. Putting tasks on a shared agenda can resurrect them from the bottom of the to-do list to the top.

People respond to different forms of accountability. A superintendent friend is famous for always asking staff members two questions, "How can I support you, and how can I hold you accountable?" When we build accountability into the work, we help ourselves (and others) to get it done.

### Get the Amount of Pressure Right

As captured in the pressure cooker metaphor, creating the right amount of urgency is necessary, challenging, and risky. While working on my dissertation, I interviewed teacher leaders in one district who frequently referenced a particularly inspiring district leader. One person summarized her influence vividly: "She's absolutely committed to closing achievement gaps and she's incredibly motivating. If she told us to get up and run towards a brick wall, we would do it."

Although I never met this district leader, she has been an informal role model. Inspiring people in this way would be a great reputation to have. At the same time, I've gotten feedback that as a result of my exhortations, staff do leap up to run full speed into brick walls . . . and sometimes they feel bruised and exhausted from the consequences! Getting the pressure cooker at the right setting—to yield a healthy rather than debilitating amount of urgency—requires listening and observing carefully. It also requires being open to being wrong.

Stress that leads to burnout is different from urgency that leads to improvement. Often the difference is the amount of work people are required to tackle. Too often, teachers are simply expected to do too much. All the district leaders send messages of equal urgency about their pieces of the pie. The science director wants to convene workshops about the use of science journals, the math director wants everyone using the new math practice standards immediately, the special education director says a schoolwide assessment of accommodations would help us differentiate better, the ELA department has identified three high-leverage strategies to improve reading comprehension, and the list goes on and on.

Each request has merit on its own, but doing it all is just impossible. A principal colleague who always seemed effortlessly on top of her game confessed that one of her biggest struggles was simply deciding how much of all the district demands she could actually do. As leaders, we have to prioritize the work that comes in and have the courage to say no. Otherwise, the pressure's going to build up, and teachers will explode.

We can't just blame the district for overload. We also have to monitor the number of demands that we place on teachers. When we need to distinguish between work avoidance and simply too much work, there's no replacement for careful listening, observing, and then more listening. Is there too much pressure? Are people stretched too far outside their comfort zone to be productive? What do people need at this moment to keep learning and take important risks? What will reduce excessive levels of stress?

These questions came up one year when I was working with two teachers who were new to a grade and who resisted the newly rolled-out data meetings. One told me that my expectations were unreasonable and unfair. "You talk about first pancakes, Sarah, but you're expecting us to do Belgian waffles and Eggs Benedict! It's too much." Feeling sympathetic but committed to firm leadership, I responded by explaining the value of looking regularly at data. This teacher continued to express concerns. At some point, I stopped talking and really tried to listen.

After I listened for a long time, it became clear that the situation with these two teachers was different from that of other teachers, and their need for more planning time was real. They were drowning in the day-to-day preparation for a grade level new to each of them and a cohort that required more than the usual amount of differentiation. They needed more time simply figuring out what to teach the next day. The answer finally became clear: we talk about differentiating for varying student needs, so shouldn't we do the same for teachers? They needed and got additional release days to work on curriculum, which they said was helpful. Their frequent expressions of appreciation served as a useful reminder: getting the amount of pressure right requires sometimes being willing to adjust.

## BECOME COMFORTABLE WITH OTHERS' DISCOMFORT

Changes cause turbulence. Learning to recognize resistance for what it is makes the rough ride less intimidating. It allows us to read people's anxiety and stress more accurately. Once we understand where it's coming from, even in the midst of upheaval, we can stay calm and hold steady.

### Hold Steady

Hard-working teachers regularly come to the principal's office to say they feel overwhelmed or to share that data meetings are stressful or to worry that there's no way to give every student reading instruction each day. Listening to their struggles prompts an enormous desire to do something to make the situation better. To take away the discomfort. It's hard to watch teachers squirm or say they're overwhelmed. At the same time, difficult experiences can prompt growth.

Sometimes, as in the preceding example, the teachers are right and they are being asked to do too much. Other times, reducing whatever was stressful only means it has to be reinstated later when we discover it's an essential part of our improvement process. For the principal, a critical role of leading improvement is becoming more comfortable with people's discomfort.

Being able to deal with others' discomfort is often hardest when people we trust and respect tell us that things are about to blow. *Stress levels are too high; something needs to be done immediately!* Ronald Heifitz and Marty Linsky point out that this is a common phenomenon. "Your allies want you to calm things down at least for them, rather than stir things up."[6] Organizations going through change—especially those like Douglass that had not undertaken substantial change for decades—are stressful places to be. It's natural for people to want things to go back to the old, familiar routine.

In these moments, it's possible—useful—to empathize with the discomfort while still holding firm. It *is* uncomfortable to look at these numbers. They don't tell us everything. Sharing feedback with a peer *is* uncomfortable. It will probably be uncomfortable many times before it gets easier. And we need to take these hard steps forward together if we're going to get better.

Acknowledging what people are giving up is also helpful. There's real loss in change. When we empathize with the full range of emotions people are experiencing and don't minimize them, people feel more respected and understood as they push through whatever is difficult.

## Don't Take It Personally; Develop Thick Skin

Defensiveness, anger, and resentment directed toward leaders can all be forms of work avoidance. Learning not to take these behaviors personally helps leaders feel real compassion for the people involved. It also makes us more effective at improving their practice.

This awareness didn't come to me right away. It has come out of sometimes unpleasant experiences. Early on, I required an independent-minded teacher to meet with a colleague to jointly determine recess rules for children at their shared grade. She was extremely uncomfortable with this request and complained bitterly. She began by criticizing the colleague but quickly moved to what felt like personal attacks about me. "No one likes the changes you're making at the school. People talk about you behind your back all the time, and they're not saying good things. You're causing divisiveness among the faculty. You just don't get it."

It never occurred to me not to take her at her word (even though she wouldn't give any specific examples). These comments didn't change my expectations for the teacher, but they did cause many sleepless nights worrying that a revolution was mounting.

Since this interaction, I've come to understand that personal attacks are one of the occupational hazards of being a leader. Some people lash out at the leader—sometimes to my face—when they are pushed out of their comfort zone. Once again, it's important to remember that it's not about me; it's about the work. I would be lying if I said that personal attacks don't feel bad. However, recognizing this behavior as work avoidance has made me lose less sleep over it. This perspective ultimately helped me view the angry teacher with more compassion and realize what a difficult thing she was eventually able to do by working with her colleague.

## Become Comfortable with Your Own Discomfort

In just a few words, an eight-year-old student summed up the disequilibrium involved in the growth process. This usually bubbly and giggling girl faced challenging work she didn't want to do. After listlessly turning the paper over a few times only to find that the problem hadn't gone away, she turned sullen and whiny. As her protestations got louder, the teacher intervened with a reminder. "Kayla, third graders tackle challenges." The only response was a louder and more obstinate whine from Kayla's corner. The teacher was firm, "Kayla, show you are a strong third grader. Whining is a sign of weakness." To this, Kayla responded in a long drawn-out wail, "Then I want to be weak!"

I can still hear Kayla's mournful wail, and I relate to it now as much as I did in that moment. Facing challenges is hard. It demands a lot from us. Kayla did pull herself together that day and, with help, accomplished her task. We can, too.

CHAPTER 6

# Building Trust

*The relationship among the adults in the building has more impact on the quality and character of the school and the accomplishments of its youngsters than any other factor.*

—Roland Barth

Over the years, the kindergarten team at Douglass has evolved into a high-functioning group of professionals. Periodically, someone comments on the quality of their work to the team's leader, Lisette, an energetic, master teacher. Upon hearing this feedback, Lisette, a veteran of many different team configurations, inevitably stands a bit taller and adopts a serious tone as if demanding her listener pay attention. She says emphatically, "That's because there's trust."

Lisette and her teammates work efficiently together to plan curriculum each week, taking turns to find texts relevant to their thematic study and then using the texts for morning meeting, literacy work, and integrated art projects. Even though these dedicated teachers are at different stages of their careers—two close to retirement, one just starting, one mid-career—and very different people, they are close. They pass in and out of each other's classrooms frequently and easily, borrowing materials, sharing ideas from lessons they've just completed, and checking in. Their fine-tuned collaboration produces terrific curriculum. And their teamwork involves more than just collaboration.

One day, Lisette walked into her colleague's room and saw kids off-task and the teacher not responding. She absorbed what was going on and left, but she raised questions after school with her colleague, "What was going on? Kids weren't getting work done in your class today. That wasn't what we've been talking about for Writers Workshop." This question and following conversation prompted a breakthrough for this colleague who had been struggling with a management issue. With Lisette's help, this struggling teacher got additional resources and addressed the issue. These teammates were able to talk to each other honestly and hold each other accountable for student learning. They were proud enough of their efforts to tell me. In this conversation, Lisette again made sure to say by way of explanation, "It's because there's trust."

Trust is necessary for all the topics discussed previously and all that follow. None of the work gets done well without trust. Building a culture of trusting relationships happens not so much through big showy events, but in thousands of small, purposeful interactions that build up over time. Setting norms, following protocols, and simply getting to know colleagues are all important strategies. In this work of culture building, leaders need to develop strategies to ensure positive behaviors continue and negative ones stop. Leaders also need to remember that building culture is not a quick, breathless sprint, but rather a long, glorious jog. It feels great when you hit your stride.

## WHY ALL THE ATTENTION ON TRUST?

Talking about trust can feel squishy. How do you see it? Can you measure it? How much is enough? It may also feel more personal than professional. How much do people in the workplace actually need to trust each other to be able to do their jobs? Being trusted may feel nice, but how much does it affect the ultimate outcome of your work? Apparently a great deal, according to the research from multiple fields.[1]

Too often, in schools, we fall victim to the "culture of nice," where the priority is maintaining adult harmony rather than tackling difficult issues that affect student learning. People in these communities are warm and caring toward each other, but they probably wouldn't take the step that Lisette did with her colleague. Imagine if they did. Imagine if all teachers trusted each other enough to have these interactions that are meaningful and honest and focused on the ultimate goal: what is best for students.

With hard work, the Douglass staff has become a collaborative community. And some, like the kindergarten team, have gone further to become what has been called an "accountable" community.[2] They not only collaborate but also feel accountable to each other for results. Like Lisette, teachers in accountable communities push each other to do better. These are the communities where student learning accelerates the most.

As I strive to push more Douglass teams to be accountable to each other, I keep coming back to Lisette's insight. This kind of work requires trust. The benefits of an accountable community can't be achieved without this bedrock.

## BUILDING TRUST DOES NOT HAPPEN BY DEFAULT

At Douglass, the process of building trust has frequently felt uncomfortable, and staff haven't been shy telling me so. Often the behaviors that engender trust are ones that don't come easily to everyone (reaching out to people you don't know well, going public with things that feel hard, etc.). As I try to tell people, if we stick to what's comfortable, we won't move beyond the culture of nice. These steps that feel awkward now are going to make a difference in how we interact down the line.

Some culture-building behaviors can be put into an action plan (community building activities for the beginning of the year, use of protocols at meetings, creating norms). Others need to be lived. Leaders do this by naming, modeling, and reinforcing them all the time.

### Personal Connection

At a very basic level, people simply need time to get to know one another, to make a personal connection. In my first year as principal, I started every meeting with time for personal sharing. People had to find a partner they didn't know well and respond to simple prompts to get to know each other. After some people grumbled about this activity and said they didn't have the energy to be social at the end of a long school day, I stopped the practice. Time was always at a premium at these meetings, so making this concession was easy.

After a rocky year for our community, however, sharing time came back. It's now a nonnegotiable. People still often complain when staff meetings include assigned tables and they have to sit apart from their teammates. However, as they share with new colleagues, they forge connections they otherwise wouldn't make. The fourth grade teacher hears about the music teacher's small victory that day in class. The special educator shares with a colleague something she'd like to learn outside school. The reading interventionist listens to an assistant teacher share about a person who is important to her. Trust gets built out of connections like these.

One long-time upper-grade teacher, Rich, conceded that the first conversation he ever had with a particular first grade teacher was during one of these sharings. Since sharing "a place that is special to you," they now greet each other in the halls like old friends. When one of the first grade teacher's students needed a tutor, Rich was happy to find one of his students who could meet the need. These relationships affect more than just the human connection and occasional cross-grade collaborations like these. When we have to hammer out whole-school agreements and compromise to provide a more coherent experience for students, people know who their colleagues are. We can argue and listen and compromise and learn better because we are connected.

## Group Norms

Most teachers habitually create rules with kids every year. Doing the same with adults is no less necessary but feels a whole lot trickier. It takes conviction and spine to create a set of explicit expectations, or group norms—share air time, be respectful, be prepared—that guide the behavior of the school staff. In addition to feeling patronizing, for a number of adults, attending to group process doesn't feel like real work. It feels like a contrived and meaningless touchy-feely activity. They would rather not participate.

As leaders, we need to confidently face the skeptics or face what can be lost when we don't.

At a staff meeting early one year, teachers met in small groups to discuss an article on building effective teams. Recommendations from the article included respecting differences of opinion, sharing the role of facilitator, and coming up with group norms to guide meeting behavior. At one team's table, an outspoken veteran teacher spoke with real disdain and frustration. She thought it was insulting to have to consider using norms. "We're adults. We know how to act. We don't have to make up rules. Nobody here needs to be told what to do. If you have something to say, just speak up about it." She was clearly irritated by the ideas in the article, and the members of her group were clearly intimidated by her sharpness.

As this teacher continued, I approached the table, listened, and decided to intervene. "Does everyone here agree with Jamie?" There was no response. People were probably weighing the risk of disagreeing with someone so heated. "Has anyone hesitated to raise a concern in a group?" Two of the three nodded yes, and one said plainly but somewhat self-consciously, "It's not always easy to speak up at meetings. It helps me when I have to take a turn."

To her credit, Jamie stopped complaining, turned to her colleague, and responded, "Really?" After a pause and a few more comments from the teachers at her table, she conceded, "Well, then, maybe I'm wrong." Probably for this gregarious, outspoken teacher, it was hard to imagine not simply speaking her mind. Later in the year, Jamie begrudgingly allowed that norms seemed to help new teammates feel more comfortable. "You're right, you're right," she said and braced herself for the "I told you so" from colleagues.

## Protocols

When a team is shifting from a culture of nice to one of honest, open feedback, it's hard to suddenly share critical feedback. No one wants to be the one to deviate from the niceties the group is accustomed to. You risk being perceived as pushy or, worse, self-righteous. Protocols can help.

A structured conversation—a protocol—feels awkward at first. Suddenly, a friendly conversation has rules, which doesn't feel natural.

However, it's the rules that help move the conversation from friendly to accountable. For example, a protocol that requires everyone to share "cool" feedback—something that could be improved, changed, that needs work—makes it easier for people unused to giving this kind of feedback to colleagues.

Some protocols allow people to share feedback indirectly (through silent "chalk talk" on chart papers hung on the walls or anonymously writing ideas on sticky notes for the affinity protocol). So if they're hesitant, they can practice the skill of being honest while still being anonymous. When people see that the group didn't fall apart, that in fact this approach was helpful, these structured interactions pave the way for direct feedback. But there's no getting around the fact that following these protocols feels somewhat strained and unnatural to many people when they're first introduced.

At first, some staff members at Douglass regularly resisted the use of protocols. They claimed the awkwardness of the protocols made it hard to bond with their colleagues. It's true the situation did feel ironic. Instead of having their usual comfortable and affirming conversations, people were required to do something more constrained in the interest of feeling closer to one another. This behavior is counterintuitive. Wouldn't we want to keep the warmth and organic nature of conversations to promote tighter bonds?

Trust, however, is not the same thing as warmth, happiness, familiarity, kindness. These are all wonderful qualities—and trusting communities usually include them—but trust is something different. When you have repeated evidence that your colleagues respectfully say what they think, tell you directly to your face when they disagree, and say honestly when they don't know something, you begin to trust them a whole lot more than when you were just exchanging niceties. When you trust that they're not pulling punches or talking about your ignorance in the parking lot, when you don't feel negatively judged—these experiences build a trust that can bear weight.

The more we use structures like protocols, the more normal they become. At Douglass, we conduct a plus/delta debrief of each meeting, use protocols to structure many conversations, use a template to take notes, and have formal roles including timekeeper. Over time, these structures have become predictable, and their familiarity makes them less awkward and even at this point comfortable. Getting there, though, required staying the course.

## NAME AND REINFORCE BEHAVIORS: MAKE TRUST BUILDING VISIBLE

People pay attention when the principal speaks. It's one of the great privileges (and perils) of the role. An experienced principal advised me to use that voice of authority sparingly and strategically. Name and spotlight what you want people to pay attention to. (More things to watch for with two-track thinking . . . ) This means looking out for behaviors that support culture change. Seize opportunities to show how positive these behaviors are for the community.

My initial list of behaviors to reinforce has grown. For example, disagreeing with the boss wasn't originally on the list, but it quickly became clear that some people were censoring themselves in meetings. So the list has expanded to include disagreeing with the boss and colleagues, in addition to asking for and offering help, giving and receiving honest feedback, and asking each other probing or clarifying questions.

Because a leader needs to hear people's honest responses, I explicitly say this at meetings and encourage what I called "pushback." At an early instructional leadership team meeting that first year, a very insightful but often quiet teacher finally spoke up. The group listened closely as she gingerly disagreed with my proposed professional development plan. After she spoke, the conversation—and the plan—took off in the direction she'd pointed us, and we came up with something much better.

This moment was pivotal for the team. If the teacher hadn't pushed back against the proposal, we wouldn't have arrived at this much stronger place. I shared exactly this feedback—named the behavior I wanted to see more of—and then asked this teacher to reflect on how it had felt to disagree. She acknowledged that it had felt hard but that she was glad she had taken the risk. At the end of the year, she wrote a note saying that she was grateful for the encouragement to push back and for valuing her opinion. Over time, more teachers came to trust that disagreements were part of our work.

If we want people to be active, not passive, members of the learning community, they need to see that their input is valued. The best way to do this, of course, is to use that input. And when we use people's ideas, it's useful to remind them at every opportunity. "Based on feedback from the ILT, we changed the timing of the Response to Intervention (RTI) meetings." "The Sheltered English Immersion team pointed out that their language assessments are not included in the progress check-in plan, and so we're going to make revisions." People hear it again and again and so absorb the narrative: we share ideas, we disagree with each other, and we do better work as a result.

As usual, what we do as leaders speaks much more powerfully than what we say. When leaders show knee-jerk exasperation at someone's response, we potentially shut down thoughtful ideas from others who are watching our interactions carefully. Even if the person responding is known by everyone to be closed-minded, even if others roll their eyes when this person has the floor, a sharp response from us communicates all the wrong messages about what kind of participation is valued.

I made this mistake during a meeting when a staff member had just one more question after we had labored through difficult topics on the agenda and were almost done. This person's aimless dithering drove us all crazy, and the group was weary and eager to leave. When I rudely cut her off mid-sentence and addressed her concern in a dismissive tone, the looks of shock on staff members' faces taught me a lesson. That person needed to be treated with respect. Our norms stated this position clearly, and if the leader wasn't going to treat this staff member with respect, then everyone else felt vulnerable, too. Even seemingly small interactions send powerful signals about what is valued and what is merely words on paper.

At least as valuable as the principal's endorsement is when staff members draw attention to what's valuable. When people name and appreciate specific behaviors from each other, this effort builds and reinforces the values we hold as a community much more lastingly than a compliment from the boss. It means that teachers, not just the boss, care about our values.

One year, we wrote down appreciations, crumpled up the papers, and threw them at each other in a mock snowball fight that ended with all of us picking up and reading the crumpled appreciations to the group. Many "snowballs" explicitly reinforced trust-building behaviors:

> I appreciate how the staff at [Douglass] take care of one another. We support each other in many ways. We are able to speak honestly at meetings and know that we will not be judged.
> I appreciate that I feel like I can go to anyone on the staff for help or advice without being judged.
> The staff's collective wisdom about and love for children has made this an amazing place to teach and learn.
> I appreciate how teachers at our school work so incredibly hard to take care of *all* our children—academically, socially, and emotionally!

It's hard to imagine a better tutorial for a new teacher learning the expectations of a new school.

When we do group debriefs at the end of meetings, staff members affirm and reinforce behaviors that helped the meeting. People aren't always tuned into the details of how trust gets built, however. This is a time to strategically use the voice of authority to focus attention. "Did anyone disagree with something today? Did you say it?" "How did the facilitator help this group get so much accomplished today?"

Focusing attention to reinforce positive behaviors is a discipline. My first reaction is usually to just say, "That was a great meeting!" It's hard to remember my job is not just to build trust but to increase our collective capacity to build trust. So instead of giving general praise, I'm trying to help all of us—myself included—reflect on *why* the meeting felt productive. If we all increase our understanding of what makes meetings good, we'll all be able to work on making the next one even better.

For most people, hearing reinforcing or reflective comments from colleagues should be enough to let you know what's expected. However, some people need more direct feedback. In one case, a teacher had a history of flying off the handle with peers and with me. A formal reprimand was not enough to turn things around. Even among adults, we can't assume that everyone has the same skills in trust building.

In the case of this teacher, very specific, positive reinforcement is helping her develop more cooperative behaviors. "When you just shared that concern, your voice was really calm. It helped me listen to what you were saying." "You were so open when Ann gave you feedback about reading books. She looked hesitant, but you made her feel comfortable sharing feedback." "Amy was really stressed at the beginning of the meeting. When you told her how much you love her morning song, she just beamed." School may be the only place this teacher gets specific feedback about her social skills.

Giving positive reinforcement that is detailed and specific—not simply "You're great!"—feels a bit awkward at first. The goal is not to be patronizing but to simply reflect back the impact of behaviors. Specific feedback about what's working helps build, reinforce, and strengthen a culture of psychological safety.

## FOLLOW UP ON NEGATIVE BEHAVIORS

Less pleasant but no less important than reinforcing good behaviors is following up about behaviors that are not positive. The staff needs to know that the way we interact as adults is as important as the way we interact with children. The two are related. When staff members exhibit behaviors that break down trust and inhibit collective learning, follow-up is needed.

This principle applies to simple things—two teachers are having a side conversation at a staff meeting, someone is chronically late for meetings— as well as larger behaviors. After several staff meetings, I noticed a pattern in the behavior of Sherry, a teacher new to our school. She had been a big fish in a little pond at her previous school. She was adjusting to having many skilled peers in her new setting. Her contributions to discussion usually involved drawing attention to her skills and being cynical of efforts to build alignment across the grades. In addition, she always offered constructive criticism for meetings led by her peers and less frequently offered positive feedback.

I met with Sherry to share my observations. The goal wasn't to stifle Sherry's suggestions for improvement, but to clarify her role at these meetings. She was missing an opportunity for learning. I told Sherry that, at the next meeting, I would watch for ways she was engaging as a learner. How would she support the learning of her peers? How would her engagement be different if she expected to come out of that meeting with a new insight?

At the next meeting, Sherry asked questions and volunteered to help with an initiative. Whether she was doing it sincerely or to satisfy me, the reason didn't matter. Her behavior had not been supporting the learning of the group or herself, and now it was. Later, after describing how much she appreciated her teammates and all that she learned from them, Sherry said that our school was very different from her previous school and that it gave her "hope for education."

## SWEAT THE SMALL STUFF

To some people, these responses and forms of feedback may seem like micromanaging. Paying attention to specific comments that people make and how they make them, observing how people engage with each other, requiring teams to follow specific procedures for leading meetings. And yet, these small behaviors over time create the culture we live in as a group. They establish trust. To build a healthy community where people can learn, we have to "sweat the small stuff."

Maintaining a healthy community requires constant vigilance. After working hard and seeing progress, we might be tempted to feel we've arrived. Hurray, no more tending necessary! I've learned this is a mistake. Staff come and go, but even if staff remain the same, maintaining trust takes ongoing work. When we think we're doing enough, we probably need to do just a bit more. The fire that is community needs constant tending.

In my first year, I engaged teachers in establishing a set of norms to guide our work together as a staff. People identified behaviors they wanted to ask of their colleagues: "What could your colleagues do that would help you collaborate and learn well together?" A volunteer committee condensed all the suggestions to a set of five:

- Assume positive intentions.
- Practice active listening and engage with each other respectfully.
- Be aware of power and share power.
- Participate in the process.
- Recognize and appreciate each other's talents and strengths; all are colleagues.

We referenced them regularly at staff meetings. "Which norm will you specifically work on during today's meeting?" "What evidence did you see of our norms being followed today?" "What norm do we need to get better at as a staff?"

At the end of that year, people said that the deliberate community building had made an impact. Teachers wrote about this change in the end-of-year survey, such as in this response: "We have become a thinking school again and you have brought the staff back together." And this one: "I think you have established a lovely tone in our school of respect, high expectations, and hard work."

A few years later, however, when district reconfiguration led to an almost 40 percent change in the make-up of our staff, I neglected to be as deliberate with norm setting and community building. Looking back on this time, it's hard to know what I was thinking. There were a lot of moving parts as a result of the reconfiguration, and I must have hoped that we could coast on the strong existing culture we had built. The result was a deterioration of trust among the staff.

Several conscientious staff members told me that they were concerned about a group of teachers who were increasingly negative and critical of others. I had observed some of this and had also heard that one staff member in particular was aggressive and manipulative and making colleagues anxious. It was easy to fall into thinking that some people were just nega-tive, gossipy, bad-mouthing colleagues, and that this small group of teach-ers seemed to be poisoning the community. I found myself lying awake at night wishing they would go away. If only we could turn back the clock to before the restructuring changes.

Finally, the concerned teachers said, "We need to do something. We can't let this continue." That's when it became clear to me that I had not actually believed that something could be done. Instead, I'd come to the conclusion that some people are just unpleasant. It's too bad they ended up at our school. The wise teacher advocates helped me realize that strong communities don't tolerate that kind of behavior. And, in contrast to my fixed-mindset belief, they seemed to think these teachers could change.

The school counselor and I made a plan. We reserved time at a staff meeting when the counselor masterfully named the problem behaviors and led a conversation about how our community wanted to address this issue. People talked about needing to share concerns face to face rather than talk behind people's backs. Colleagues had an opportunity to say what they hoped for in our community. People agreed that we all probably felt tempted to engage in negativity at different points, but knowing how hurtful it could be held us back.

After this meeting, the A-team revisited the whole-staff norms, made suggested revisions, established a few new norms about talking to each other directly, and posted them in the staff room, near all photocopiers, and in the office. Everyone agreed that the staff meeting marked a shift in the dynamics in our community.

The staff meeting was a turning point in that it engaged the full staff in taking ownership of the problem and doing something about it. The meeting was also a catalyst for me to step up and take action. I made ap-pointments to speak with several of the negative teachers individually. I named their behaviors, pointed to the standard for professionalism on the teacher evaluation rubric, and let them know that they were not meeting that particular professional standard and would be rated as unsatisfactory in that category unless there was a change in their behavior.

These individual meetings were difficult. While I prided myself on high standards for teaching practice, I hadn't expected to have to hold people accountable for interpersonal interactions. My definition of instructional leader hadn't included that kind of feedback, and it felt intrusive and personal. It was helpful to remember that the feedback was not a critique of personality. The feedback was sending a clear message that (a) collegial expectations need to be met and (b) I fully believed that people would meet them.

These teachers did change their behavior that year. No one would say they became angels, but they learned where the line was and not to cross it. They held back more. Importantly, they lost some of their audience as people gained the confidence to resist the negative talk. With clear expectations stated from both colleagues and from me, our community got back on track in our ongoing work building a trusting culture.

A few months after that staff meeting, as a few of us waited for a meeting to start, an assistant teacher demonstrated what the work of culture building looks like. She confessed to feeling nervous. She had decided to address a colleague who was bad-mouthing people, and she was planning to do it that day at lunch time. "It's what we talked about at that staff meeting," she said. "We all know it's not right, and I need to say something to her." The people around the table affirmed her courage and the importance of her plan. Implicitly, they also affirmed this teacher's belief that the offending teacher's behavior could change and that she could play a role in that.

## TAKE SMALL STEPS OVER A LONG TIME

Teachers usually build trust with each other more quickly than with the principal. They plan, meet, and interact much more frequently with colleagues than with me. It makes sense that our trust trajectories are on different timelines. Even knowing this, I wish someone had shared how long it takes to build significant trust between principals and teachers in a large organization. I knew it would take time . . . but *years*? Not the time frame I was expecting.

Of course, not everyone requires years to build and achieve trust with the principal. Some teachers form relationships with the principal more quickly than others, and certainly a general sense of reliability and respect grows much sooner. But for me, it wasn't until the end of the fourth year when things shifted. That's when most staff members easily took me at my word, felt comfortable disagreeing with me as their boss, and had a sense of where I was coming from as a leader. It's when I could make the April Fool's announcement canceling recess over the loudspeaker and not worry that people would get uptight about it. Building trust from the position of the boss requires perseverance and perspective. And patience.

Simply knowing that trust will develop over time is helpful. As principals, we don't need to take it personally when staff members take our words the wrong way or assume negative intent when there is none. Building trust—especially with the boss—takes time.

CHAPTER 7

# How to Listen, When to Speak

Being listened to is so close to being loved that most people cannot tell the difference.

—David Augsburger

At the end of my first year as principal, I was invited to speak to a class of principal interns. While I was preparing for the session, it became clear that the most important lesson from the year wasn't an improvement strategy or protocol or plan for evaluation. It was a single word that I wrote on paper and held up repeatedly through my presentation. The word was *listen*.

In this class we talked about using data. *Listen to learn: how people assess student weaknesses, what people are worried about with the process, when people grow silent.* The aspiring principals asked about teachers resistant to change. What can you do to make them buy in? *Listen to understand why they resist. Listen to hear their worries. Listen to see what they value.* We talked about the role of the leader. *Listen because it disrupts people's expectations when they go to you for answers. Wait for them to speak and own their expertise. Listen for the most basic reason: you can't know it all. You need help.*

Communication—both speaking and listening—is inextricably wrapped up in trust and deserves special focus. As leaders, we need to explore different ways to listen and speak. Effective listening helps me accurately diagnose a concern and know how to respond. Effective speaking is a way to provide support and decrease the vulnerability that many parents, teachers, and children may feel. Together, these skills communicate that we, as leaders, value members of our community. Thoughtful, reflective listening and speaking deepen trust.

## LISTEN TO LEARN

Educators are usually viewed as good listeners. We really attend, don't drift when someone is talking, and try to wait until the person has finished before formulating a response. However, is the person speaking aware of all this effort? How does that person know we're listening attentively and not spacing out or bringing significant skepticism or bias to the interaction? All the speaker knows is that we're not talking. In addition, how well do we actually understand what the speaker wants to communicate?

Listening is one of the most common and yet—as the opening quote indicates—one of the most powerful acts we can perform each day. People regularly come to the principal with concerns. For the teacher who shares a frustration, the student who expresses resentment at the way she was treated, or the parent who shares disappointment with a school policy, the way the leader listens is pivotal. It's likely that all of these people will harbor some anxiety that the principal is misinterpreting what they say. And often they're right. Too often, the speaker and principal enter an interaction with an idea of what each person is going to say and leave without much new information. The consequences are missed opportunities to understand and solve problems and a gradual eroding of trust.

This job requires going deeper in listening. It requires constantly striving to hear what the person means and not just what the person says. Leaders build trust and have more productive conversations by saying out loud how we're making sense of what a person shares. We need to make our listening audible.

### Listen for the Meaning Behind the Words

Author Barry Jentz uses the term *reflective listening*.[1] His work frames communication skills in entirely new ways. Essentially, he teaches leaders to put aside assumptions and preconceived ideas and listen to the meaning be-hind what another person is saying. Then he asks us to check our assump-tions: *Is this what you're saying? Is this what you're feeling/needing/resenting/wishing?* As leaders, we need to discern the root cause of any concern.

While this kind of listening sounds straightforward, it is challenging to put in practice. The main reason is the usual one: as leaders, we want to jump right into solving the problem, to take action right away. Instead, we need to make sure we fully understand the problem. We need to ask questions and explicitly check our understanding to get a clearer picture of the problem and our role in relation to it. The other reason this is so hard is that it feels awkward at first. Checking understanding midconversation is not the usual mode of communication.

One of my best instructors in developing reflective listening was Lau-rie, who frequently came to talk about her struggles in the classroom. It was during a year when this incredibly capable and talented young woman had a challenging student whose emotional needs were eventually con-firmed severe enough to place him in a therapeutic setting. During this year, Laurie would regularly come by the office afterschool and describe difficult interactions she'd had. The situation in her classroom was taxing for everyone involved. Staff members at both the school and district level were pursuing all avenues of support for this student and teacher, but determining the right services for any student takes time. During these af-terschool conversations with Laurie, I felt concerned and wanted to reduce the stress and make things better. It felt natural—necessary—to offer as-sistance or brainstorm solutions or otherwise look for ways to improve the situation. A pattern developed. I would offer suggestions; she would explain why they wouldn't work. We would both end the conversation feeling frustrated.

One day, Laurie told me that sometimes she just wanted to share what was going on and didn't need us to come up with solutions. She wanted me to know what she was doing and how she was doing. It would be reas-suring, she explained, to know that I understood her situation. Her gentle but direct guidance was what I needed. It was time for me to demonstrate reflective listening.

"It sounds like you're working hard to show you care about him," I would offer. Laurie would nod her head, give a relieved sigh.

"You're worrying about the other kids and how you can give them what they need, too." This was testing the waters; was this the concern beneath what she was sharing? Or was I missing her main concern?

"You're wondering if you're pushing him too hard. But you're also worried about not pushing him enough." This summary would either satisfy Laurie—yes, Sarah understands the crux of the issue—or she would shake her head and explain further what it was she couldn't figure out.

When Laurie shook her head or politely said, "Not really," that was my cue to listen harder to try to better understand the knotty problem she faced. It was incredibly difficult not to problem-solve. I felt awkward just sharing back what I was hearing. However, the results were meaningful. With our new approach, after ten to fifteen minutes together, Laurie usually rose from her chair looking less weighed down. She would thank me sincerely for listening before picking up her coat and bag and heading home.

In these small one-on-one interactions, people either feel heard or misunderstood by a leader. Think of what a relief it is to feel truly known by your boss. Asking for help, taking risks, and proposing off-the-wall but innovative ideas are all easier when a deep level of trust exists. By the same token, when this level of understanding doesn't exist, relationships and the work are strained.

Another small but telling example of the importance of reflective listening came during a progress check-in meeting. The meeting had not gone well, people felt frustrated that we hadn't addressed all the issues, and we were wrapping up with plus/deltas. Connie, the teacher facilitator, who also was clearly disappointed with the meeting, said one of the reasons the meeting had gone poorly was that we hadn't taken the time to create an agenda. I was taken aback and immediately defensive—and truth be told, judgmental. At just the last meeting, I had named the same issue, and together we had drafted an agenda for the meeting we were just now ending. Connie's comment was baffling; she seemed to be grasping for something or someone else to blame for the lackluster meeting she had just led.

In frustration I blurted out, "But we do have an agenda." I quickly realized how unsupportive this statement must sound and instead tried to use inquiry to truly understand what Connie was saying. Slowing myself down, I pointed to the list on our laptop screens, "Is this what you mean by an agenda?" Connie replied right away, "No. It doesn't have times next to the topics. At ILT meetings, agendas have goals for the meeting, times for each topic, and we're really consistent and refer to them all the time."

Aha! So she wasn't throwing blame around; she was reflecting on what could help her do a better job next time. And Connie was right. What had sufficed as an agenda for our small group bore no resemblance to the sophisticated agendas we made for our instructional leadership team meetings. Checking for understanding—"Is this what you mean when you say 'agenda'?"—prevented a misinterpretation of her remarks. Slowing down to ask that one question helped her articulate exactly what she—and our committee—needed.

When I first tried reflective listening, I worried that interactions would feel contrived or stilted. Asking so many clarifying questions is not the way we normally interact. Maybe people would feel manipulated. In fact, people don't seem aware of anything unusual in a reflective response. They just feel heard. When people hear a summary of what they've said and respond with an emphatic "Exactly," it's immensely satisfying for both speaker and listener. A solid plank has been laid in the building of trust.

At that point in the meeting or conversation, when they feel truly heard, people are usually ready to brainstorm solutions or own responsibility. Feeling confident that their perspective is understood, they can relax and move forward. Reflective listening has done its work.

### Listen to Dissenting Points of View to Strengthen Relationships

The principal's office sees a steady stream of people coming in to request something, share a worry, or make a demand. In the context of schools, individual needs have to be considered alongside the needs of the larger group. For this and various other reasons, a principal often has to provide an answer that disappoints the other party. Over the years, many situations have required my saying no or otherwise disagreeing with requests. I used to think in these interactions that people wouldn't be satisfied unless we ended the conversation in agreement. Knowing I couldn't possibly please everyone made me feel doomed to alienating members of the community.

I've found it interesting to learn that while people would clearly prefer to get their way, that's not the only outcome of the meeting. If a leader can clearly demonstrate having heard opposing viewpoints or a concern, relationships emerge stronger rather than weaker from the interaction. People realize that the leader has not discounted their opinions and will listen again in the future.

This insight hit home after I stood in front of what seemed certain to be a fierce firing line. The district was considering implementing a system of tracking, which would separate students by academic performance. In deciding to speak against this proposed policy at a televised school committee meeting, I knew my position would disappoint some parents. Their resentment (or outright hostility) seemed inevitable. I began by explaining the reasons I heard people say they desired tracking. Then I explained why I could not support the issue.

A parent organizer who supported academically tracked classes later told me that she had been sitting at the edge of her couch at home watching the broadcast of the meeting. When she heard me acknowledge her concerns, she said she sank back into her couch in relief. Someone had fully and accurately understood her perspective.

Again, I was surprised but also heartened to know that this wasn't a zero-sum game—you're either with me or against me. This mother wrote a thank-you note saying that even though we were on opposing sides, she respected me. When people feel heard, they are more able to move on— and importantly, to continue to work together. It's the quality of listening in these interactions that makes the difference.

### Listen to Understand What's Behind the Anger—and to Receive It Well

Receiving anger is another form of listening. With reflective listening, even when someone is upset, the results can be surprisingly affirming.

Someone is always mad at the principal. It comes with the job. Sometimes the anger is based on something you've done. Other times the anger is aimed at the institution, and you are the figurehead that represents that institution. And other times the anger has nothing to do with the school, but it's no less fierce or pointed or unpleasant.

One winter, Ahmed, a first grader, missed the bus home—a mix-up at the end of the day resulted in the teacher not taking him with the rest of his bus group. This child had just arrived at our school a few months earlier—and while Ahmed's English was proficient, his mother spoke limited English since her family had moved here from Somalia only about a year before that. Even with her limited English, Amani was able to communicate her outrage quite clearly the following morning.

Ahmed's mother stood in the door of the office and spoke accusingly to me and the secretary and anyone else in earshot. "He's just first grader! He needs help. He's just first grader!" At first I tried to explain that a mess-up happened, that it was highly unusual, and that it wouldn't happen again. With other parents standing nearby, it was easy to feel defensive. Her son hadn't listened to the announcements, he was regularly off-task, and he had followed the routine plenty of times before. After he missed the bus, we had found Ahmed a ride that got him home at about the same time the bus would have. It didn't seem reasonable that this mother was yelling so publicly and so vehemently. When she kept repeating her statements, however, it was clear that this tack wasn't productive. She needed to know she had been heard.

"You think that we leave Ahmed on his own to go to the bus."

"Yes! He's just first grader."

"You're right. First graders need help. His teacher needs to help him leave for the bus."

"Yes," Amani said, but she was still agitated.

It was time to listen beyond the words to the feelings and what might be behind her anger. "You trust us to take care of your son. When he didn't come home on the bus, you were scared."

She nodded vehemently and said yes several times. Her response indicated that I had hit upon something important.

"I would be scared, too. I am so sorry."

Then I tried to extrapolate what an immigrant mother would be thinking at this time of extreme vulnerability. "Amani, you trust us to take care of your son. It sounds like you were scared that something had happened to him and that we didn't care."

She stopped yelling and in tears said that, yes, she was so scared. I empathized with how she must have felt. We continued for a few minutes and then she left, quietly, asking as she left, "You'll put him on the bus today?" I assured her that we would.

At the time, in the heat of the accusations, it seemed certain that Amani would never forgive the school or me. She had been so angry, had yelled so publicly. She would probably never make eye contact with me again. What happened instead surprised me and taught a valuable lesson. Amani became one of my staunchest supporters. She speaks highly of me to other parents and teachers, frequently stops by to say hi, and tells her children to respect me because I am a "good principal." She trusts me. In large part, I think the reason is that early interaction. Out of this feeling of betrayal came a feeling of trust.

Ronald Heifitz and Marty Linsky point out that the way someone receives anger is often an opportunity to build trust.[2] This behavior isn't intuitive—in fact, quite the opposite. When someone is yelling at us, our instinct is to get into a defensive position and deflect what's being thrown. Instead, we need to let the anger sink in. The moment when someone is fuming mad is usually also when someone feels desperately vulnerable. If we can receive that anger with understanding, we reduce that vulnerability and build a needed bridge in the relationship.

This practice proved similarly helpful with an incredibly distraught teacher in the hallway one day. This teacher and I had not had many positive interactions, so I approached her with caution. She had just escorted a challenging student to the school counselor and was agitated and angry and in no shape to return to working with either this student or the rest of her class. The judgmental voice in my head started running through all the ways this teacher needed to grow in classroom management, and the administrator voice started running through the list of who could cover for her class until she cooled down. As I came up to her, she blurted out, "That kid needs to be in %$#&ing therapy! I don't know what else I'm supposed to do!"

Seeking to use reflective listening to help her calm down, I said, "You've worked really hard to help him." Her response came quickly, "You don't even know the half of it. He takes up every minute of my day." She went on to describe some of the challenges. This was the time to sense what was behind the heated words. Pushing back judgment, I tried to listen for meaning. "It sounds like you do so much that no one knows about. You've been working hard with him, and people don't even know how hard it is because you just do it every day."

Her tight shoulders began to relax. Her voice grew more controlled. The challenge wasn't going away, but she felt heard. Someone understood her situation. We spoke for a few more minutes, and I asked if she needed a break. She said she was ready to go back up to class, and her tone and behavior indicated this was true. After hearing herself thank me, she looked a bit surprised, as if unsure why she was left feeling grateful.

How lonely this teacher must have felt in her classroom. She faced this significant challenge every day, and part of the difficulty was feeling so alone with it. Reflective listening not only allowed this teacher to return to class but also shed light on the internal struggles I hadn't seen and the support she would need going forward.

## LISTEN TO REDUCE PARENTS' VULNERABILITY

All parents have a certain degree of vulnerability in the parent–school relationship because they entrust their children in our care. However, some have more vulnerability than others. When children do something wrong or in any way struggle, many parents feel this behavior reflects poorly on them. This sense of shame manifests in different ways. Some parents try to avoid talking about it because it's too painful, others get defensive because they assume the school is judging them, others deny that anything is wrong. When the principal listens beyond their defensiveness and demonstrates compassion for their pain, parents are more likely to engage as partners. Building this trust requires more reflective listening to understand the source of their hurt.

Examples may look different, but with practice, the pain is easy to recognize. Sometimes it's on the surface. One parent said to me when we met about her child who had hit a teacher, "Sarah, I ask myself all the time, 'What did I do wrong?' Why is it so hard for him?" This heartbreaking comment reminded me to say explicitly to this parent, "I am not here to judge you or your child. We're meeting to figure out how to help your child be successful."

Other times, the pain masquerades as anger. The mother of a child who was transferred to our school in eighth grade regularly came to meetings swinging. Before we could explain why her son had been called to the office again, this mom would start flinging accusations of how horribly the school was treating her son. A special educator who attended all of these meetings commented on both the intensity of this mother's angry attacks and also how quickly she calmed down after she felt respected.

Listening behind this mother's accusatory words, we realized she needed reassurance that we weren't judging her as a bad parent. She was an immigrant mother with a strong accent, so it's fair to assume she wondered if staff members, including me, were biased and judging her. "He's feeling like no one in school listens to him. Like everyone judges him and that people think he's a bad kid." She would nod and stop yelling. "You are working hard to make sure your son gets a good education. You come to school whenever we need to meet, you sacrifice a lot to make sure he gets to school each day. You know that education is important."

After hearing that we were not condemning her and in fact appreciated her hard work and understood the concerns of her son, she would calm down. Then we could proceed with the needed problem solving to address the concerns raised at the meeting and get this child the help he needed. A few years after graduating from Douglass, this student returned to visit the school office (a place far too familiar to him from his very short time as a student here). He came up to the door with a huge grin, received and gave hugs all around, and proudly told us about his classes in high school. In the end, this boy and his family felt our respect.

At Douglass, families who are low income, families who aren't fluent in English, families whose children have significant special needs, and families of color deserve extra affirmation and the knowledge that they receive our full respect. While some of these groups are substantially sized minorities, not one of these communities forms the dominant group in our larger school community. Because in our society (and in schools), these families are more likely to be overlooked, treated inequitably, or otherwise get the short end of any deal, schools have a greater obligation to ensure these families feel welcomed, heard, and valued.

Even small steps in listening make a difference in building trust with families. Before beginning my first year, I called all the families that lived at one particular city housing project and invited them to meet to let me know how Douglass could support their children in school. A group of mothers from Ethiopia, Haiti, Eritrea, and Guyana met in the small community room of their tall apartment building. As their children ate pizza and cut construction paper, these moms used their developing English to its fullest extent, telling me they wanted their children to be challenged, they wanted good teachers, and they wanted to know that their children would do well in high school.

After the mothers spoke, I repeated what I heard and promised to do my best so Douglass would meet their expectations. In subsequent years, when we saw each other at curriculum breakfasts or school celebrations, they greeted me warmly; we had a meaningful connection. They also never hesitated to tell me how the school was doing to meet their expectations.

For years, I reaped trust from this one meeting. At classroom and school events, these parents felt they knew me and brought over friends and relatives for introductions. Several of these parents came personally to ask for help arranging after school care or summer programs. That early act of reaching out and listening—as small as it had been—had signaled to these families that their opinion was valued. They responded by granting their trust. A father whose children joined our school several years later and who participated in a later, similar meeting with families off-site wrote to me, "At other schools, Ethiopian families don't know what's going on at the school. Here we do because of you."

Like educators everywhere, we know that the home–school connection affects student achievement. The staff and I invest time and energy improving this connection. We plan workshops and outreach and home–school summer initiatives. These important and valuable activities need to continue. However, when we are trying to institute a new sense of partnership with disenfranchised families, large-scale efforts may not be enough to turn the tide. Communicating sincere caring and a desire to listen to individual families also plays a significant role in family engagement.

## COMMUNICATE MORE THAN YOU THINK YOU NEED TO

As the preceding examples show, knowing when to talk and what to say comes from good listening. Instead of waiting until there's something to say, respectful leaders tune in to what people need to hear. The more leaders can listen to and empathize with what other people are thinking and feeling, the better they'll be at anticipating questions or concerns. In general, a lack of information causes people to worry, so the key is to communicate—much more than we think we need to.

### Silence Speaks Loudly

I've learned—sometimes painfully—that no communication is, in fact, communication. People read into a nonresponse just as much as—possibly more than—they read into a response. When a parent or teacher doesn't get a reply to a complaint, she may feel that the leader is dismissing her concerns, has a personal vendetta against her or her child, or has a prejudice against teachers/families of color or families who don't volunteer enough or . . . you get the idea. There isn't space enough to list all the possible ways that someone could read into a nonresponse.

These inferences can prompt a range of actions from the concerned party. A superintendent once warned, "If you ignore someone knocking on the door, they may break the door down." A clear response—even if it's not the one people are looking for—goes a long way to helping them feel heard and valued. Lesson in a nutshell: reply to people's concerns.

Over the years, patient parent volunteer Mary-Ann has expanded my definition of this principle. When something happens at school that is unusual, Mary-Ann reminds me not to wait for a query but to proactively communicate with whomever is involved. Anticipate the concern or question that hasn't yet been expressed. This advice may sound obvious, and perhaps everyone else already does this. But after a long day of work, with a to-do list the length of the gymnasium, it's easy to downplay the need for writing a proactive letter or making another phone call. Can't people just trust the school?

When I stop thinking from a tired principal perspective and understand the vulnerable parent perspective—*What's going on at that school with that new leader?!?*—the need is clear. For example, by sheer coincidence, we had a fire drill and a lockdown drill on the same day. Lockdown drills are new to our school and still cause anxiety, so parents got a letter about this double dose of drills. Another day, the cook exploded in anger at students and made a number of them cry. I sent an e-mail to families and called parents who didn't have e-mail addresses. This fall, we're implementing a new strategy of assessing students' progress. It gets an explanation at Back to School night.

If we want more than the usual parent-school relationship—if we truly want to be partners—well, then we need to go beyond the usual amount of communication. We can't just say, "Trust us."

Similarly, when we went through the district restructuring and possible teaching reassignments, I learned that simply writing in the staff e-mail "We don't have any new information right now" was better than saying nothing. In an information vacuum, any tidbit makes people feel less adrift and lets people know that their concerns and questions are known. When we're hiring, getting new technology supplies, or about to start a new process, communicating regularly makes a difference. Once reliable and thorough communication is established as a precedent, people trust that they'll be kept in the loop and stop worrying about what they don't know. They won't spend valuable energy fretting that there's something out there the leader isn't telling them.

### Repeat, Repeat, Repeat

A leadership guru asked a group of principals, "When should you talk about your vision?" and then answered himself, "ALL THE TIME. As part of everything you say." It's only slight hyperbole. As leaders, we need to repeatedly give context and purpose for what we're doing.

The reason for repetition isn't that people are dense and don't get the point. It's that for the majority of their day, people are focused on their individual teaching responsibilities. They need help making that transition to whole-school thinking. As leaders, we can easily forget that our perspective is not the same as everyone else's. Meetings or conversations with teammates or the principal are miniscule blips in a teacher's incredibly jam-packed, busy day. We have to expect that things won't always sink in.

In addition, people invariably—and especially under new leadership—worry they're being excluded from something important. This leads to a sense of vulnerability—something's going on and they're not part of it. They ask warily, "Where did this action plan come from?" *[We created it together last spring.]* or "We were never told that the indoor recess schedule changed." *[You got a paper copy in your box and two e-mail reminders.]* "Since when do teachers have to sign up to use the computer lab?" *[Since the A-team recommended it at a staff meeting last month.]* Grumbling can turn into assumption of negative intent. "She's trying to sneak something past us." "She must have something to hide; otherwise, she would have told us about this earlier." "What's coming next?"

Being frustrated about how often things get misinterpreted or need to be repeated doesn't pay. It's just the nature of large organizations of busy people. So now, each time we begin an action step from our school improvement plan, for example, we briefly review the purpose, the truly inclusive creation process, and the nine previous steps that got us to where we are. Each time. People need reminders of where something came from, and they need to hear it multiple times. (The general rule of thumb is nineteen times.

Give or take a few.) This repetition allows people to focus on the message itself rather than feeling anxious about where the message came from.

## Be Transparent About Your Assumptions

Particularly as a White person, I need to frequently state my beliefs about equity, inclusion, and racial bias. I can't assume that people, particularly people of color, will give me the benefit of the doubt. Why would they? Unconscious racial bias is ubiquitous and just that—unconscious. So if I want people to know that I care about equity, I need to speak up about it regularly.

Early on I asked the staff to read an excerpt about different cultural expectations around discipline from Lisa Delpit's book, *Other People's Children*. Once the handouts were passed out, we broke into small groups for discussion. It was startling to learn that some teachers of color questioned why we were reading the excerpt and wondered if I was communicating that our African American students were problematic behaviorally.

On the contrary! I wanted to raise a discussion of culturally responsive discipline at our school. I thought the article would prompt people to think about how their own racial identity and background influences what they expect in student behavior and how they manage discipline. In particular, I wanted teachers to improve their work with our African American boys, whom teachers referred to the office too frequently and often inappropriately.

The problems that seemed obvious to me were ripe for misinterpretation. Simply stating these intentions clearly at the beginning would have helped all teachers and particularly teachers of color know that I wasn't recycling pervasive and pernicious stereotypes about Black boys. In fact, my goal was to expose and address these biases. Of course, it would be nice to assume that I'm presumed innocent until proven guilty. But in a world where stereotypes are rampant, it's not unreasonable that teachers would remain skeptical, or even suspicious, until there's clear evidence that their leader sees the fallacy of racial stereotypes.

When asking the staff to read this book excerpt, I had naïvely assumed that people knew my perspective and trusted my intentions. This early blunder taught important lessons. Never miss an opportunity to communicate purpose and intention, and always communicate more than you think is necessary.

## Reveal the Information You Didn't Know You Were Hiding

A principal needs to always remember two basics of communicating. First, understand that people can't see your thinking; they can't read your mind. Second, try hard to read the minds of others.

People can't read a leader's mind. They don't know when we're confused, what we're wondering, how we're weighing different decisions, and whether or not we're concerned about something. Sharing all this information puts people at ease. They can (almost) stop trying to guess what's going through the leader's mind.

At the same time, as leaders, we need to anticipate what anxieties, fears, and unspoken questions other people bring to the table that may need to be addressed. Doing this proactively can prevent misunderstandings that later have to be repaired. Empathy goes a long way in any interaction.

This lesson was brought home one year after we had launched our new Response to Intervention process. We were about to hold a series of meetings mid-fall to see if reading interventions were up and running in each grade or if anything needed adjusting. It was my first time running this round of meetings, and it was important that each team of teachers feel the meeting was efficient and worthwhile. Facilitating these meetings was complicated. I had so many butterflies in my stomach that I couldn't eat breakfast on the morning of the first meeting.

Before school started, I called a thoughtful colleague to review the agenda and ask if I had forgotten anything. I was focused on what the principal should say. She focused on how teachers might be feeling. She helpfully pointed out that the principal wasn't the only one who might feel nervous and that she always told people that these meetings were not about judgment or "hand slapping."

I followed her advice to the letter. After giving my planned overview, including that the meetings were intended to be helpful, I reminded everyone that the meetings were not about hand slapping. We were all still learning the process. No one was being judged based on whether plans were up and running yet. At each meeting, after they heard this, teachers looked visibly relieved, and in almost every debrief, teachers mentioned this specific phrase and that it was helpful to hear so directly.

What was most surprising about teachers' reaction to this framing was that none of this was new information. All of this had been described by the leadership team, shared via written agendas, and explained at the first round of these meetings earlier that year. Plus, did people really think that a goal of the meeting was to get them in trouble just as we were all learning this new process?

It's easy to forget that people bring a range of reactions to meeting with their boss. It continues to be surprising what people read into my actions. When people don't know what's coming next in a meeting, they may feel as though they're not on level footing, and this isn't conducive to listening and learning. Restating explanations, intentions, and goals—and the fact that I'm a learner, too—is never redundant.

## COMMUNICATE TO AFFIRM PEOPLE'S EFFORT AND WORK

When asked why her staff trusted her so much, a principal colleague replied quickly, "Because I don't think I'm better than they are." This principal appreciates the complexity of teachers' work. And, importantly, her staff members know it. The simple act of recognizing and acknowledging people's hard work helps people feel known and valued. In broad brush strokes, it's based on listening again; individual stories are heard.

### Know Teachers' Practice

One of the most straightforward ways of communicating respect to a teacher is to be familiar with her work. Infrequent observations can be stressful because they show only a slice of a person's practice. Many teachers are actually reassured when the principal visits regularly enough to know the classroom routines, recognize when units are changing, and identify the small victories in student behavior and learning. Teachers pour energy and effort into their lessons and students every day. It's easy to take this work for granted. After all, it's what we do; we're a school. However, when you're a capable teacher, it feels good to know that your boss knows the specifics and the quality of your work.

At regular intervals, I've made the common administrator decision to stop visiting strong teachers so that I could focus time on struggling teachers. Some would assume teachers would feel respected by this decision—their boss feels confident in their skills. Probably some teachers don't mind at all. However, plenty of teachers prefer that their boss knows their work well. After one period of not making regular classroom rounds, I returned to visiting all classrooms. One particularly strong teacher went out of her way to say she had noticed. "I like it when you come by my class more. I like it when you know what I'm doing." She wasn't looking for approval. She wanted her teaching to be known, her story to be heard.

## Use Affirmations to Communicate Respect

A survey of Douglass teachers early in my tenure showed near unanimity about two aspects of my practice. One hundred percent of the staff agreed that I had high standards for student learning and teacher practice, and almost everyone said that I didn't affirm people's hard work enough. Since getting this feedback, I've tried to be more conscious of sharing strengths.

A lot has been written about the potential and pitfalls of praise. There's a fine line between helping people feel that their efforts are valued and creating praise-junkies, who depend on other people's approval to feel effective. The research shows that effective feedback is specific, oriented toward outcomes rather than approval, and sometimes comes in the form of questions that prompt reflection. "How did you introduce the vocabulary wall that I see your kids using so much?" "Tell how you get [a struggling writer] to do so much writing in one sitting?"

Like many leaders grappling with twenty-first century norms, I'm cautious about overuse of e-mail as a means of providing feedback. This initially meant a strict personal policy of never giving feedback via e-mail but instead seeking out the person for face-to-face feedback. However, it's hard to track people down. Plus, with a busy schedule, priority always goes to sharing concerns, and as a consequence, the positive feedback often gets forgotten. So now I don't hesitate to share affirmations in e-mails although in-person sharing is always the goal.

Another characteristic of effective feedback is that it happens! Periodically, I realize that I've been nose to the grindstone with meetings and evaluation follow-up and problem solving and not looking up to notice and recognize all that's working well. And at every school, there's a lot to recognize even just from a single stroll down the hall. "I saw how welcoming you were to that new family. They just beamed." "You must have put a lot of work into this newsletter; I bet families appreciate getting all of this information." "The essays your kids wrote show so much growth. It's clear you've taught them a lot."

Verbal affirmations are just one means of showing respect for someone's work. But there is more than one way to affirm people's efforts. For example, arranging the snacks on a tray for a meeting rather than throwing a pile of bags on the table makes some people feel honored. Spending a few minutes talking about a personal connection makes a difference for someone else. At conference time this year, teachers got care packages in their mailboxes. After receiving one, a teacher who was often critical made a point of seeking me out in a rare visit to the office. "That was so thoughtful of you!" she exclaimed about the simple baggie of granola bar, gum, sticky notes, permanent marker, and encouraging note to the whole staff. For someone else, the gift probably didn't mean much. For her, that baggie made her feel appreciated in a way that wasn't happening through verbal feedback.

## Communicate Support

Teachers' work moves at a very fast pace. Out of respect for teachers' nonstop sprint during the school week, we administrators need to adjust our pace to theirs, not vice versa. Responsive leaders attend to the details of a teacher's work—whether it's approving a field trip request, moving quickly to sign a maternity leave form, or responding to a call for help. These tasks may feel tedious and inconsequential in the scope of a principal's day, so it's tempting to push them aside in favor of more leader-like tasks. We risk a lot more than delayed paperwork in doing so.

Years ago, when I was working as a staff developer with teachers, one complaint came up at every workshop: principals didn't understand the challenges of a teacher's daily work. As a consequence, teachers didn't feel supported by their principals; they didn't feel principals had their back. In particular, one universal story repeated itself with only slightly different variations: *I was struggling with a student; I called for the principal's help; and thirty minutes later when it was too late, he showed up.* In every case, the feeling of abandonment quickly led to a larger sense of betrayal. At these workshops, after hearing colleagues share their versions of this story, teachers around the room would immediately empathize. Many said they had been there.

For the principal involved in each story, this interaction may have felt like a small thing. Or perhaps the principal perceived the call as unnecessary. Whether or not that was the case, in that moment, for the teacher, it was the difference between feeling able to do her job and feeling ineffective—and, often, humiliated—in front of her class. Teaching can be an isolated and lonely job. Teachers need to know that administrators support them.

These teachers' stories and their strong emotional response have stayed with me. For this reason, if a teacher calls for help in the classroom, I drop everything to respond immediately. Our school secretary also has internalized this priority. People joke that if Cheryl is at the copier when an incoming call comes from a classroom, she practically leaps over her desk to answer the phone. As I've explained to the custodians, the lunch crew, and the office staff, we don't work at an ordinary institution. At our workplace, teachers are the surgeons performing incredibly complex and challenging work transforming minds. There isn't anything we could be doing that's more challenging than teaching a group of children well. Our job is to support that complex work.

But what about those situations in which the teacher is making an unreasonable request or when the anxiety appears to be unmerited?

As a principal, I have definitely had times when I question the judgment of the teacher or feel that another way of approaching the situation wouldn't require administrator intervention. The bottom line is: it doesn't matter. In that moment when the teacher is with children, she feels vulnerable and is asking for help. That is a trust-building or trust-destroying moment. Do I hear her or don't I? Later, after responding and addressing the need in that moment, the principal can meet with the teacher to discuss the situation and come up with an alternative plan going forward.

## COMMUNICATE RESPECT FOR CHILDREN

How do principals win the respect and trust of children? In all the same ways they do with adults. Listening behind the words. Showing respect for their work. Noticing and affirming their contributions to the school community and their individual growth. Recognizing ways they may feel vulnerable and proactively seeking to address those. Helping them feel known and valued. Again, small actions reap big rewards.

Administrators meet with students for a variety of reasons on a regular basis. For the principal, the meeting is routine. For a student, this meeting is a significant event. Sometimes a situation calls for a swift and firm reprimand and redirection. Other times, problem solving will produce the best long-term results. In every case, the way we listen and speak is what makes children leave that meeting either feeling heard or feeling invisible.

One day in September, four girls were sent to my office. These second graders took their seats around the office table with great solemnity. Once they sat down, their heads and shoulders were only a little higher than the table top, and their legs dangled above the floor. They looked nervously up at me as I closed the door and found my chair.

Rachel, the smallest of the children, had been spitting on the others at recess, and for some reason (the teacher was sick? the lunch supervisors were busy? perhaps this was a recurring behavior?), this issue ended up in my lap. The details of the meeting and the situation are fuzzy now, but I followed my routine of teaching the girls to be reflective listeners.

After each child took a turn to speak, another repeated back what she had heard.

The room was quiet as they earnestly listened to each other. When one girl had to try again because she hadn't caught the meaning the first time, the speaker repeated herself right away without any change in conviction or emphasis. After agreeing to a resolution (perhaps it was that they would include Rachel in games and that she would make cards showing she understood how they each wanted to be treated), the students shook hands and left the office with the same seriousness with which they had entered.

The next day, Rachel paused before walking through the front door to give me a big hug, promising to treat her classmates the way they wanted to be treated. A few moments later, after walking his daughter to class, the father of one of the other girls came back to my post at the front of the school. He told me that his daughter had always wanted to be a teacher, but after our meeting the previous day, she announced at dinner that now she wanted to be a principal.

Even a difficult conversation can feel affirming when you feel heard. And even young children sense the power of listening well. It is one of the purest acts of kindness we can perform.

Another way I've learned to build trust with children is through greeting them by name each morning at the front door. At first, this effort felt purely symbolic: the principal welcomes you to a day of learning. Over countless mornings of summer sun, slick rainy streets, and piles of snow, however, the students and I have built relationships. Years of watching them grow up allows me to know their stories in some small way. When I notice missing teeth, haircuts, proud smiles, or dragging feet, they feel known.

A recent example brought together many lessons of listening and trust. A teacher called for help with a stubborn first grader on the playground who angrily refused to return to the classroom at the end of recess. This child had been in the United States for only four weeks at this point, so he was likely exhausted on a daily basis from straining to understand everything going on around him. In his distress, he was biting and hitting anyone who came near him.

As I approached where he was sitting on a bench, his scowl deepened and I could tell he recognized me from mornings at the front door. He must have understood the severity of the situation (the principal had to be called), and he tensed, turned his back, and pulled his clenched fists around his hunched-up, taut torso. I sat a few feet away on the bench and wondered what to say. Underneath all his show of anger, his eyes showed fear.

Somehow, I dredged up three words in his home language—"Now . . . we . . . together"—and walked two fingers together down the bench to show the meaning. At the sound of the first two words, the boy's shoulders lowered and he turned around. He looked intently at me, wanting to be sure he had heard right. I repeated the words and gestured toward the school. His body relaxed, and together we stood up and began walking toward the school. Despite the scowls of a moment before, it didn't seem surprising when he instinctively reached up to hold my hand. With relief, he let out a torrent of words in his native language as we slowly made our way to the office hand in hand. Once there, he sat on a chair calmly as I began the process of calling his parents and addressing the situation.

In this case, there was no master plan, just a series of intuited steps and those key three words that miraculously came to mind in a moment of need. The child's immediate response surprised me as much as everyone watching. It also felt like a significant lesson in how listening and speaking help us all trust one another.

Like this student, adults, too, can feel that they are adrift and no one understands them, that everything has changed for the worse and nothing is familiar. The carefulness of a leader's listening and speaking can make a powerful difference: a simple gesture of understanding; an effort to communicate in a manner that the adult understands; a willingness to listen to the torrent of words and attempt to make meaning

## CHAPTER 8

# Naming and Addressing Racial Bias

If I love you, I have to make you conscious of the things that you
don't see.

—James Baldwin

While issues related to race infuse every aspect of school improvement,
here I want to directly address racial bias. If we, as leaders, want to disrupt
the status quo of unequal outcomes in schools, we have to start with a
deep look at inequities in schools—and for White leaders like me, this
includes examining our own role in perpetuating them.

I'm prejudiced. On a national test of implicit bias, like the vast majority of White people in the study, I show a preference toward people who
look like me.[1] That's hard to face and harder to tell people. Especially as a
leader committed to ending racial inequalities in education (let alone as a
member of an interracial family), I am horrified by these results.

This prejudice isn't about burning crosses or flinging around racial
epithets. Nothing so obvious. I'm naming the racial bias buried deep in
unconscious thinking that subtly and insidiously informs people's actions
and belief systems. It's this unconscious prejudice that makes people assume attributes about a stranger before even saying hello or that informs
split-second judgments about a child or parent before anyone could possibly know enough to do so. Assumptions and responses like these aren't
intellectually thought through. They're from deep in our unconscious.

When they bubble to the surface, they remind us of the work we need to do to root out what society teaches.

It's scary to admit that I can't trust my instincts to be fair. However, this is exactly why it's important to honestly face up to this truth. Especially as a leader, I need to watch my thinking and decision making all the time. Do I file reports with the state for child neglect quicker with a family of color than with a White family? Am I judging a low-income family as pushy, whereas if a White family did the same thing I'd see it as advocacy? Do I shake my head and move on when an immigrant family neglects to show up for a conference but feel worried for a White family that does the same? How do I make sense of the data when a White teacher's Black students all failed the state exam? Would I react differently if all of her White students failed?

Unfortunately, racial bias is the norm in our society. The vast majority of White people demonstrate racial preferences in a variety of studies. Research continues to pile up confirming the ways we unconsciously assign positive attributes to people who look like us (or sound like us or have names like ours) and negative attributes to those who don't.[2] Owning this bias is the first step toward changing it. Owning our part in larger systems of inequity is the next step.

Community institutions and policies reinforce and perpetuate inequitable outcomes. As principals, we have the power to disrupt this status quo in the organizations we lead. We do this by redefining what fairness means in our community, naming race in conversations with people, presuming bias even from wonderful people, and being willing to be uncomfortable—or make others uncomfortable—regularly.

I need to acknowledge up front that the dynamics around naming race, presuming bias, and experiencing discomfort are going to be very different for leaders of color, who are subject to different perceptions and biases than White principals. I'm acutely aware of the limitations of writing from my own experience but also hope that, by reading one principal's perspective, readers from all backgrounds will be encouraged to reflect on the roles they can play in increasing racial equity in their schools.

## REDEFINE FAIRNESS

The concept of a level playing field is a recurring image in American conversation. In sports scenarios, even people who desperately want to win don't want a head start. It wouldn't feel fair. This was evident a few years ago in Illinois after a tornado wiped out much of a town just before students were to compete in the state high school football playoffs. The opposing team and community donated food and workout gear to the football players and paid for transportation for fans to be present to cheer on their team.

"We definitely want to win, as do they," one of the mothers from the opposing team said. "But you know, there's also human kindness. . . . If it would have happened to us, we'd hope that our opponent would try to make it as level a playing field as you possibly could under these circumstances."[3]

This mom couldn't ignore the circumstances that put another team at an unfair disadvantage. She and her neighbors felt compelled to address the inequities of the situation—to provide extra support to other people's children. To these football parents, fairness meant redistributing resources to ensure everyone's needs were met.

How is this circumstance different from the circumstances children face in schools each day? The child whose mother isn't literate. Or the twins whose parents' income is below the poverty level and who come to school hungry and stressed. These children and others arrive at school with an unfair disadvantage purely through circumstance. Any truly fair system should do as the parents in Illinois did and provide *extra* to make up for the unfair disadvantage. This *extra* includes being taught by the best teachers, receiving extra resources, having a longer school day, whatever it takes to make sure all our kids get the opportunities that learning provides. This is the definition of fairness.

When the word *equity* gets bandied about in education, does it mean the same thing to all of us? Two frameworks have influenced my definitions of equity and fairness in schools. The first defines the historical context, which we have to understand before moving forward. The second points to a practical solution for what we should do right now.

Gloria Ladson-Billings argues for a paradigm shift in how we think about achievement gaps. She distinguishes between the achievement *deficits* that exist for too many students of color and the education *debt* that has accumulated over centuries as a result of our country not serving communities of color fairly.[4] Achievement gaps don't occur in a vacuum. There's a long history that has to be understood and addressed to be able to adequately disrupt inequitable educational outcomes. This framework helps me analyze our responses at Douglass. Are we just addressing the surface deficits in student performance, or are we thinking critically about how to address the deep-seated debts that result from long-term inequity?

The other framework establishes a practical way of achieving equity. Over the years as a teacher, I came up with a demonstration to share this framework with my students. I would balance a piece of chalk on the top of the blackboard and ask the tallest and the shortest students to each come up to the board and retrieve it. The tallest student would reach up and take down the chalk, but the distance was too great for the shortest student.

To these preteens, there was no question: the situation was unfair. Inevitably, someone would suggest that the shorter student should get a chair or a stool or some other resource to allow him or her to reach the chalk. The lesson students took away was one that many elementary school teachers impart to their students: fair doesn't mean equal. It means giving everyone what they need to reach the goal.

Political scientist John Powell describes this concept for the university set.[5] He coined the term *targeted universalism* to describe what fair should look like. As with the chalk example, targeted universalism recognizes that giving the same amount of support to everyone can in fact produce inequitable results. To achieve equity, we first determine the goal that people must achieve and then differentiate our resource distribution to get everyone to at least that level. Leading for equity means integrating this approach into instructional improvement, our work with families, and everything we do.

As a new leader at Douglass, I thought the challenge would be convincing teachers and parents that fair doesn't always mean equal. And that has been some of the work. But much more challenging—and humbling—has been learning that in fact I sometimes don't see the inequity around me. Sometimes my biases prevent me from recognizing when something is unfair.

## What Does Fair Look Like in Schooling?

Initially, simply redistributing resources seemed like the whole solution to the issue of fairness in schools. When he was mayor of Newark, New Jersey, Cory Booker frequently described what this might look like. With his usual passion, Booker pilloried the status quo in schools, where we have historically held time constant (everyone goes to school for the same amount of time) and allowed achievement to vary (not all kids achieve proficiency).

Instead, he urged, we need to hold achievement constant (all kids will reach or exceed proficiency) while holding time variable (extend learning time for those who need it). This follows the idea of targeted universalism. Some kids get more of the resource—in this case, time—to pass the threshold of proficiency.

I shared Booker's framing with teachers and families at Douglass, and we took some good steps to redefine fairness at the school. We repurposed an afterschool homework help session to provide an additional ninety minutes of instruction for our lowest-performing students. I insisted to classroom teachers that when they assigned reading groups, the lowest-performing students had to be taught by the teacher with the greatest level of expertise in the room. No longer should student teachers be assigned to the lowest-performing groups (happening in some but not all classrooms). And, like many schools, we at Douglass began an extensive process of monitoring student growth throughout the year and designing interventions for students who were falling behind. Our commitment to increasing opportunity for the lowest-performing students seemed clear.

A pattern quickly surfaced. The same group of students came up below grade level in more than one subject and repeatedly throughout the year.

These mostly low-income and mostly Black students weren't learning the material the first time it was taught. They did poorly on assessments and then required reteaching of the material in order to catch up.

The staff and I prided ourselves on taking responsibility for these students' achievement. When assessments showed them below grade level, we designed remediation for them to learn the material they hadn't mastered. This approach frequently involved pulling students from class to give them targeted remediation. Once they had learned the skill, they would no longer have to leave the classroom. Many students made progress. However, underlying this approach was a bias that wasn't being addressed.

We had fallen into what is a fairly typical cycle in American schools. We lamented but didn't question the fact that the same kids—mostly kids of color, mostly low income, many nonnative English speakers—were repeatedly falling behind. We were 100 percent committed to helping these kids catch up each time, but we never questioned the fact that they weren't understanding the instruction the first time around. What if the deficits weren't in the students but in the general instruction, the way we structured learning, and my expectations as an administrator?

Working with Elliot Stern, my leadership coach, I came to realize that we needed to assess our basic instructional methods. Were we providing enough differentiation from the get-go so that more students could get their needs met during the general instruction? Shouldn't the goal be for students to access learning along with their peers rather than repeatedly falling behind and then being pulled from class for catch-up? Why was I comfortable with some kids—the same kids, the majority of whom were kids of color—repeatedly needing to be pulled out for remediation? Why didn't this data cause me to examine the instruction that led to this inequitable outcome in the first place? Have I grown so accustomed to inequitable results that I expect them at this point? Do I think the status quo of racial achievement gaps is normal?

These are the kinds of questions a principal colleague asked at a recent administrator meeting. We were in the midst of evaluating a district curriculum. She asked if our assessment of the curriculum would be different if large numbers of White students regularly fell below grade level under this approach to instruction. Would we think differently if large numbers of White students regularly needed remediation? Why is it different when the group of students consistently falling behind is Black? When we're analyzing the data, why aren't we more shocked when large numbers of Black students underperform? Why, she asked, would we continue to consider the curriculum viable with results like those?

At my school, changing our perspective about our goal led us to change the agenda for our data meetings. We realized that we needed to use the results not just to determine who needed extra support in the short term but also to determine what we could do instructionally so that fewer kids would be off-track next time around. What could we learn from the needs of the students in front of us that would help improve the general instruction they were getting every day? We needed to design an intervention to improve *teaching*.

Thinking about how to adjust our overall approach to instruction prompted teachers to rethink routine patterns. One teacher said, "I realize I need to provide more reading time in my schedule so that students don't have to go outside of class to get additional reading instruction." Another reflected, "I need to do more explicit grammar instruction in class to address these gaps." As a school, we determined we needed to explicitly teach language development because of the high number of English language learners in all our classes, not just our Sheltered English Immersion classes.

After we discussed this new framing of looking at data, a team leader said at an ILT meeting, "I think the data is telling us that we need to really look at the way we teach. There shouldn't be so many kids who need remediation. We need to rethink the model." Another said, "Maybe we need to rethink how we do pull-out special education services. Some kids are missing quite a few whole-class lessons." This has raised a larger question that we're investigating now: how does our instructional model support or not support all students? How could we be using it more strategically? These questions won't be easy to answer but are compelling us to dig deeper into how to level the playing field in school.

## What Does Fair Look Like in Curriculum? Windows and Mirrors

One February, I sent an e-mail to the staff explaining my mixed feelings about Black History Month. Truly multicultural curriculum incorporates Black history, along with the cultures and histories of all different backgrounds, into the ongoing curriculum of the classroom. Black history should be taught every month, not just relegated to a single month each year.

Within minutes, a Black teacher sent a reply to everyone that immediately made me regret my e-mail. Yes, we should incorporate Black history throughout the year. *And* we should give it extra time in February. With the norm so far skewed in our society, we've got a long way to go before the scales are balanced. I realized she was right.

Educator Emily Style describes multicultural curriculum as a combination of windows and mirrors.[6] We all need to see ourselves reflected in the content of our curriculum, and we also need windows to see into the experiences and cultures of people different from us. Mirrors validate who we are in the world; windows broaden our view of how the world looks to others. Poet Adrienne Rich described the importance of curricular mirrors vividly, "When someone with the authority of a teacher describes the world and you are not in it, there is a moment of psychic disequilibrium, as if you looked into a mirror and saw nothing."[7] We want students to feel affirmed—not absent—within the curriculum.

Most staff members at Douglass embrace this thinking and make efforts to have read-alouds, word problems, wall displays, research assignments, units of study, and morning greetings reflect the cultural diversity of our school. The kindergarten team used to study China every year. Now they've adjusted to teaching about whichever country outside the United States is widely represented in their classes that particular year. Last year they studied Ethiopia. This year, with a significant number of Bengali children, they are studying Bangladesh. One day I walked into class as children tried on traditional Bengali clothes that one of the students had brought in to share with her classmates. She beamed with pride as her peers oohed and aahed over the wardrobe from her home country.

Children of all grades swell with pride at our all-school assemblies, which frequently incorporate affirmations of our cultural diversity.

Some individual teachers have needed prompting, however. "You have a number of kids from Haiti in your class. Have you been able to find books about Haiti or immigrant families to read to your class?" "How do you choose songs, writing, and art projects to provide mirrors for more kids in your class?" Without this awareness, we risk marginalizing children, devaluing their home culture, or making them feel invisible in the life of the classroom.

I saw a poignant example of this when I joined a school mid-year as an interim principal. Before vacation at this school, several hallways had been filled with Christmas displays, children had completed Santa wish lists for homework, and several teachers had used their own money to buy their students Christmas presents to take home "to put under the tree." On my first day in January, I visited a second grade classroom where children were returning from December break and sharing about their vacation. When it was her turn, one little girl said with her eyes looking down, "I had a bad vacation." Surprised, her teacher asked why, and the little girl, who was Muslim, said as if stating the obvious, "Because I didn't celebrate Christmas." I can still picture her dejected slump.

Schools have the power to help children feel accepted and valued for who they are or to reinforce marginalization, a feeling of being "other." This teacher gave a warm and sympathetic comment to the student, but it failed to heal the child's or my broken heart at such evidence of not belonging. Several years later, I was prepared for this situation and didn't hesitate to respond.

During one lesson at Douglass, I observed a sixth grade teacher define several vocabulary words using middle class references. "You know, it's like that feeling you had when you went on a plane for the first time." "Imagine when you go to a restaurant with your family." At another point she held up a coffee cup from a K-cup coffee maker and expected kids to recognize it.

Once again, I could feel myself get queasy. Looking around this teacher's class, I saw a student who lived in a homeless shelter, another who had only recently gotten her first bed after sleeping on a couch for many years, and other children whose families' income likely prevented them from being exposed to any of these situations first-hand. In debriefing the lesson with this teacher, I pointed out this issue and asked her to think of examples more accessible to all students, including those whose background was different from hers. She was surprised but did so and was more conscious of her approach in future lessons.

As a beginning principal, I hesitated to give this kind of feedback, fearing that it was nitpicking about small issues and that I risked being perceived as a micromanaging principal. I've come to see that the reason these issues make me so uncomfortable is that they are *not* small issues. Affirming each child's identity is not nitpicking; it's essential to creating a school where all kids succeed. When teachers understand that their background and perspective are not universal, they become more skillful in valuing and validating the experiences of all their students.

For White, middle class educators like myself—members of the dominant group in our society—we have the privilege of experiencing our culture and daily routines as normal. When we ensure children of all backgrounds feel validated for exactly who they are, we begin to change what normal means in our school and our community. We also build trust between families and school. Like other principals committed to multicultural education, I want teachers at my school to feel this power and use it to increase, not diminish, students' sense of belonging.

### Redistribute Principal Time

Time is the most valuable currency in schools. How time gets allocated signals what is valued—and what is not. At Douglass, as at many majority-White schools, the status quo has long been that the White, middle class, and more affluent families participate and advocate the most and consequently have most access to the principal's time. This may be true for various reasons. The people in authority look like them, the school sends messages that affirm their experiences so they feel welcome and included; their work schedules allow it; or they have had positive past experiences talking to authority, asking for resources, or advocating for their needs to be met so they don't hesitate doing so again.

For a variety of reasons, our families of color, our low-income families, and immigrant families—those families who aren't part of the dominant group—historically have not participated as much. The reason may stem from a cultural expectation that schools are to be trusted and not questioned. It may be due to busy work schedules, or it may stem from not feeling welcome or affirmed at the school. Leaders are responsible for ensuring that all parents feel powerful at school.

Books and articles on increasing family engagement suggest leading workshops on literacy, conducting focus groups to understand parent concerns, and engaging families in conversations about homework and how to advocate for their children in parent conferences. At Douglass, we strive to follow these suggestions, and they've all been productive ways for us to engage with families across our community. We also started a Family Cultural Exchange Program (FCEP) to partner domestic families with immigrant families to create greater interconnectedness at school and among families. We hold support sessions (on reading to children or supporting academics over the summer) for parents at school and at local housing projects. We held an evening session for all of our Ethiopian families to learn about literacy with translators and plan to do more for our other large immigrant groups.

These programs are useful, and we need to do more of them more frequently. However, another strategy is unexpectedly powerful, reaches our historically underserved families, and requires time but little planning: simply reaching out personally one-on-one. This small step has made a noticeable difference at Douglass. Over months and years, it shifts the balance of power. Once again, it's leveling the playing field by giving some families extra. In this case, the "extra" is time.

I invest extra time in cultivating relationships with families outside our dominant cultural group. For example, every year, I learn the names of all students at the school. While I don't make the same promise to learn parent names, I do put effort into learning names of parents of color and immigrant parents. (This sometimes requires writing down phonetic pronunciation guides on the clipboard I carry around at drop-off time in the morning.) Through phone calls and in-person solicitation, I personally recruit these families to serve on our hiring committees and school council.

Most importantly, at school events, when these mothers or other parents whom I've recruited for committees arrive, we greet each other as friends. It's been surprising to see that even single instances of reaching out make such a difference. Because I am the figurehead of the school, every act I do carries extra weight. Simple acts like reaching out personally make people feel they're part of the inner circle. In fact, over time, I've come up with a deliberate strategy of seeking out our most underrepresented families at school events and greeting them personally. This step is born of experience—finding out what happens when I'm not so deliberate.

At my first school event, I approached the potluck dinner casually and spoke to those who happened to be standing near me or who approached me. By the end of the night, I realized two things. The first is something all brides and grooms know: you don't get to eat when you're the host of the party. Second, all the people I'd spoken with had been White, English speakers. Without any deliberate effort or intention on my part, I had reinforced the status quo of who gets the most access to power.

Now I'm more strategic at community dinners and performances. I've learned to scan the venue as I approach, seeking out our historically underrepresented families. In this way, I can more strategically share the spotlight that follows me everywhere in this role of leader. With greater awareness, I can make sure that families of color and immigrant families receive the majority of my time.

Sometimes small acts such as shifting the distribution of time can affect who feels a sense of agency at school. As with my experience at these school events, if we just stand still—let things unfold on their own—we reinforce the status quo. This leads me to ask myself, How much time is spent meeting with families who already have power at Douglass versus time with those who don't? Things are unlikely to change if I wait for our underrepresented families to make an appointment with me; I need to seek them out.

After several years, I am reaping the benefits of these connections as many of these families now seek me out to introduce a visiting grandmother, tell me something they noticed about the curriculum, ask for help finding a summer program, or tell me what they appreciate about their child's teacher. And now, at our annual World Foods Dinner, an Ethiopian mom regularly saves a plate of her homemade injera and okra so at the end of the night, I have something for dinner.

My actions alone aren't enough to create a more inclusive culture, however. So I've been looking for ways to "teach" the community that we are stronger when we hear from everyone. Annual publicity about the Family Cultural Exchange Program, teachers' messages home, and the principal's note in the monthly newsletter all send a clear message that intercultural relationships are valued. However, some people need more than messaging; they need actual practice reaching across boundaries.

Times when we get together as a school community for meetings or events provide opportunities for this kind of practice. Now some of the limited time at Back to School night is reserved for people to practice stepping outside their familiar circles and actively participate in our racial, economic, and linguistic diversity. During the school day, we teach children to do this, and I finally realized that we also need to be explicit about this behavior with adults. So when the families of each grade level gather in the cafeteria, I invite all the attendees to stand up and introduce themselves to someone whom they don't know and to make a commitment to do this at every school event.

Because these introductions are sometimes new for people, I've learned to offer suggested topics to talk about ("Ask about your children. What's their favorite part of school? Least favorite? How has the transition to the school year gone?"). In response to my directions, people put down their handouts and slowly stand up from the plastic cafeteria tables. Moms, dads, grandmothers, and aunts look around and, after an awkward pause, turn or walk to a stranger and reach out a hand. What begins tentatively evolves into a chorus of animated conversations as people lean in to hear a name a second time, nod their heads at shared experiences, and invest in their new connections. It's always hard to interrupt and bring people back to their seats. Parents have said that these few minutes affect the tone of the evening and sometimes the school year for them.

Evidence suggests these strategies are helping. More low-income families—many of whom are immigrants or families of color—now choose our school within our district's controlled choice system than in years past. And many more families of color and immigrant families attend school events; an immigrant parent says she thinks the numbers have at least doubled. At the most recent teacher appreciation potluck, we had easily triple the number of immigrant parents and parents of color volunteering than we have had in the past. More parents of color ran for school council this year than have in any of my previous years, and more volunteered to be room parents.

Informally, I've also seen more connections across race, class, and language lines as people reach out to families different from their own. When parent Hodan from Somalia and American-born Emily greeted each other with a big hug in the school lobby, I asked how they knew each other so well since their children were in different grades. Hodan answered with exuberance, "She's my [FCEP] buddy!" They both beamed, and I felt the foundation of our community knit stronger in their shared smiles.

## NAME RACE

A few years ago, I was part of an administrator group conducting instructional rounds at another school. We observed in a second grade classroom where the teacher read aloud a biography of Wynton Marsalis, the famed trumpet player. At the first picture of Marsalis, who is African American, a child excitedly called out, "He looks like Martin Luther King!" The teacher looked carefully at the picture and said, "You're right, he does. His hair looks the same. And his eyes are the same color. He does look a lot like Martin Luther King." Then she continued to read the story.

I stood on the side of the room dumbfounded, struggling to follow the ground rules of our silent observation. I wanted to interject, "And his skin color is brown just like Martin Luther King's skin. You're right; they both have that beautiful chocolate-colored skin." Isn't that the most obvi-ous thing the child was responding to, especially since the two men don't otherwise look much alike? What message did the children get when the teacher so carefully avoided naming skin color? Later that day, the other observers and I shared this class exchange with the principal, but I was left feeling that something much larger than this individual teacher's avoid-ance had surfaced.

We don't talk enough about race in schools. Or rather, White people don't talk enough about race in schools. Most White people don't talk about race at all. I've heard some say that they don't see race. They believe erasing any recognition of racial differences is the most constructive way to fight inequities. And if you say you don't see racial differences, then you don't talk about them either.

The facts, however, are clear that overall our society is most definitely not color-blind; people of color *are* treated differently from White people in this country. Personal beliefs can't erase this fact. Additionally, color isn't something to be feared. Would we say in the same way that we don't see gender? What's the problem with race that makes people feel they shouldn't see it? Our racial identities are complicated and socially con-structed and often wrapped up in cultural identities that shape us in pro-found ways.

For other White people, this conversation feels awkward and uncom-fortable and therefore is to be avoided. I've heard many White people say they're anxious about saying something wrong. I can empathize with this anxiety and feel it even more acutely in my position of authority. In his research on stereotype threat, psychologist Claude Steele describes this common fear among White people of saying something racist and the self-censorship that results.[8] It's painfully ironic that White people tend to avoid the very conversations about race that would provide the experience and learning necessary to counteract their unintentional biases. This lack of conversational experience maintains ignorance. Many people of color have had to endure a whole lot of discomfort talking about this issue with mainstream White America. It's shouldn't be too much for me and other

White educators to push ourselves to be uncomfortable more regularly. Naming race is a critical way to disrupt the status quo.

### Make Race Terms Normal

I'm increasingly aware of the times when I and others neglect to name race in our conversation and the adverse impact this can have on our work. Similar to the earlier second grade teacher example, when describing a student or someone else at our school, many people will tell everything about the child except skin color. Wouldn't that be an important descriptor if we need to quickly and easily picture the child in question? When describing anyone, I've taught myself to include race as a normal descriptor like hair color or height. It's interesting how disconcerting this can be for many White people.

I used to name race only for people of color until I realized that doing so reinforces the status quo that White is "normal" and everything else is "other." So I name race for White people as well. "You can find the fourth grade teacher in the cafeteria this period. She's tall, White, has long brown hair in a ponytail." "Can you give this to Evan? He's the small, Black kid with the backpack standing outside the office right now." "Do you know Susan's mom? She's White, blond hair, usually hangs out with her son in the park after school." Naming race shouldn't be taboo. For many people, just this act of including race in descriptions of people is a first step toward normalizing naming race.

Race is clearly relevant when describing someone's appearance, but what about other times in conversation? Sometimes we don't need to know the race of a person to understand the situation. Other times we do. When describing the fact that three kids were left off the field trip list, is it important to say they were all Black? What about when describing a distraught parent at the concert? Is his race relevant to the story? And when we're developing interventions, should we attend to race when we assign groups? Whether or not we name race in these situations reflects whether we think it has bearing on the situation. And this in turn reflects the range of associations we have with race. We learn a lot about ourselves by observing our own inclinations and those of others and analyzing the thinking behind them.

## Make Talking About Racial Bias Normal

I've also learned the importance of naming potential racial bias. Most White people want to believe that bias doesn't exist. Or certainly that we ourselves are free from it. We may be tempted to insist "There's not a racist bone in my body" or to think of racists as obviously bad people, usually wearing white hoods. It's true that we've come a long way in reducing conscious, overt racism. Institutional racism, however, persists and unconscious bias continues to seep into our thinking from a host of sources around us. Bias is part of what we absorb in this country like unseen pollution in the air. All of us carry unconscious prejudices. Denying that we do demonstrates a level of ignorance.

For people of color, racial bias is a reality, a part of their daily lived experience. So whether or not it's conscious, whether or not it's brought up in conversation, it's present in people's thinking. Acknowledging it can go a long way in building trust across racial groups.

A brief interaction with a parent helped me see this point. A Black parent from Haiti called me one summer to request that her son skip a grade. He was advanced in math, on grade level in literacy, and she was insistent that I do this. I wanted to be responsive to this parent, to reinforce her engagement with the school and with me. However, for a variety of strongly held principles, double-promotion isn't something we practice at Douglass. Therefore, I had to decline the request much to this mother's anger and frustration.

In reflecting on this situation much later, I realized an important piece of information might have made a difference in our interaction. Perhaps this mother had assumed that race was a factor in how I considered her request—that a White principal had a prejudiced view of her Black son. Or that I harbored prejudices about immigrants.

Given the stereotypes that are alive and well in our society, this assumption certainly would have been rational. This parent may even have had past personal experiences of people treating her inequitably. In fact, what evidence did this mother have to reassure her that prejudice was *not* informing my decision? The preponderance of evidence indicates that a White person is more likely to be prejudiced than not, so the logical assumption would be to distrust my decision.

What I neglected to share with this parent was that just a few months earlier, I had declined a White family's request for the same thing and had given the same explanation. In retrospect, I wish that I had shared that example and had named race and potential bias as factors in our interactions. "You may wonder if I'm refusing to promote your son because he's Black. I would understand if you had that worry. So I want to share another example in case that is helpful to know." I wish I had seen outside my own White lens to understand and empathize better with this mother's possible perspective.

In contrast to our school's policy about promotion, we feel many young kindergarteners benefit from a second year in kindergarten. This is a challenging topic to present to families, however. Many parents worry that we are suggesting retention because we don't see their child as capable. This concern is understandably amplified for children of color whose parents may feel that our view of their child is biased because of racial prejudice. Bringing this concern into the conversation helps address what is otherwise an unspoken and therefore unaddressed fear.

One year when a younger than average kindergartener who was Black struggled to connect with her peers developmentally and was also behind academically, we recommended a second year of kindergarten. Her mother was furious, said that we were judging her daughter incorrectly, and took steps to request a transfer to another school across the city. This single mother, Jasmine, was herself barely literate, was struggling to find work, and was desperate for her daughter to excel in school.

After hearing about her response, I reached out to Jasmine to suggest that she speak to another mother whose child was going to repeat kindergarten. This other mom was White. I told Jasmine that two years of kindergarten was a practice that we thought was valuable for kids of all races and not just something we recommended for Black students. It was drop-off time at school, and I ran to find the second mother. While their kids played in a classroom, the two mothers sat in the teachers' room weighing the pros and cons of kindergarten retention and sharing their children's experiences in school. After this conversation, Jasmine reluctantly decided to keep her child at our school.

In her second year of kindergarten, this girl blossomed. She gained confidence and academic strength, and said she loved to read. By the end of first grade, she was on grade level and displaying a wonderful voice in her writing. Jasmine began volunteering at school events and periodically would come to the office to ask if there was anything she could do to help. Four years later, after moving to another town, Jasmine made a special trip back to our school to say thank you for "everything." She came to trust that we had her child's best interests in mind.

## Call Attention to Our Potential Bias

Mica Pollock's book *Colormute* lays out a framework for thinking about the ways people do and do not name race in schools.[9] According to her research, we either suppress, use, or contest the use of race names. In her research at a school, she found that people most often suppressed—or did not want to name race—when they might be personally implicated in a situation. In each of the examples described previously, naming race could feel like opening up the possibility that I was being prejudiced. In actuality, this is the view from a White lens. I might have feared that naming race would introduce this possibility into the situation. For most people of color, however, this possibility is *always* present.

Unlike in these two examples, I don't always have a parallel situation to point to so that I can reassure people that they are not being singled out because of their race. So how can I reassure a parent that the school is not treating her child unfairly because she is a child of color or doesn't speak English or in whatever other way is in a group that often experiences discrimination?

The bottom line is that I can't. Unconscious prejudices may always creep in to our decision making. Bias will likely always influence the way we interpret the situation. As products of a society rife with messages of

White as normal and everything else as other, we can't escape that fact. However, I've learned that it can help to acknowledge that we at the school are aware of and actively working to recognize bias in our thinking and acting.

The value in naming potential bias became clear when we worked with the mother of a child with extreme behaviors. When this child, Jaylen, was in fifth grade, he had come close to being expelled from another school in the district, and communication with his mother had deteriorated to the point that a mediator was involved. Instead of being expelled, Jaylen was transferred to our school. At our urging and with his mother's reluctant agreement, Jaylen began working with a psychiatrist who was then in close touch with the school. At the end of a year, this psychiatrist joined our school team, Jaylen's mother, and a social worker to discuss whether Jaylen should remain in our school or attend a special therapeutic program.

As we discussed the situation, Jaylen's mother was visibly tense and on guard. She appeared to brace herself for threats from multiple directions. As staff members shared their experiences with her son, the mother immediately shot down each concern. With this mindset, she wasn't going to be able to hear our observations or requests for collaboration let alone discuss placement recommendations.

It was hard not to be acutely aware of race at this meeting. While our school psychologist and occupational therapist are Black, the teacher and I are both White. Jaylen, as well as his mother, social worker, and psychiatrist are all Black. We all knew the reality that most of the children referred to the therapeutic program were Black boys. Overall, the school system was not serving Black boys well. And yet, here I was at this meeting feeling as though this child had psychological needs beyond what we could service in a general education setting. His behavior was increasingly aggressive, and his impulses conformed to what several mental health practitioners informally diagnosed as severe mood disorder. His previous school's team report also confirmed this diagnosis.

How could we diffuse the tension so that we could have the frank conversation we needed to understand this child and his needs better? How could we build the trust that we desperately needed to help Jaylen make progress? It seemed right to vocalize the unspoken thoughts in the room. I described the racial make-up of the therapeutic program and my feelings about that. None of us wanted to be the school that fails and sends another Black boy away because of his behavior.

I spoke directly to Jaylen's mom, "I'm guessing that you desperately want to keep your son out of this program and you're wondering if this school just wants to get rid of him. I'm White, his teacher is White. You may be wondering if we see your son with prejudice, if we are judging your son as incapable because he's Black. If I were in your shoes right now, that would definitely be a worry going through my head when White people are assessing my son."

No one responded directly to my comment; no one said "thank you" or "yes, that's what I was thinking." There was no dramatic change in the meeting at that moment. However, the discussion slowed down a bit. The psychiatrist and social worker brainstormed additional strategies that hadn't been on the table, and we all agreed to try them. We continued to work with Jaylen for two more years before the full team agreed that he needed a more therapeutic setting.

Almost a year after this meeting, the psychiatrist was at our school and pulled me aside to talk to me about my comment. He confirmed that racial bias was in fact a recurring topic of conversation with this family as it was with most of the Black families he worked with around the city. He said that he had never heard a White principal make a comment like mine and he felt it had helped both him and the family have a better relationship with the school. The social worker who worked with other families in our school approached me at one of our graduations to say the same.

In her article "Cultivating the Trust of Black Parents," psychologist Beverly Daniel Tatum describes the experience of parents of color at meetings like these between White educators and Black parents.[10] As she explains, when a White educator names race, it is reassuring *not* because it means the person is free from bias but because it indicates that the person may be aware of her own prejudices. Recognizing the pervasiveness of bias and our vulnerability to it is an important first step. Parents will still reserve judgment until they can assess actions, but it can be reassuring to know that a White person with authority in this situation at least understands this underlying problem that so many families of color face.

Often, just naming race or potential bias in conversations has symbolic positive impact. It signals that these are not inherently scary topics and talking about them is not taboo in this meeting. At the same time, talk is not enough. When White people acknowledge the potential for racial bias, we need to be ready to own our role in that. Am I not seeing something in this situation? Or am I doing something that could be reinforcing the problem?

Talk is only the means; it is not the end goal. Talking about race is productive to the degree it helps us identify and dismantle our unconscious biases so that we are better champions of equity.

## DO ASSUME POSITIVE INTENTIONS; DON'T PRESUME HIGH EXPECTATIONS

When I entered the job as principal, I thought low expectations would be easy to spot—teachers clearly favoring White students over students of color, ignoring the needs of students of color or dismissing them outright. As a leader for equity, I anticipated fearlessly confronting these prejudices, showing these uncaring teachers how they were wrong, and insisting that they change or leave. In fact, the situation is not so straightforward. Low expectations show up in more subtle ways—ways that are critical for school leaders to recognize in teachers and in ourselves.

Like teachers most places, the adults at Douglass care deeply for our students. Every day is full of countless demonstrations of this caring. Teachers follow up when Susie looks sad, bake cakes when they know a family isn't able to send in birthday cupcakes, and buy books to send home over the summer and new jeans for Louis whose ankles are showing. Teachers spend their lunch time providing extra help and drive students home after tutoring them after school. Teachers ask about Francine's new baby brother, provide hugs and nurturing when Ryan's grandmother dies, and celebrate academic growth with sincere delight. Administrators see only the smallest fraction of all that teachers do to help their students.

They don't do these things because someone's watching; they do it because they love their students.

We can easily mistake this kind of caring as having high expectations. They're not the same. Caring alone is not enough, and in fact, caring alone may stunt student achievement, particularly for our students of color. Harvard professor Ronald Ferguson's research identified two characteristics of effective teachers for students of color: high help (a commitment to provide unwavering support and assistance to a child) and high perfectionism (an insistence upon reaching the highest standards for performance).[11] High help combined with high perfectionism was found to produce the greatest results in student achievement for students of color, including African American, Latino, Native American, and Pacific Islander. High help alone—without an equally high expectation for results—was found to produce positive outcomes for White students and the lowest outcomes for African American students. One administrator at a majority African American school ruefully noted this pattern, "We're loving our students to mediocrity."

Other researchers have used the phrase *warm demander* to describe this combination of skills proven to be highly effective with children of color in particular.[12] The warm part of that equation comes easily to most educators. When they need to insist on high performance, the unconscious bias creeps in. To be a warm demander, you have to carry a deep-seated conviction that every child in front of you can achieve at high levels. You have to be able to insist on that even when meeting resistance from a student—especially when meeting resistance from a student. Warm demanders approach all children, and particularly the lowest-performing children, with confidence, never pity.

Even the best intentioned, most caring White teachers may have internalized low expectations for their students. I've had to confront my own resistance to this idea. Racial bias is something I expected to find only in bad people. If a teacher cares about her students and is really good in so many ways, how could she have low expectations for a particular group? Realizing that caring educators can have low expectations and unconscious prejudice feels particularly unsettling because it means my own warmth and devotion to all students doesn't make me immune to unconscious racism.

Therein lies the problem of ascribing intentionality to bias. More often than not in schools today, bias is not a deliberate act. Rather, it's a slow, steady, subtle brainwashing. It stems from the images and distorted or false narratives that bombard us. If White people don't consciously seek out other narratives, we unconsciously absorb the prejudice and are blind to it. When White people think they're free from racism, we're less likely to check ourselves and potentially more damaging to the children we seek to serve.

In a compelling and funny TED Talk, commentator Jay Smooth describes a way to respond to the racism none of us wants to be stuck with.[13] He explains we wouldn't think twice telling someone we respect that they have spinach in their teeth before they enter a high stakes arena. We know they don't want it there; they didn't put it there on purpose. It's just part of what happens when you're ingesting food. The natural response is to alert the person to what we've observed, let her address it, and move on. Leaders need to be able to take the same approach when we see subtle forms of bias in schools. If we can separate the bias from the person's identity, it's easier to address. No caring teacher wants to harbor low expectations.

Inevitably, these low expectations translate into low student performance—either in academics, behavior, or both. These teachers aren't consciously prejudiced. Rather, they're allowing unconscious, unchecked bias to influence their decisions. And teachers make a lot of decisions. How to respond to student questions, who gets pushed to do higher-level work, what to share with parents, what to expect from homework, how to respond to misbehavior, and so on. It's been important to question my own decision making and judgment of students. Am I truly seeing all students as full of potential, or have I unconsciously written off some students as those who just aren't going to make it?

I was forced to confront my own bias one year when staff member Christine, who is Black, raised a concern. Christine is one of those amazing people who anchors a school, with a strong connection to most of the students (and adults) at Douglass. She was worried that a Black student had been disengaged from academics for several months. From junior kindergarten on, Keon had been one of our most challenging students. This year, after starting fifth grade with daily, aggressive outbursts and disruptions, he had been granted a pass to take a break in the office or library to collect himself before returning to productive work. This system had reduced the outbursts and gotten him back on task most days. Now, months later, he showed signs of decline—staying out of his classroom for longer periods of time, half-hearted engagement with his work. Keon's learning was suffering.

Christine's concern revealed the blind eye I had been turning to Keon's decline. I'd noticed it peripherally, felt that queasy feeling, and moved on to the seventy-three other things on my to-do list. If I had dug into the root cause for my work avoidance, it would have been clear that I didn't immediately know what to do. If we assumed that Keon's teacher had done everything possible, maybe this was as good as it could get. Maybe we should celebrate the success of eliminating outbursts and claim victory. He no longer disrupted the class and most often cooperated with his teacher, who gave him snacks and frequent hugs of encouragement. (In fact, he even gave handwritten notes to the teacher telling her she was his favorite and asking if she would be his mom.) When I did eventually dig into my internal response, I also found doubt. I wasn't confident Keon could do any better.

Christine's concern made me identify and face my doubt. Spurred to action, I set up weekly meetings with the teacher and determined that together we would raise our expectations for this student. When I investigated further, it became clear that the teacher hadn't called Keon's mother or increased accountability for academics on the existing behavior plan. Perhaps, like me, she had been satisfied with meeting the low bar of decreased behavioral trouble. I committed to being a warm demander. I let her know that at each week's meeting we would follow up on our previous week's plans and look at Keon's academic work for the week. I offered whatever help I could provide and pledged to keep meetings under thirty minutes.

Holding these meetings wasn't easy. The teacher was stressed and felt she was working very hard with Keon, who had given many skilled teachers in the building a run for their money. I resisted the impulse to simply offer support and forced myself to hold her accountable for academic results. And she got them. At the next meeting, she reported that she had gotten some support from Keon's mother, had recalibrated the classroom plan to raise the bar on academic output, and had met with Keon to alert him to new expectations. While this result took several weeks, these meetings proved to be a turning point. During the last half of the year, Keon was out of class far less and, more importantly, completed all of his work to standards.

The teacher confessed that our meetings felt hard. No matter how much I offered support, she couldn't help but feel that she had messed up and was being called to task by her boss. But the role of a warm demander isn't to coddle, and in fact the teacher and I had both messed up. Keon's low performance was the proof. Our meetings held both of us accountable for demanding high-quality outcomes. We needed to expect as much from this student as we would from our own children. To do anything otherwise is to fall short of our commitment to equity.

Lessons like this one have alerted me to the range of ways that low expectations may persist in a classroom and a school by the best-intentioned educators, including administrators. Teachers may pity a student, feel concerned about being perceived as mean, or want to avoid potential resistance because it's hard to hold steady. In addition, some teachers feel they've done everything they can when they've run through their repertoire of strategies and just need help seeing outside the box of their familiar practices. And often, a teacher inadvertently lowers expectations out of her desire to help a child succeed: "I helped the child every time he raised his hand . . . explained the vocabulary so that he could understand the piece . . . told him he could write less because he looked frustrated" and so on. What some of my staff call *coddling* has been referred to as *dysfunctional rescuing* and is a serious problem stemming from the best of intentions.

Teachers like the one I described here sincerely want all their students to succeed. Unconscious biases interfere with their best intentions. When we, as school leaders, see through our own biases and can help teachers do the same, we disrupt inequity and everyone benefits.

## BE WILLING TO BE UNCOMFORTABLE

As I work on disrupting my own biases, I continue to make mistakes along the way. Missteps can be painful, humbling, and with conscious effort, ultimately helpful. More and more I'm learning that staying in the discomfort—continuing to ask questions, delving into the roots of my thinking—is what leads to necessary learning.

After hearing that all the members on a newly appointed hiring committee were White, two teachers came to my office to express concern. I acknowledged that I had cut corners this time. When all the initial volunteers were White, I hadn't personally recruited people of color to serve on the committee because I was so busy. However, I shared with the inquiring teachers my thinking that everything would be fine because everyone on the committee was committed to increasing the racial diversity of our staff. "They're all on board," I assured the concerned teachers.

Then one of the teachers, who is Black, pointed out what I hadn't considered—the perspective of the people of color interviewing at our school. What message would those candidates get about our school from an all-White hiring committee? How would they interpret that leadership decision? These teachers were right. I recruited a parent of color. We didn't end up hiring a person of color for that role, although we did for several other roles that year. However, this parent turned out to be a critical bridge for our new hires in ways we couldn't have expected.

Another example occurred as I was facilitating a series of committee meetings about increasing the achievement of our African American students. This committee's goal was to engage the faculty in talking about race and to make sure these conversations felt emotionally safe for everyone. After brainstorming ideas, we moved on to the next topic. A White staff member pointed out that we had attended solely to the ways we could make these conversations comfortable for White people to express their honest thoughts and feelings. We hadn't considered what a person of color would need to feel ready to join in the discussion.

Once again, I had forgotten to recognize my own lens in the conversation. What I assume is a universal perspective is not; it's a White perspective. Hearing that teacher's calm but pointed observation initially sent me into a tailspin. *Again*, I'd forgotten to check my assumptions. How had I let it happen again? How could I call myself an ally if I kept forgetting to consider views different from my own?

In these moments, I've felt the gamut of responses of shame, embarrassment, defensiveness, and defeat. Like many leaders, I strive to always be prepared and to have the right answers, so knowing that I'm missing part of the picture is deeply disconcerting. Increasingly, however, I'm realizing that shame and guilt about this gap inhibit growth and simply aren't helpful. As a consequence, my emotional response is changing. I've come to terms with the fact that, as a White leader, I realize countering and addressing my own unconscious bias is ongoing work, and sometimes I'll make mistakes. Over time, I'm learning to embrace rather than resist (or try to hide) this disequilibrium as a natural and necessary part of learning. With this growth mindset, working to expand my view is a rewarding and empowering act, not an apologetic one.

What happens if we don't do this work? If we get defensive or otherwise send the signal that we don't want our mistakes pointed out? Or that we don't want to learn about the impact of our words and actions? We maintain the status quo. We meet the needs of people who are like us, but we don't hear all voices. We walk around blind to the experiences of some of our students and families. We inhibit growth, both theirs and ours.

As my colleague Marco says, this work is hard, demanding, tiring, *and* never-ending. The goal isn't necessarily for the conversations to get easy, but for us to get more skillful having them. Like building a muscle, the more we do it, the stronger we get.

CHAPTER 9

# Supervision and Evaluation

The truth is that everything that can be accomplished by showing
a person when he's wrong, ten times as much can be accomplished
by showing him where he is right. The reason we don't do it so often
is that it's more fun to throw a rock through a window than to put in a
pane of glass.

—Robert T. Allen

Discussing supervision so far toward the end of this book may seem
strange. If improving instruction is the goal, shouldn't observing teachers be up front and center? The fact is, these topics are all intertwined.
Supervision is effective only when trust exists. A culture of continuous
improvement maximizes what teachers take from supervision. Principals
need to understand their own work avoidance tendencies to be able to
follow through with ongoing classroom observations. It's all part of an
interlocking system.

Courses on supervision are based on the premise that teaching is a
practice that can be taught. It's more science than art. Theoretically, this
concept makes sense, but as an entering principal, I still felt deep down
that teachers were born and not made. A new teacher might struggle, but
you could tell that she had what it takes—you could recognize her potential. In the same vein, it seemed logical that you could recognize when
someone just didn't have what it takes to be a good teacher.

In fact, in what a colleague has described as a BFO—blinding flash of the obvious—it has become clear to me that teachers are not so easily divided into the categories of good and bad. Teachers with incredible instincts for motivating kids may have no understanding of how to differentiate tasks. Others excel at building caring communities but have low-level expectations for academics. Some people with the most rote approach to teaching math are thoughtful curriculum designers when it comes to literacy.

The complex skills of teaching require development and refinement over the course of a career. This growth happens both collectively and individually. Principals can accelerate teacher learning with colleagues using strategies such as developing a strong school culture of improvement, internal coherence, and internal accountability. Principals also can support the individual progress of each teacher through supervision.

In this role of supervisor, administrators are often blamed for not firing bad teachers, and it's true that too many principals don't follow through with this step when it's necessary. Determined not to fall into this category, I did not shy away from evaluating people out of the job. However, while dismissing teachers is necessary, you can't fire your way to closing achievement gaps. Firing someone may take courage, but the more ongoing work of supervision takes something potentially much harder.

Effective supervision requires principals to understand that learning is developmental, to use data with compassion and curiosity, to build trusting relationships, and to hold ourselves accountable for doing rigorous, compassionate work. Ongoing supervision takes enormous skill, effort, and persistence. If we, as principals, don't shoulder *that* responsibility, we will never make the improvement our students need and deserve.

## SHIFT FROM A MINDSET OF FIXING TO GROWING

While observing in new third grade teacher Mrs. Bailey's classroom, the principal notices young Johnny struggling to learn multiplication. What is the principal's job in this moment? If you're like most educators, you probably have an instinctive impulse to do whatever it takes to make sure that Johnny learns the math. There's a strong desire to intervene directly with the child right then—to "fix" the problem.

You also may want to advise Mrs. Bailey about what went wrong with the lesson so she can make immediate improvements. "You didn't model the skill before you sent kids off to do it independently." "The kids didn't know how to record their data in an organized way so they didn't learn the pattern." That's certainly where my mind goes right away. It's a classroom teacher's mindset: figure out how to improve that lesson then and there. Get that child to learn multiplication.

Like many educators, I love figuring out the best way to teach a particular lesson. Getting deep into the weeds of pedagogy has immense appeal. *Is it better to model the strategy first or have kids mess around with the problem to get them hooked and then share some strategies? What's the perfect sample text to help kids see the writer's strategy we're focusing on?* Answering these questions is where I naturally go in conversations with teachers. Sometimes explicit directions of what to do and when to do it are exactly what a teacher needs to grow (or simply survive) in her teaching. Often, however, this can be the equivalent of simply telling the learner the answer. It's not going to produce much growth over the long term. As a result, in Mrs. Bailey's class, Johnny might end up learning multiplication the next day, but fractions and long division are right around the corner. How can I be sure the teacher won't make the same mistakes there? Who's to say that she'll be able to design and implement effective lessons for those units?

Good supervisors need to have a long-term view of each staff member and see their job as developing each teacher's skills. *What does this teacher need to learn at this moment? What habits of planning and assessing and reflecting are needed across the staff?* We must develop a mindset in the teacher so that she will be able to solve future instructional problems on her own. As principals, if we influence how a teacher plans, implements, and reflects on her teaching, we've had a profound impact on the learning that will happen in her classroom in the weeks, months, and years ahead. Allowing the teacher to problem-solve, experiment, and observe the results will teach these skills so they stick.

This approach feels slower. It feels less direct and sometimes frustrating. It involves juggling a lot of variables. Most of all, it requires continually holding those "fix" impulses in check and cultivating an instinct to coach for long-term skills. When this approach is done well, tomorrow's lesson *will* go better. The same struggle applies here: balancing the sense of urgency about day-to-day instruction with a disciplined focus on improvement over time.

When we are helping someone learn and grow, it's important to figure out when the learner just needs some information and when she needs to grapple with a problem and figure out her own solution. When someone is drowning, it won't help to stand on the dock and show her different strokes. On the other hand, repeatedly diving in to rescue someone without ever helping her learn and practice basic strokes isn't going to build a strong swimmer either. Diagnosing a teacher's developmental needs as a learner is critical to good supervision and one of the biggest challenges.

Coaching gurus Laura Lipton and Bruce Wellman recommend three different strategies to help teachers improve practice: coaching (asking targeted questions to prompt problem solving, reflection, and analysis), collaborating (coplanning or assessing side by side with the teacher), and consulting (providing specific strategies and skills).[1] A beginning teacher often needs more explicit consulting. However, as teachers gain more skill and experience, the authors recommend asking questions that prompt them to learn from an experience and then generalize from that to other situations.

These questions might start out with some scaffolding. *I noticed you used fair sticks [cold calling] for the opening discussion and didn't use them in the final reflection. How do you decide when to use that strategy for calling on kids?* Whether someone is ready for coaching or consulting might also be more dependent on her learning style than years of experience. A struggling veteran teacher might need more direction. Beginning teachers benefit enormously from reflective questions. Or sometimes the most helpful thing might be just adding tools to the toolbox. *I saw that kids took a long time moving from whole group to small group work. Have you learned transition strategies? Let me suggest a few, and you can choose some to try.* The principal's job is to toggle among these various strategies and use the one that prompts the most growth.

Sometimes the people who are hungriest for me to tell them what to do *most* need me to hold back and ask the reflective questions. These are the teachers who need to learn to do their own thinking and cultivate a habit of reflection so that their work has more purpose and intention.

It's not just increased experience with these conversations that improves the practice. Taking time to reflect on these debriefs—or ask the teacher to reflect on them with me—helps identify which strategy seemed helpful and which led to a dead end. Real-time conversations move fast and require relatively quick decisions. Thinking back over a meeting often helps pinpoint the cues in the conversation that should have been signals for choosing a more effective strategy. Reflecting helps me figure out which questions got the most traction from our discussion or when too many suggestions stifled reflection.

A significant learning moment happened by happy accident while practicing these new skills. I was meeting with a teacher after an observation. I had prepared a few reflection questions that the teacher responded to thoughtfully but briefly. After this exchange of no more than ten minutes, I thought to myself, "Well, that didn't feel substantive." I was gearing up to share some insights of my own when we were interrupted. One of us—I don't remember which—had to leave suddenly, and the meeting ended.

Much to my surprise—and edification—shortly afterward, this teacher referenced our conversation and the significant insight she'd had as a result of my questions. She thanked me sincerely. In her classroom, she made deliberate changes in how she structured whole group conversations based on the questions she had thought about at our meeting. All I did was provide the time, space, and some focus for her to reflect on her practice and learn something new. Thankfully, I didn't get in the way by offering my own solution to someone so capable of designing her own.

With practice, the long-term focus on growth becomes more instinctive and is replacing my fix-it mentality.

## USE DATA TO FACILITATE REFLECTION

In all cases, having concrete, incontrovertible observational data helps to ground a supervision conversation. Usually, when an observational debrief is not feeling meaningful, the reason is that the principal launched the conversation by looking for a solution rather than starting with the observational data.

For example, in the first observation of one veteran teacher's class, I was alarmed. Mike lectured during the whole lesson, and his checking for understanding strategy was straight out of the *Ferris Bueller* movie— "Anyone . . . ? Anyone . . . ?" During our meeting following the lesson, I shared my concern that the lesson had been all lecture style and that teachers are expected to design lessons that engage students in the work, to have clear learning goals that are compelling, that classroom tasks need to require higher order thinking. . . . I'm afraid this list may have gone on for too long. He dutifully jotted notes in a spiral notebook and seemed extremely disinterested. He seemed to be mentally counting the number of different administrators he'd had and thinking "This too shall pass." We weren't getting any traction in our conversation. It was, perhaps, a bit too much like his lesson.

Finally, I said that his students appeared lethargic during his class and that none of them raised a hand or had any flicker of response to what he was saying. Mike perked up and leaned forward with interest. "Yeah, they were really flat, weren't they? I don't understand it. I just can't seem to get this group interested." Aha! Rather than start with the observational data, I had jumped several steps ahead to my own analysis of the problem. He didn't know how I got there and wasn't with me. I needed to start with what we both saw in the students. From there, we could jointly make inferences about what this data meant for teaching and learning.

This meeting didn't result in a miraculous transformation; Mike did not leave with a newfound passion for inquiry-based learning. The meeting did end, however, with a shared sense of the problem. The data about his students was indisputable. He was interested in working on this issue and had opened up to brainstorm reasons why his students might be so bored, which included things like needing a learning goal that mattered to them, needing opportunities to talk to each other, needing to read or interact with information rather than just listen to the teacher explain it. This experience was a good reminder for me to slow down, start with the data, and build teachers' understanding of the problem as well as their ability to come up with a solution.

## Focus on Students and Student Work to Learn About Instruction

Good teachers always look for evidence of whether and how a child understands a concept or skill. They know it's not enough to say, "I taught it." These teachers constantly look for evidence that the student learned it. More and more, I measure my effectiveness as a supervisor by the extent to which teachers have adopted this outlook.

When we operate from this standpoint, data has to be present at the table when discussing teaching practice. Data might be the observation notes from the lesson, the journals that kids were writing in, the test they just took, exact quotes recorded from class discussion, or the words copied from some students' work. This is the material we analyze and discuss to figure out how students are making sense of what's being taught. When teachers aren't meeting with me, I want them to use this same method to evaluate lessons on their own. Modeling this practice in our meetings is a deliberate strategy to build and reinforce this habit. It's also, of course, the best way to know what students learned.

Data at the meeting can shift the discussion away from the teacher and toward learning. A post-observation meeting might start with the teacher sorting student work by how well the students understand the material. After sorting the set of papers, the teacher and I sit side by side examining the student work, analyzing it to learn more about student thinking.

In this way, the two of us are allied, shoulder to shoulder, in our joint goal to improve what is on the table in front of us. I ask the teacher why she thinks the student papers in the first pile didn't include evidence in their responses and the student papers in the second pile did. Do the first-pile students have anything in common? What does she think they need to understand better to be able to accomplish the task? What do the students in the second pile need to learn next? How will she push their learning as well? As we lean forward to look more closely at one or another of the pieces, we're reflecting and reinforcing the culture of the school: collectively oriented toward the same goal—improving student learning. *I'm your warm demander keeping you focused on the goal, offering support to get you there.*

Looking at data is particularly useful when a teacher seems stuck or pushes back on feedback. "I don't think I'm talking too much." Or "The students do understand the material. I can tell they're all following along as I read." Rather than get into a debate about teaching practice, I can defer to the data. We act like scientists investigating a theory and look for evidence in the student work to see whether the kids are in fact meeting the learning objective.

During my first year, after meeting a few times, a teacher remarked, "You seem to like looking at student work." "Yes! And I want you to as well," I replied. "How else will we know how your kids are learning?" The good news was that he had noticed this practice. His comment also indicated that he'd not yet internalized it. We had more work to do.

Focused observation of individual students serves the same purpose. In one classroom, a child was repeatedly off-task during lessons. Stevenson was a small boy whose family recently emigrated from Haiti and who frequently looked out the window for long periods with a dejected look on his face. Other times, he sat at lessons with his arms folded across his chest, brows furrowed, and face in a defiant "I'm not participating!" expression. I shared these observations of him with Gabby, his teacher. She responded, "Yes, he is moody and doesn't like to participate, and it just doesn't help to get in a power struggle with him about it."

When I first entered the role as principal, I might not have pushed Gabby right away. I might have given her the benefit of the doubt and assumed that she was doing all she could do. Now I don't make assumptions and am more assertive. In this case, I shared with Gabby that in fact Stevenson had paid attention in an earlier grade. He had loved learning. In addition, his success in school depended on her helping him access lessons and get that love back.

Gabby was surprised that he'd had success and talked to his previous teacher, who affirmed this and shared some of Stevenson's strengths. A few observations later, Stevenson still struggled to engage but attended to the directions in a way I hadn't seen previously. I went over to him to give him a big thumbs-up—and to model for Gabby the importance of affirming his efforts as she raised her expectations. Stevenson's big smile radiated pride. He tucked into the work in front of him with fresh determination. After each visit, I shared observations of Stevenson. Gabby came to understand that her lessons would be measured by this student's level of participation. She paid more attention to him during lessons.

She began reporting on her successes. "Stevenson stayed on task for the whole reading lesson today." "Look what Stevenson wrote in his story!" She learned she was accountable for his engagement in class. Maybe this was just what she did to please her boss, but the results are the same. She learned to be responsible for his engagement and through doing so saw that her behaviors made a difference in his learning. I don't have enough data to claim a radical transformation in Gabby's belief system; there's still progress to be made. But this is the kind of work she and I need to do to get there. Sometimes actions come first and beliefs change afterward.

Some teachers benefit from knowing that a few specific children will be the focus for all observations and debriefs. Teachers might need to grow in their practice with children with special needs or children who speak very little in class or Black boys about whom there are too many pernicious, damaging stereotypes. Focusing attention on specific children can raise debilitating biases and beliefs to the surface so the teacher can address them. In one case in which the teacher and I together designated specific students to observe, he began looking first to those three children's work to assess his lessons since he knew I would bring them up at our meetings. He would arrive at our meetings with an analysis of these students' needs at the ready. He was beginning to build the habit of using student learning to assess his teaching.

## Use Standards to Contextualize Data and Depersonalize Feedback

My heart sinks when a new teacher says something to the effect of "Just tell me what you want me to do." It's an indictment of the overall evaluation system that supervision is so often perceived as arbitrary, up to the personal judgment of administrators. Few things undermine a sense of professionalism more than this inconsistency. There shouldn't be mystery about what constitutes effective teaching and learning. It's not Sarah's judgment against the teacher's.

When a new teacher asked this question, I pointed to the shelf in my office that holds the state standards for teaching and the subject-specific standards for student learning. It's all in there. My job, I tell teachers, is to ensure that all students reach or exceed the learning standards. That happens when teachers meet or exceed the teaching standards. Teachers will get help to meet these standards, but the bottom line is that everyone—students and teachers—must meet this goal.

One teacher in particular taught me to use the standards. She started the year very defensive about feedback and portrayed my comments as stylistic rather than substantive critiques. I learned to ground all of our conversations in the standards. This made the process transparent so she could feel on equal footing at the meetings. When planning or reflecting on individual lessons, we looked at both learning standards and teaching standards. We examined student work side by side with the learning standards. When we talked about her communication with families, collaboration with colleagues, or differentiation for students with special needs, we looked at the teaching standards to clarify expectations.

After several meetings, this teacher began referencing both the learning and teaching standards in our meetings. When it came time to submit her evaluation, I asked her to do a self-assessment using the standards. Our ratings, including several areas below proficient, came out almost identical. She said the process felt fair and helpful—a striking difference from the way we began the year together. The standards focused our work and helped both of us track and feel proud of progress.

# PLAN FOR OBSERVATION DEBRIEFS AS IF THEY WERE LESSON PLANNING

If we're serious about wanting to improve teaching practice through supervision, we need to go about this work as deliberately as any good teacher preparing for a lesson. We need to know the work of teachers, know the standards, and lesson plan for our meetings: what's our objective? How will we achieve it? How will we check for understanding? Otherwise, any feedback we give is just throwing darts in the dark.

## Make Time to Know Teachers' Work

In most formal evaluation systems, the required number of teacher observations is either laughably or insultingly low, depending on your mood. Two to four observations is not sufficient to know a teacher's work well enough to help her grow professionally. These observations need to be accompanied by more frequent, although not necessarily as lengthy, classroom visits. It goes without saying that being in classrooms and understanding the teaching and learning needs of the staff constitute the most important work of leading schools. However, even with a strong conviction about the centrality of this work, I still frequently fall short of my goals in this area. Why is it so hard?

We all know one reason it's easy to fall short of goals: time. We're busy. Like most principals, if I ever stop moving, the to-do list weighs me down, pinning me to my office chair. However, knowing a teacher's work well is essential to knowing what she needs to learn. Principals have to get out of the office. One method is to get into classrooms first thing in the morning before becoming immobilized in front of e-mail or in meetings. Without a plan in my first year, however, my track record was spotty. Frequently, I got bogged down in the office and didn't make the rounds. Regularly, my rounds were interrupted after visiting only two to four classrooms. Even after changing my regular route a few times, I still tended to unconsciously favor one hall or a few classrooms over others.

Then I read Kim Marshall's book about supervision, felt re-inspired, and copied his schedule template for "mini-observations" from the appendix of the book.[2] On a staff list, I marked when observations happened and then when subsequent follow-up conversations took place. I organized my schedule so that I would get into every classroom about once each four to six weeks. Brief, frequent observations of about five to seven minutes were the goal, followed by an equally brief interaction about the observation. This approach seemed short and doable.

Finding time to follow up with people was surprisingly challenging. Following up during prep periods felt uncomfortable even though I did it sometimes. I carried my list at all times and caught people in the copy room or the hallway before school. I sometimes sent out affirmations by e-mail when I hadn't gotten to talk to someone in person, even though the in-person conversations were still the goal.

After a few months, this strategy fell by the wayside because of the intense feeling of failure every time I looked at the list and saw how many follow-up conversations were left unchecked. Frequently, too much time would pass for me to talk to the teacher about a brief observation from three weeks earlier. Marshall's philosophy of mini-observations continued to be the goal, but I just couldn't make the complete cycle work.

So then came shorter lists of high-priority teachers (new teachers and teachers of concern) to observe and check off when they were complete. This approach was an improvement. However, it too didn't always pan out smoothly. At one point, a teacher couldn't help laughing when I arrived to observe and her students were leaving for a specialist. It was the third time in a row that I had arrived only to miss observing her teach.

The next logical step was to simply look at teachers' schedules and re-serve times in my calendar. This step of preparation was time consuming to do each week and wasn't infallible because teachers changed their schedules or the student teacher had a takeover week or a visiting parent was reading a story or things came up elsewhere in the school that had to be dealt with immediately. And it was still a struggle to track down people to talk about the teaching. However, the process was inching closer to the goal.

I've finally landed on a hybrid version that includes the most helpful step of all: prescheduled debriefing meetings. The school secretary schedules every-other-week meetings with about seven to ten of the teachers who are the highest priority to observe. These are nontenured teachers, teachers new to the school, and teachers about whom I have concerns.

With a meeting on the books, I no longer have to chase after someone to discuss what I noticed. And because the debrief meeting is locked in, the observation just *has* to happen—whether it's scheduling it in my calendar or just being persistent in dropping by more often, sometimes just before our meeting. Some debrief meetings do get cancelled, but because the next one is already on the calendar, it's less of a worry. When an experienced teacher new to our building complained to a union representative that I was in her classroom too much, that felt like a sign that this was the right system; observations were happening more regularly. The union rep declined to file a grievance.

With the rest of the staff, I do my best to get into classrooms as often as I can. Monthly mini-observations and follow-up conversations are still the goal, but I don't beat myself up if the follow-up doesn't happen. The observation still feels important. Even when it's just a matter of passing through for a few minutes in each room, it's possible to notice a great deal from those tiny visits. They form the basis for understanding strengths and weaknesses in our children, staff, and school overall. They help teachers feel like their work is known and help me understand individual learning needs and patterns across the school.

## Prioritize

My current strategy reveals that it's not just the scarcity of time that makes it hard to get into classrooms. It's also a matter of prioritizing. When I'm faced with a full e-mail inbox, a budget proposal deadline, a parent meeting to prepare for, and data to review before the next progress check-in, it always feels tempting—sensible even—to postpone a classroom observation. The classroom will be there tomorrow. Will there really be much that's different from the last time I visited? And sometimes I feel that the effort to extract myself from the work of the office to go upstairs into a classroom for just five to ten minutes isn't commensurate with what I'll gain.

The challenge is similar to other disciplined commitments that need to be sustained over time in order to see any benefit: exercising, gardening, saving money, practicing the cello. The hoped-for result comes not from a single incident but rather from the accumulated benefit of repeated incidents over time. It's always possible to justify missing an individual day of cello practice or observing in classrooms. Weighing that individual instance on its own will never tip the scales. It's the regularity itself that makes the difference.

Prioritizing this way is the reason the scheduling strategy works for me. It removes the in-the-moment decision. On Monday at 11:45 a.m., I'll face a teacher in my office and will need observational data for us to talk about. I've got to get into her classroom this week. Rigging the system in this way makes it harder to wiggle out of an individual instance of observing. In case conviction isn't enough, the meeting accountability will keep me disciplined.

## Prepare

Many of my interactions with people about their teaching are informal conversations. "I noticed your chart about growth mindset. Tell me more about how you use that, and do you see kids internalizing the concept?" "Elias seemed really distracted in math today. Do you think something's going on for him?" Or a teacher may follow up, "Sarah, I want some advice about Ruth. She's been really mean to Alex recently, and I'm feeling at my wit's end."

While this kind of debrief may suffice for some teachers in a busy principal's schedule, other situations require a more in-depth conversation about a teacher's practice. They are typically new teachers, teachers on professional improvement plans or about whom I have concerns, and teachers whom I am evaluating that year. Working with a teacher to improve instruction is a form of teaching and therefore, as with any good teaching, requires planning. At first, these meetings were more free-ranging, with only observation notes on the table and just a general sense of what to address as a guide. As I reflect on this precious use of time—particularly the meetings that don't go well—I've come to prepare and create clear structures for them. As a result, they're producing more meaningful improvements in practice.

Planning requires knowing the standards well—both the standards for student learning and the professional practice standards for teachers. What does high-quality writing look like for a third grader? What skills should fifth graders be working on in their reading? Which teaching standard do I think is the most critical for this teacher to work on right now? Frequently, before meeting with a teacher who is struggling, I review the learning standards for that particular grade and content area so our conversation about student work, lesson plans, and next steps can be very specific.

A parallel exists between the basic principles of supervision and teaching here. When a teacher supports a developing reader, one of the critical skills is figuring out the reader's zone of proximal development—to determine which of many complex reading skills will most boost that reader's growth. Is it inference? Fluency? Word attack? Usually, the lesson can go in several directions. Teachers have to deliberately choose the focus that will most support their student's growth.

Similarly, in supervision, principals need to select an aspect of practice that will most boost a teacher's growth. Is it questioning? Checking for understanding? Choosing clear lesson objectives? Delivering feedback? Usually, a teacher could work on multiple skills fruitfully. A principal needs to think carefully and specifically about a teacher's development to answer the question, What's the most important skill for this person to develop with these particular students at this point in her career?

For example, recently I saw a young teacher dutifully following a district-provided math lesson plan about equivalencies. The classroom ran smoothly; children dutifully followed all the teacher's directions. In small groups, they placed different weights on a balance and noted what combinations made the balance level. However, the lesson didn't feel meaningful. The problem wasn't the district plan; that was actually relatively thoughtful. There just wasn't evidence from the observation that the children had learned the deeper concepts behind the activity.

In preparing for our debrief meeting, I first thought that the focus should be about questioning and what types of questions could prompt children's deeper thinking. After thinking about the lesson further, however, I realized that there wasn't evidence that the teacher had in fact understood the mathematical concepts the plan was intended to teach. She didn't draw out understanding, highlight a specific skill, or ask children to make connections that they could then apply to new material. "Why do you think the scale isn't balanced now? What could you do to make it balanced? How could you write this as an equation?" Instead, she simply marched students through the lesson plan. Perhaps this lack of understanding of the mathematical goal of the lesson was the root cause of her weak questioning during class. Perhaps this should be the focus for our debrief.

Before meeting with this teacher, I read through the curriculum material along with the learning standards so that I would be well versed in her grade level and prepared to talk about the underlying concepts behind the larger unit. At the beginning of our meeting, I shared data about specific kid behaviors and asked questions about the lesson's goals. Her responses showed thoughtful attention to details but overall a failure to connect the individual lesson to a larger skill set.

Our brief exchange confirmed the learning objective for our meeting. This teacher needed to leave our discussion with a commitment to digging into lessons and standards to understand the larger goals: for example, the pre-algebra skills involved in understanding the elements of an equation or the concept that fractions represent a relationship of part to whole or the idea that geometric shapes can be classified by sides and angles. By the end of the meeting, she said she understood for the first time why students were using weights and balances and what these specific lessons were about. She also realized why following the steps of an outlined lesson was not enough. I offered help from a coach and the teacher readily accepted. Identifying the underlying mathematical concepts connecting each activity became the focus for coaching as well as our conversations about lessons for the next several weeks.

Often it takes multiple observations to identify what the most important issue is. For example, a tense teacher escalated conflicts with students regularly. Finally, I figured out that she was afraid of conflict, and this anxiety led her to approach it with too heavy a hand. In another case, a skilled teacher's students were regularly snippy and frustrated with each other. After I watched closely to understand the problem, one issue that surfaced was that this teacher periodically reacted to minor misbehaviors with intense irritation, and kids picked up on this response and did the same. An exuberant teacher had students who loved her but produced low-quality work. After looking at student work and asking questions, I figured out that she wasn't confident with the appropriate level of rigor to expect and didn't want to demoralize students by having them redo their work. Once we named this as the problem, we could set her up with anchor papers and exemplars and work to address the issue. Like solving a complex puzzle, identifying a knotty problem of practice feels immensely satisfying. It's also necessary if we want to make long-term improvements in instruction.

## DECIDE HOW MUCH IS REASONABLE TO EXPECT FROM NEW TEACHERS

Anyone who has been a teacher has great empathy for that first year. The learning curve feels unthinkably steep and endless. Strangely, we treat all teachers the same throughout their careers, even though we know this not to be true. The job description is identical for the first-year teacher and the thirtieth-year veteran. Of course, it's unrealistic to hold these two teachers to the same expectations. But wait a minute—there are still children in that first-year teacher's class. What are the right expectations for a new teacher?

As a beginning principal, I worried so much about overtaxing new teachers that I didn't have a clear strategy for how to supervise them. I set them up with mentors, coaches, and supportive colleagues; held periodic group meetings for new teachers; and other than that tried not to take up too much of their time. I frequently gave them chocolate along with lots of affirmations and a reassurance that things would get better. Not a robust strategy. My fear of overwhelming them was preventing them from getting important information. They need to know which of the ninety-seven important things on their to-do list should be priorities.

The importance of messaging explicit priorities wasn't apparent to me at first. I assumed that people heard my vision at meetings, came to the profession with a commitment to all students, and would feel their colleagues' sense of mission. Sometimes this was the case, but not always. This point became clear one year when I was talking to a new teacher about a struggling student and asking what she had learned from the recent parent conference. She said she hadn't had it and further along in the conversation that she hadn't called to follow up when the parent didn't sign up for the conference. She said slowly as if testing the conclusion, "That was bad. . . ."

This behavior came as a surprise. I had e-mailed all staff clear expectations about needing to persist until reaching 100 percent participation in conferences. In fact, this message had gone out multiple times. Was she ignoring schoolwide expectations? Probably not. She was drowning in things she had to do; messages in her inbox were piling high. She needed very explicit guidance about where to direct her attention.

Principals can't assume that teachers share our priorities around how to work with families and our most struggling students. Sometimes this mindset needs to be taught. So now I'm more explicit about the highest priority areas to focus on. *I will closely observe your struggling students during classroom visits. They are an important gauge of teaching effectiveness. I will look at student work and expect you to do so with me. I expect all kids to know what they're learning and why.*

I'm also learning that it is possible, even necessary, to communicate that a teacher isn't proficient in the teaching standards and at the same time communicate confidence that she will get there. This is the warm demander approach to supervision. "I expect you to meet these standards and will do everything possible to help you meet them." A teacher friend told me that in her first year, the principal shared four formal, written evaluations with her within the first two months of school. They highlighted many areas for growth as well as areas of proficiency. I haven't achieved this frequency of written feedback, but it's a good goal.

Instead, I now meet with beginning teachers to review the teaching rubric, share feedback about their overall practice, and discuss together areas of focus and a plan for growth. No doubt, this meeting is overwhelming for new teachers. Teaching involves a complex set of skills. However, the alternative—not alerting them to concerns, assuming they'll be taken care of over time, sharing only praise—is not helpful. A year later, when a teacher still hasn't focused on the right skills or hasn't identified the areas of concern on her own, there's a harder conversation to have about how she isn't meeting standards and is closer to being let go. Being transparent from the beginning helps everyone.

## BUILD TRUST; OTHERWISE, EXPECT LIMITED TRACTION

None of the learning described here will happen without trust between teacher and principal. It's impossible to overstate this point. Earlier I described the critical role of trust that allows teachers to invest in and increase each other's professional growth. The same is true in the relationship between supervisor and teacher. Building a trusting leader–teacher relationship requires the humility to place the other person's learning first. Ego has no place at the evaluator's table.

One way to build this trust is through talking about the process and inviting in the teacher as a partner. I often share that I am striving to get better at helping teachers improve. For example, when practicing the Three Cs strategies (coaching, collaborating, consulting), I told some teachers about this approach and about my struggle, in the midst of our feedback meetings, to determine the right next step. With everyone, I have tried to regularly ask for feedback about these debrief meetings. We do a quick plus/delta periodically so we can each share what is helping the meetings feel effective and what could make them more helpful. The plus/delta alone doesn't build trust. Acting on it does. When the principal takes feedback to heart and follows through with it, she demonstrates that the leader sees herself as a learner, too. That willingness to make changes in practice and to join the teacher in continual improvement builds trust.

Trust can be hardest to achieve with the teachers who struggle the most. It's hard not to show frustration or anger when kids aren't being well served. This is the point at which the warm demander mindset comes in. This isn't personal; it's not about whether someone is a good person. As teachers hear me say many times, my job is to make sure all of our students learn. Because that's my job, I insist on that happening. And I can do this warmly and compassionately *and* absolutely firmly.

## HOLD YOURSELF ACCOUNTABLE

Effective supervision is time consuming, and time is a scarce resource for principals. Tasks can easily slip through the cracks. Who is the warm demander for the principal? Who insists on high-quality supervision, and who provides support for this to happen? In most districts, no one. No one checks to see how often principals observe; no one asks to see records of visits. And no one monitors whether the supervision is actually improving student learning. Quality control is usually left up to individual principals, and the problem is that we may unintentionally supervise some classrooms better than others.

Some classrooms demand our attention. Teachers who struggle with classroom management are in this category. Following up with misbehavior can take a bite out of an administrator's schedule, so there's a personal stake in improving that teacher's management skills. Teachers who get lots of complaints from parents typically get closer supervision than their colleagues. Teachers who administer state tests that ultimately are published in the newspaper may get more attention as well. These are the pressing needs that we can't escape because they make themselves known, often loudly.

How do we make all classrooms feel as urgent as these? If a kindergarten teacher isn't performing well, her students lose important ground. Shouldn't that be as urgent as the classroom with the kid throwing chairs? When the science teacher successfully teaches all but the children with special needs, that small number of failures may not show up on aggregated test scores, but the implications will most certainly show up in those students' science skills. As principals, we have to make sure that these critically important needs aren't overshadowed by whatever seems to be more pressing. We need to pay disciplined attention. Without disciplined attention, we let what's urgent take precedence over what's truly important.

So how do we do this? How do we ensure our supervision addresses the most important problems? We can't wait for a parent to complain. If that were our sole barometer, it's clear our focus would be skewed and almost certainly would not be equitable. We can't expect that teachers with low expectations will always reveal themselves in obvious ways. Like most teachers, these underperformers usually have the best intentions. Occasionally, an accumulation of low test scores over time will point us to a problem in performance. We all know, however, that context matters, and so this is rarely a straightforward or reliable route to identifying a struggling teacher.

The bottom line is that allocating our time and energy correctly requires ongoing, careful observation of teacher practice. External pressure from parents and test scores or first impressions based on personality should not determine how we focus our supervision. Our own internal sense of justice and motivation needs to guide our examination of instruction.

For all these reasons, in this very important work, we principals need to hold ourselves accountable. We need to feel a personal commitment to follow up with that kindergarten teacher and to observe frequently in that science teacher's classroom. In these cases, we need to feel morally compelled to act.

## FIRING . . . WITH COMPASSION

Being a warm demander sounds admirable, but what if a teacher just isn't willing to put in the work to improve? Or she's trying and it's taking a really long time and kids' learning is suffering? Is there a point at which the principal stops being the warm demander and has to get mean and fire people?

Every year, I have fired people. Few things have felt as hard, and this task hasn't gotten easier with time. However, the first two people I fired taught me a lot about how to do it with compassion. One lesson was to allow the process to feel messier. The other was about how people hear feedback and respond.

In the first case, it was close to the evaluation due date. I spent the better part of a Sunday afternoon laboring over the evaluation of a teacher I planned to fire. Peter had neglected to put in the effort to help his lowest-performing students improve. Thinking about the situation made my jaw tighten with frustration. Despite hours of meetings about how to help his students, he hadn't followed through and had continued to express impatience with student behavior rather than take responsibility for learning.

The evaluation didn't mince words and included comments about Peter not caring enough for underperforming students and lots of sweeping words like *never, always,* and *none.* After proofreading it one last time, I printed the document in preparation for our meeting the next day. Then I set aside work and headed out to an event at a local community center that evening.

In a moment of both coincidence and awkwardness, with hot beverage in hand, I found myself talking with a woman who turned out to be Peter's wife. As she described why she was there, it became clear we shared a commitment to a particular cause and had similar interests. The conversation was lovely. And, after my afternoon's work, it was also jarring. This was a caring woman, married to the teacher I'd just been excoriating in text. Perhaps he was more complicated than I had allowed.

After participating half-heartedly at the event and upon arriving home, I tore up the printed evaluation and returned to the computer to make revisions. In truth, Peter wasn't sarcastic *all* the time. In fact, he had developed relationships with the students; they just weren't the warm demander relationships that would maximize their learning. But that didn't mean that he didn't care about them. And he had a good sense of humor, which came out in some of his creative assignments.

Working into the evening, I dialed back the harsh tone in my writing and acknowledged more of Peter's skills. None of this changed the outcome of the evaluation—Peter was still fired—but it changed the tenor of the writing and the next day's meeting. The evaluation was a more accurate picture of Peter and his work, and this enabled him to recognize himself in the write-up rather than dismiss it out of hand. Having glimpsed a fuller picture of Peter through his wife, I was able to enter our meeting the next day with compassion rather than disdain. I sincerely did wish him the best after letting him know he wouldn't be returning. Using this approach made the meeting more complicated; it was harder to see his disappointment and dismay with the knowledge that he was probably a good guy in many ways. But it also somehow felt better to view him more fully and have him know that.

Other aspects of giving negative evaluations were surprising even though they shouldn't have been. My dissertation examined Peer Assistance and Review, a careful and complex process in which teachers support and ultimately review their peers' proficiency in meeting teaching standards. For this research, I interviewed dozens of people who regularly recommended people for dismissal. These brave peer reviewers frequently used the phrase *no surprises* as a reminder that teachers should get regular, clear feedback so that they know when they are not meeting job expectations, know exactly what to do to meet them, and know what performance level they will receive on their evaluation. Despite my personal research, I still made plenty of mistakes. More than that, I felt shaken to my core about the emotional toll of these conversations.

Early on, I worked with a teacher in her seventh year who struggled with classroom management and rigor. She agreed with some of my feedback and disagreed with other parts and was always respectful in our interactions. Despite conversations about the fact that she wasn't meeting standards, she was shocked when she read her first written evaluation. People absorb feedback differently when it is in writing. She sat up and took notice. I did, too—and made a mental note to share feedback in writing earlier.

This teacher worked to improve but still needed to be put on a professional improvement plan, which we all knew could lead to dismissal. I felt ready. This was the hard work I had prepared for in grad school—of being a principal with high standards and the moral imperative to back them up. When this young teacher heard about the PIP and the possible consequences, she absorbed the information slowly and then stood up from her chair as if backing away from the news. Her words will forever be burned into my memory. "But Sarah, I'm raising two kids on my own. This is all I know how to do. How will I support my family?"

I didn't know what to say and was utterly unprepared for the effect of her words—and her look of helplessness—on my emotions. The full significance of my actions and decisions suddenly felt like a guillotine, and it was impossible to pretend it didn't affect me. I managed to get through that conversation—and subsequent conversations with other people I dismissed—but it was no walk in the park.

People cry. Others get angry. In all my visions of sharing hard truths, the scenarios always ended at the point of sharing the final hard news. They never included what would come next. How do you end this meeting? When the person on the other side of the table is suffering, the educator instinct of wanting to help kicks in. But what is the right thing to say?

I've learned to prepare for the end of this conversation now as much as for the beginning. I move to next steps and an effort to preserve the teacher's dignity within the community. I reassure the teacher that the decision is confidential, I act with professionalism, and I will allow the teacher to decide how the news should be shared with colleagues. Sometimes the teacher waits until getting another job before announcing she is leaving. Other times, the teacher writes a letter explaining a reason for needing to move on. Our meeting usually ends with the teacher agreeing to take some time to think about this next step.

Increased experience has not lessened the intense discomfort of these moments. However, my bold, brash attitude coming into the job has been tempered by the complex reality of working with human beings. In the challenging realm of school, they deserve a humble, respectful leader.

# CHAPTER 10

# Permission to Be a Learner

"My teacher said she learned something new today. She said we taught her something that she never knew."

—Mustafa, grade 3

Describing leadership, people often talk about the *messiness* of the work. Before I became a principal, that term always seemed overly ambiguous and somewhat pretentious—like a code word that only insiders understood. What exactly did it mean? Plus, messy seemed unnecessary. Surely, with enough preparation, effort, or focus, the leader could ensure a relatively clean process. Now, after several years in this role, I can confidently confirm that *messy* is a terrific way to describe what improvement looks like in schools.

The initial plan is tidy with clean lines and clear explanation. As soon as it hits the reality of school, the unraveling begins. People start to interact with the plan in unpredictable ways. New ideas and questions come up that hadn't been anticipated. Now we're spending time on unforeseen issues, and we must make a host of additional decisions. Do we abandon the original plan or just tweak it? Or can we even go forward without addressing all the other concerns that have come up?

Suddenly people's emotions are in the picture. As people then respond to others' emotions, the process becomes more tangled. And this is just one issue; in fact, six others are in play at the same time. I can't think of a better way to describe it: messy.

Improvement in schools depends on interconnected variables that are unpredictable and ever shifting. Managing a process like this is challenging enough for an experienced leader. When you're new to the role, you're learning to juggle and ride the unicycle at the same time. There's just no way to prepare for every variable. To successfully navigate this terrain, leaders must have resilience, a strong mindset, and a tenacious sense of humor.

As leaders, we might be tempted to feel embarrassed when we lead a meeting poorly or to hide the fact that we don't know what to do when facing a dilemma. We don't want people to know we're beginners. And while it's true that leaders need to communicate confidence and poise, the truth is, everyone already knows we're new. People already know that we're not perfect and don't know everything. Acknowledging this is not a big reveal.

A better approach is to communicate what kind of beginner we are. We're self-possessed, unafraid of challenges, receptive to feedback, and constantly striving to get better. When people see that we act on that— that we incorporate suggestions and do better the next time—they're likely to cut us some slack.

As has come up earlier, a growth mindset is a prerequisite to leadership development. We have to be able to fearlessly tackle unfamiliar work, make progress and mistakes, reflect on both, and apply lessons learned to the next unfamiliar task. In this regard, it's similar to the on-the-job learning that happens for all first-year teachers.

An important difference exists between the first-year teaching experience and the on-the-job learning that happens as a principal, however. When I was in the classroom, the only witnesses were nine-year-olds who loved and trusted me enough to overlook the fact that they were confused by a lesson or two. On the other hand, now that I am principal, mistakes are often painfully public and the audience considerably more intimidating (and less inclined to be forgiving). There's no getting around it, though. No matter how much book learning, planning, or role playing you do, when the rubber meets the road, the job is a brand new experience. You have to experience growing pains publicly to get better. Experience is when real learning happens.

Or rather, this is when real learning *can* happen, under the right conditions. Simply surviving the experience will not make you a better practitioner. Once again, as John Dewey so wisely put it, "We do not learn from experience . . . we learn from reflecting on experience."[1] A leader needs to view reflection not as a pause in the work but as a strategic step in the work. You have to find time to build it in. Without it, progress will be slow.

Reflecting in writing about my experience is a useful way for me to mine lessons from the day. Most often I dig into interactions that went poorly or systems that aren't working. Journaling usually surfaces whatever it is that's holding the organization or me back. Defensiveness, pride, lack of foresight, a particular form of resistance.

As I write (often about things I'd rather forget), I discover the steps I need to take to prevent such an interaction again, to repair a broken system or relationship, and I try to see the patterns. Why am I regularly triggered by the Spanish teacher? Why does she threaten me? Teachers keep pushing back about release time from class; what is it I'm not understanding? Or, once again I'm noticing that I have given out more critical feedback than positive. What is behind this tendency? What will help me internalize the need for a better balance?

Occasionally I remember to reflect on what's going well. I bask in the affirmation of the handwritten note from the first graders of Room 110, "We love you as our princibl," and the poignant note from the graduating eighth grader, "Thank you for not giving up on me." Sometimes journal entries include these details I never want to forget. Morning greetings from Frantsis who knows few English words but gives a very fluent hug. The union rep thanking me sincerely for constructive critical feedback. Teaching seventh graders the Gotcha game and watching them try to hide their smiles when they realized they were having fun. Understanding where these stories come from needs to be part of the reflection time, too.

At the end of a long school day, however, it's hard to muster the energy to write (let alone think deeply). Knowing this about myself, I have sought out opportunities to talk to trusted colleagues about the work. Principals share job responsibilities with no one in their work space. We've got to find time to meet with other school leaders. This is when we get to ask colleagues how they work with coaches, how to negotiate with central office personnel, what to write in tricky evaluations, and the pros and cons of joining staff members at the local drinking hole. As trust builds, the harder, self-reflective issues come up as well.

Once again, the principles of learning are familiar. As with teachers learning to trust their teams, being the first among colleagues to share a question or struggle is hard. What will other people think? Should I be the first to reveal a weakness? What if honest reflection makes colleagues change their opinion of me? Do I trust that these colleagues will respect me even though I don't have it all together?

A wise colleague said she's learned to reframe this last question. Rather than ask if she trusts her colleagues enough, she asks if she can trust herself enough no matter what her colleagues think. Can she trust that she will not judge herself harshly for not knowing all the answers? Can she trust that she'll still feel strong even if people think she made a wrong decision? That she will be fine even if others do judge her negatively? As principals, we need to grant ourselves permission to be learners.

We also need to take care of ourselves as learners. Our school counselor talks emphatically about self-care. She once reprimanded me for answering e-mails in the middle of the night when I couldn't sleep. "If nothing else, at least you can see that it's not good modeling!" She's right. So I've learned some alternate strategies. One is the notepad I keep by my bed so I can quickly jot down ideas and then put them out of my mind instead of lying awake worrying whether I'll remember.

On weekends, I spend time with family and friends who make me laugh and release the workweek tension. During the school week, I deliberately visit kindergarten classrooms when I'm feeling overwhelmed. There I see Mohan, Ashyana, and Will co-constructing their block structure with all the vision and confidence of the most seasoned urban planners. In the writing corner, always-busy Soliyana unselfconsciously and loudly voices the words of her story as she figures out what letters to use. Nelson excitedly counts the tiles, delighted to find the number matches his prediction. Observing these young children's unmatched resilience, openness, and joy in learning is usually just the inspiration I need to go back to a meeting or a memo with perspective and peace.

One other form of self-care relates to the mental approach we bring to the work. Our work has consequences for people's lives. Leading an organization that affects hundreds of people each day can feel like a heavy, stressful responsibility. And in many ways, it should. But once this stress becomes paralyzing, we're no good to anyone. Managing the struggle between urgency and patience has been a particularly hard challenge. I hold myself responsible for achieving results *and* somehow need to feel strength and resilience even when my efforts haven't yet borne fruit.

This need comes back to a discipline of maintaining the long-term view. Like that conductor who is constantly aware of what her musicians just played, are currently playing, and are about to play, the leader has to keep moving the organization forward. We have to trust that the small daily steps will, over time, take us to our destination. My superintendent urged me to trust myself to do my best. As long as that "best" includes a commitment to continually improving myself, I can settle into that approach. I can go home each day with a fair assessment—not whether we, everyone at the school, accomplished every goal we needed to reach, but whether I did my best today. Did I earnestly pursue learning—for all of us? And am I returning tomorrow committed to doing the same?

Another part of a leader's mental approach involves managing responses to other people's stress, anger, or anxiety. This book has described strategies for not taking things personally. *Remember that people are responding to the role and not the person in it. Step back and get the view from the balcony to understand how people are feeling. Develop thick skin.* Another strategy—potentially the most effective—is to cultivate greater empathy.

When people are mad at the principal—as is inevitable in a job as large-scale and public as this—a powerful response that defangs the anger is to temporarily release our own perspective and take on theirs. Anger often stems from fear or discouragement. When we discover the root of what that person fears or why he might feel deflated, we open up to compassion. When I remember to do this and am successful, my face relaxes, my shoulders drop, and my peace returns. With this approach, I'm freed to greet that person with genuine warmth the next morning. Empathy removes the barb and allows healing.

And finally, it's important to laugh. A wise organizational consultant said that the health of an organization can be measured by the quantity of laughter found there. Principals have the privilege of working in buildings with hundreds of children. This atmosphere is ripe for laughter. After school, the fifth grade teacher has everyone hooting at her description of sweet Christopher's reaction to the Sex Ed video. During recess, two kids race into the office asking for straws and tape to build a house for pillbugs. And third grader Micky amazes us all with his unexpected and vigorous dance performance. Laughing brings us together. In addition, I never lose an opportunity to join a classroom game or song or chant. This is another great privilege of schools. We sing and dance every day! How many other organizations can say that?

Periodically, when I stop to look up from my work, I marvel at the miracle of school. Each day, children and adults come through the school door with varied life stories, worries, hopes, needs. We join together to do some of the hardest work that exists—to learn to do things we haven't done before. In the process, we laugh and care about each other. We learn and grow.

# Principal's Bookshelf

The following is a short list of readings that have helped me understand the role of principal and how to carry out improvement work. The list is far from comprehensive. Many books have influenced my thinking; those listed here are the ones I return to again and again. They have become reference books that remind me why I do this work, what I value, and how to lead.

1. *Courageous Conversations About Race: A Field Guide for Achieving Equity in Schools*, by Glenn E. Singleton and Curtis Linton (Thousand Oaks, CA: Corwin Press, 2006)

   This essential book describes the challenges of having conversations about race in schools. The reflection questions and exercises embedded in the chapters make this book immediately useful for anyone who wants to start the practice of developing cultural proficiency and increasing equity in schools.

2. *Leadership on the Line: Staying Alive Through the Dangers of Leading*, by Ronald A. Heifitz and Marty Linsky (Boston, MA: Harvard Business School Press, 2002)

   The authors' concept of adaptive leadership shapes the way I think about improvement. I find new lessons in this book each time I read it. The examples in the text feel startlingly familiar and remind me that I am not alone and that my challenges are not personal but are in fact the work of leadership.

3. *Data Wise: A Step-by-Step Guide to Using Assessment Results to Improve Teaching and Learning*, edited by Kathryn Parker Boudett, Elizabeth A. City, and Richard J. Murnane (Cambridge, MA: Harvard Education Press, 2013)

   This book describes the approach I used for inquiry cycles. It provides a clear, practical eight-step process for examining data and instruction to improve student learning. The process described here is not formulaic; rather it's an overall approach to improvement efforts in schools.

4. *Everyday Antiracism: Getting Real About Race in School*, edited by Mica Pollock (New York, NY: New Press, 2008)

   Each article in this collection includes a single strategy educators can use to create more inclusive, antibiased classrooms and schools. The short, practical articles are a useful format for team and whole staff meetings. Discussion questions at the end of each article make them actionable.

5. *School Reform from the Inside Out: Policy, Practice, and Performance*, by Richard F. Elmore (Cambridge, MA: Harvard Education Press, 2004)

   Richard Elmore's writing and work have defined my personal understanding of effective school improvement as well as the national conversation about this topic. This collection of essays forcefully makes the argument that shouldn't have to be made: schools should be places of learning.

6. *Transforming Ineffective Teams: Maximizing Collaboration's Impact on Learning*, by Alexander D. Platt, Caroline E. Tripp, et al. (Acton, MA: Ready About Press, 2008)

   The authors describe situations that you will swear came directly from the staff at your school. They understand the challenges school leaders face and, from decades of thoughtful leadership, they know exactly the steps to advise without oversimplifying any of the complexity of public schools.

7. *Mindset: The New Psychology of Success*, by Carol S. Dweck (New York, NY: Random House, 2006)

Dweck's research on how we think about intelligence not only will influence the way you think about what teaching should look like but also will help you reflect on your overall strategies for supervision, professional development, and how you reflect and learn from your own work.

8. *Why Are All the Black Kids Sitting Together in the Cafeteria? And Other Conversations About Race*, by Beverly Daniel Tatum (New York, NY: Basic Books, 2003)

This important book clearly describes different stages of racial identity development for White people and people of color in the United States. Tatum describes ways to talk about race and racism that further our own and others' racial identity development. This book was a central text in my understanding of how to be a White ally opposing racism.

9. *Leverage Leadership: A Practical Guide to Building Exceptional Schools*, by Paul Bambrick-Santoyo (San Francisco, CA: Jossey-Bass, 2012)

In this how-to book for principals, Bambrick-Santoyo uses many practical examples, videos, and supporting digital materials from high-achieving schools to lay out his strategy for effective leadership and a compelling argument for why you can't afford not to follow it.

10. *Power of Protocols: An Educator's Guide to Better Practice*, by Joseph McDonald, et al. (New York, NY: Teachers College Press, 2007)

When I was in graduate school, this book convinced me of the value of protocols, and I've been hooked ever since. The authors explain why to use them and how to facilitate them, and describe many common protocols in detail.

11. *Teaching Children to Care: Management in the Responsive Classroom*, by Ruth Charney (Greenfield, MA: Northeast Foundation for Children, 1992)

    As a teacher, I looked to this book to define the rigorous, safe, joyful learning that I wanted for my students. As a principal, I returned to this book and found that all of the principles—and the humility modeled by the author—apply equally well to building a learning community with adults.

12. *The Behavior Code: A Practical Guide to Understanding and Teaching the Most Challenging Students*, by Jessica Minahan and Nancy Rappaport (Cambridge, MA: Harvard Education Press, 2012)

    Every principal's job includes working with children who have challenging behaviors. With their considerable expertise, the authors teach how to support some of the most difficult students in schools. They teach how to approach these students with the compassion and inquiry that will enable them to make progress.

13. *The Skin We're In: Teaching Our Children to Be Emotionally Strong, Socially Smart, Spiritually Connected*, by Janie Victoria Ward (New York, NY: Free Press, 2000)

    Ward describes strategies for combatting the "new racism" and how to teach Black children to combat it. She offers a useful four-step model—read it; name it; oppose it; replace it—that helps children (and adults) think critically and counteract racism.

14. *Finders and Keepers: Helping New Teachers Survive and Thrive in Our Schools*, by Susan Moore Johnson and The Project on the Next Generation of Teachers (San Francisco, CA: Jossey-Bass, 2004)

    The compelling examples from this longitudinal study of new teachers bring the important research findings to life. The book includes clear examples of what leaders should do to support the next generation of teachers and cautionary tales of what happens when leaders don't attend to new teachers' needs.

15. *How the Way We Talk Can Change the Way We Work: Seven Languages for Transformation*, by Robert Kegan and Lisa L. Lahey (San Francisco, CA: Jossey-Bass, 2001)

When you can't figure out why you want so badly to change your behavior and can't seem to do it, this book has the answer. You'll learn how to support your own and others' transformational learning. It's my go-to book for descriptions of how to build and maintain a healthy organizational culture.

16. *Strategy in Action: How School Systems Can Support Powerful Learning and Teaching*, by Rachel E. Curtis and Elizabeth A. City (Cambridge, MA: Harvard Education Press, 2009)

This book provides clear and practical guidance for improvement at the district level; however, the lessons apply equally well to every level of an organization. In particular, I have flagged pages and implemented helpful ideas from the section on effective teams.

17. *Leaders of Their Own Learning: Transforming Schools Through Student-Engaged Assessment*, by Ron Berger, Leah Rugen, and Libby Woodfin (San Francisco, CA: Jossey-Bass, 2014)

The authors describe a thorough process for engaging students and teachers in meaningful assessment. The balanced view of multiple forms and uses of assessment in this book provides a much-needed counterpoint to the overemphasis on standardized test data.

# Notes

## Introduction

1. "Douglass" is a pseudonym for the school.
2. The district uses a "controlled choice" policy of school assignment rather than neighborhood assignments.
3. Alvin Chang, Matt Carroll, Anil Nathan, and Jack Schneider, "Dreamschool: Top 15 High Schools in Massachusetts Overall," *Boston Globe*, December 4, 2013, http://www.boston.com/yourtown/dreamschool-top-high-schools-massachusetts-overall-top-high-schools-mass/gnPZP70FeTPhlRKQvhRbwK/article.html#slide-1.

## Chapter 1

1. Doris Kearns Goodwin, *The Bully Pulpit: Theodore Roosevelt, William Howard Taft, and the Golden Age of Journalism* (New York, NY: Simon and Schuster, 2013), 571.
2. Kathleen McCartney, interview by Kai Ryssdal, Marketplace, American Public Media, March 19, 2014, http://www.marketplace.org/topics/economy/education/smith-college-president-talks-affordable-education.
3. Jerome T. Murphy, "The Unheroic Side of Leadership: Notes from the Swamp," *Phi Delta Kappan* 69, no. 9 (1988): 654–659.
4. Ronald A. Heifitz and Marty Linsky, *Leadership on the Line: Staying Alive Through the Dangers of Leading* (Boston, MA: Harvard Business School Press, 2002), 11.

## Chapter 2

1. Brian Rowan et al., "What Large-Scale Survey Research Tells Us About Teacher Effects on Student Achievement: Insights from the Prospects Study of Elementary Schools," *Teachers College Record* 104, no. 8 (2002): 1525–1567.
2. See Kay Merseth's course called "Dilemmas of Excellence and Equity in K–12 American Schools" at the Harvard Graduate School of Education.
3. Susan Moore Johnson et al., "Ready to Lead, But How? Teachers' Experiences in High-Poverty Urban Schools," *Teachers College Record* 116, no. 6 (2014): 1–50.
4. Kathryn Parker Boudett, Elizabeth A. City, and Richard J. Murnane, *Data Wise: A Step-by-Step Guide to Using Assessment Results to Improve Teaching and Learning* (Cambridge, MA: Harvard Education Press, 2005).

5. Ariana Huffington, "Rule 4: Fail," *Inc.*, February 2013, 52.
6. John Dewey, *Experience and Education* (New York, NY: Simon & Schuster, 1997).
7. Kathryn Parker Boudett and Elizabeth A. City, *Meeting Wise: Making the Most of Collaborative Time for Educators* (Cambridge, MA: Harvard Education Press, 2014*).*

## Chapter 3
1. Ronald A. Heifitz and Donald L. Laurie, "The Work of Leadership," *Harvard Business Review* 7 no. 1 (2001): 124–134.
2. Greg J. Duncan and Richard J. Murnane, *Restoring Opportunity: The Crisis of Inequality and the Challenge for American Education* (Cambridge, MA: Harvard Education Press, 2014).
3. Amy C. Edmondson, "The Competitive Imperative of Learning," *Harvard Business Review* 86, no. 7 (2008): 60–67.
4. Paul Bambrick-Santoyo, *Leverage Leadership: A Practical Guide to Building Exceptional Schools* (San Francisco, CA: Jossey-Bass, 2012), 37.

## Chapter 4
1. Gary Klein, "Performing a Project Premortem," *Harvard Business Review Reprints*, F0709A, September 2007, https://hbr.org/2007/09/performing-a-project-premortem.
2. Kathryn Parker Boudett, Elizabeth A. City, and Richard J. Murnane, *Data Wise: A Step-by-Step Guide to Using Assessment Results to Improve Teaching and Learning* (Cambridge, MA: Harvard Education Press, 2005), 191–192.
3. Ronald A. Heifitz and Donald L. Laurie, "The Work of Leadership," *Harvard Business Review* 7, no. 1 (2001): 124–134.
4. Elim Chan, interview by Rachel Giese, *Q*, CBC, December 22, 2014, http://www.cbc.ca/radio/q/schedule-for-monday-dec-22-1.2926416/elim-chan-on-how-conductors-conjure-musical-magic-1.2926421.

## Chapter 5
1. Ronald A. Heifitz and Donald L. Laurie, "The Work of Leadership," *Harvard Business Review* 7 no. 1 (2001): 124–134.
2. Robert McKain, quoted in Kim Marshall, *Rethinking Teacher Supervision and Evaluation: How to Work Smart, Build Collaboration, and Close the Achievement Gap* (San Francisco, CA: Jossey-Bass, 2009).
3. Marshall, *Rethinking Teacher Supervision and Evaluation*, 44–45.
4. Robert Kegan and Lisa Lahey, *How the Way We Talk Can Change the Way We Work* (San Francisco, CA: Jossey-Bass, 2001), 47–66.
5. Carol Dweck, *Growth Mindset: How You Can Fulfill Your Potential* (London: Robinson, 2012).
6. Ronald A. Heifitz and Marty Linsky, *Leadership on the Line: Staying Alive Through the Dangers of Leading* (Boston, MA: Harvard Business School Press, 2002), 141.

## Chapter 6

1. Amy C. Edmondson, "Psychological Safety and Learning Behavior in Work Teams," *Administrative Science Quarterly*, 44, no. 2 (1999): 350–383.
2. Alexander D. Platt, Caroline E. Tripp, et al. *The Skillful Leader II: Confronting Conditions That Undermine Learning* (Acton, MA: Ready About Press, 2008), 29–36.

## Chapter 7

1. Barry Jentz, *Talk Sense*: *Communicating to Lead and Learn* (Acton, MA: Research for Better Teaching, 2007).
2. Ronald A. Heifitz and Marty Linsky, *Leadership on the Line: Staying Alive Through the Dangers of Leading* (Boston, MA: Harvard Business School Press, 2002), 145.

## Chapter 8

1. Project Implicit, "Implicit Social Cognition: Investigating the Gap Between Intentions and Actions," https://www.projectimplicit.net/index.html.
2. Sendhil Mullainathan, "Racial Bias, Even When We Have Good Intentions," *New York Times*, January 3, 2015.
3. Amanda Vinicky, "Rivals Help Level Playing Field for Tornado-Shattered Team," *National Public Radio*, November 23, 2013, http://www.npr.org/2013/11/23/246872437/rival-high-school-helps-tornado-shattered-team.
4. Gloria Ladson-Billings, "From the Achievement Gap to the Education Debt: Understanding Achievement in US Schools," *Educational Researcher*, 35, no. 7 (2006): 3–12.
5. John A. Powell, "Post-Racialism or Targeted Universalism?" *Clearinghouse Review: Journal of Poverty Law and Policy*, May–June 2010.
6. Emily Style, "Curriculum as Window and Mirror," *Social Science Record* 33, no. 2 (1996): 35–45.
7. Adrienne Rich, *Blood, Bread, and Poetry: Selected Prose 1979–1985* (New York: Norton, 1986), 198–201.
8. Claude Steele, *Whistling Vivaldi : How Stereotypes Affect Us and What We Can Do* (New York: W. W. Norton & Company, 2011).
9. Mica Pollock, *Colormute*: *Race Talk Dilemmas in an American School* (Princeton, NJ: Princeton University Press, 2004), 8–9.
10. Beverly Daniel Tatum, "Cultivating the Trust of Black Parents," in *Everyday Anti-Racism*, ed. Mica Pollock (New York: The New Press, 2008), 310–313.
11. Ronald F. Ferguson, "Helping Students of Color Meet High Standards," in *Everyday Anti-Racism*, ed. Mica Pollock (New York: The New Press, 2008), 78–81.
12. Elizabeth Bondy et al., "Becoming Warm Demanders: Perspectives and Practices of First-Year Teachers," *Urban Education* 43, no. 3 (2012): 420–450.
13. Jay Smooth, "How I Learned to Stop Worrying and Love Discussing Race," TED Talk, Posted November 15, 2011. https://www.youtube.com/watch?v=MbdxeFcQtaU.

## Chapter 9

1. Laura Lipton and Bruce Wellman, "How to Talk So Teachers Listen," *Educational Leadership* 65, no. 1 (2007): 30–34.
2. Kim Marshall, *Rethinking Teacher Supervision and Evaluation: How to Work Smart, Build Collaboration, and Close the Achievement Gap* (San Francisco, CA: Jossey-Bass, 2009), 41–88.

## Chapter 10

1. John Dewey, *Experience and Education* (New York, NY: Simon & Schuster, 1997).

# Acknowledgments

A friend compared the principal experience to purifying metal in a black-smith's fire, weaknesses burning off, heat making us stronger. The job is certainly a crucible of learning. Experiences like this remind me how fortunate I am to have strong people to lean on and learn from. Friends, colleagues, teachers, and family members have provided enormous support through the steep learning curve of this job. The learning described in this book—and the demanding process of figuring it out and writing about it—could not have happened without them.

First and most important, I want to thank the members of my school community. Their daily actions taught me how to be a better leader. When the parent–teacher steering committee continued to meet in the dark even after the electricity went off; when student alumni regularly returned to school to thank their teachers; when the teachers went to enormous lengths to make learning relevant, rigorous, and joyful for children—and children similarly invested and engaged and created beautiful work as a result; and when the entire student body cheered on the dancing faculty at an assembly, I knew I was part of something unusual and extraordinary.

Every staff person taught me valuable lessons. (This includes the greatly missed junior high staff.) Many modeled leadership in supporting the growth of their colleagues, the larger school community, and me. They are too many to name. However, several people need to be individually recognized. Coaches Kathy Greeley and Claire Dahill worked tirelessly and brilliantly to support instruction, the well-being of teachers, and me. School Counselor (and breakfast doppelganger) Karen Haglund's wisdom and support were instrumental. Nurse Ronnette Capehart was simply a godsend. Parent volunteer Mary-Ann Matyas deserves special thanks for her leadership, advocacy on behalf of all children, and many acts of kindness and deliciousness. Assistant Principal Barry McNulty and School Secretary Cheryl DePasquale were absolutely the best partners I could ever hope for. Hands-down. No question. I am indebted to them forever for their hard work, excellent humor, deep compassion for kids, and uncanny (and invaluable) understanding of adult behavior.

Several other schools have shaped my vision of effective leadership and learning. My own principal, Lynn Stuart, and many stellar colleagues at the Cambridgeport School formed the intense laboratory that defined effective teaching for me. The principles I learned from my colleagues and Lynn in those years have been my reference point in all of my teaching and leading since.

Wise and generous professors at Harvard Graduate School of Education expanded my learning in ways I'd never planned. Barry Jentz taught me how to listen using strategies that changed me professionally and personally. Richard Murnane taught me that areas of disagreement and discord are often the places where the important learning occurs. Richard Elmore not only taught me how to pursue continuous improvement at an organizational level but also personally models this quest for ongoing learning. Lee Teitel practices learner-centered leadership by holding up a mirror to help me see what I need to learn. Susan Moore Johnson continues to be a role model for me with her skillful leadership, personal high standards, and strategies for (seemingly effortlessly) shaping high-quality collaborative work. Like many of her former students, I regularly ask myself, "What would Susan do?"

Thaly Germain and the faculty and fellow principals in the Lynch Leadership Academy provided the right combination of useful theory and on-the-ground practice. My LLA coach, Elliot Stern, effectively shook up my entire sense of leadership. His thoughtful, probing coaching prompted much of the learning this book documents and makes me realize how much more I have to learn. I will always feel grateful to Thabiti Brown, who, in the midst of hosting a gaggle of administrators at his school, took the time to refer me to LLA, which led to so much personal and professional growth.

Superintendent Jeff Young allowed me to take time off to write, and I could not have written this book without this precious window. He and central office administrators Barbara Allen and Carolyn Turk (who have watched over my career for the past twenty years) and many other district and school administrators provided important encouragement and guidance throughout my principalship. I am grateful to Tom Fowler-Finn, who took a risk and appointed me as an interim principal, launching this phase of my career.

I want to thank the following wise educators and leaders (and educators of leaders) who read and gave feedback on the first draft of the book: Denny Buzzelli, Irwin Blumer, Christina Brown, Mark Conrad, Rachel Curtis, and Elliot Stern. They shared useful feedback and equally helpful encouragement. Marco Curnen also provided careful feedback at a critical time for the book. I would love to get this group in a room together to see how they could revolutionize school leadership.

For planting the seed for this book (and persistently watering it), I am indebted to Caroline Chauncey. Early on, she encouraged me to take notes that were invaluable both for writing the book and also for building a discipline of reflecting on my learning along the way. Caroline consistently provides the highest quality feedback. Her balance of push and support inevitably makes me want to strive harder. I thank her for infinite patience and great modeling.

David Jacobson was a dedicated thought partner throughout both the principalship and the writing process. His clear thinking and commitment to educational equity along with his considerable expertise proved invaluable for both endeavors. I sincerely thank him for his detailed feedback, helpful advice, and kind cheering.

I'm grateful to my extended "family" for their support. Emily, Kevin, Maya, Alex, and Calvin Qazilbash have kindly opened their tent and included me in their energetic, loving, and generous family. They regularly push my learning around life balance, all things education-related, and Minecraft. I also send a special thank you to Laurie and Tom McDonnell, who are unparalleled in their ability to inspire and feed me, push and support my learning, and make me laugh and feel cared for.

Other people whose wisdom helped shape this book are Tracey Benson, Sarah Bruhn, Cesar Cruz, Emily Glasgow, Annie Sevelius, Rolandria Justice, Kathy Boudett, Liz City, Len Solo, Stephen Lapointe, Liz Drury, Tony Byers, Lori Likis, Pat Gold, Carole Learned-Miller, Robin Harris, Katie Charner-Laird, Paula Denton, Ruth Charney, and the members of SLP 2015 BCE. Years ago Ben Mardell came up with the excellent pancake metaphor that I've been using ever since. Cornelius Lee described building the skills to have difficult conversations as exercising a muscle. I'm grateful to both for these images I like and use so much. Vanessa De-Guia is the colleague I reference who speaks eloquently about not waiting until she trusts others but instead learning to trust herself to take risks. I'm also indebted to the deep thinkers at Expeditionary Learning for providing compelling examples of what thoughtful leadership and excellent schools look like.

My uncle, John Tyler, regularly supports my work with insight, grace, and humor. My thoughtful sister, Rebecca Fiarman, gave sage advice on chapters, and even more importantly she reminded me to pause for gratitude. My deepest gratitude goes to my parents, Janell and Sidney Fiarman. It's not just that these former educators spent countless hours reading drafts, giving critical feedback, being sounding boards, and reminding me to journal. They are also inspiring role models of humility, community involvement, continuous learning, and joy. They are my anchor. I am blessed to have such selfless supporters as family and am ready for the celebratory apple pie.

# About the Author

Sarah E. Fiarman is a Lecturer at the Harvard Graduate School of Education, where she teaches instructional leadership for elementary, middle school, and high school principals. She is a former public school teacher and principal. Across her work, she is committed to building powerful learning communities through developing teacher leadership, examining teaching and learning in a collaborative context, and surfacing and addressing unconscious racial biases. Her coursework, consulting, and writing focus on increasing educational equity for all children, particularly children of color and other historically underserved student groups.

While serving as a public school teacher, Sarah was a National Board Certified Teacher, Responsive Classroom Consulting Teacher, and facilitator with Seeking Educational Equity and Diversity. As a principal, she was awarded a Lynch Leadership Academy Fellowship, and in 2013, the Boston Globe rated her school the "#1 Dream School in Massachusetts."

Sarah has consulted on improving instruction at the classroom, school, and district level. She is a coauthor of *Instructional Rounds in Education: A Network Approach to Improving Teaching and Learning* with Elizabeth A. City, Richard F. Elmore, and Lee Teitel. Sarah is also contributing author to *Data Wise in Action: Stories of Schools Using Data to Improve Teaching and Learning*, edited by Kathryn Parker Boudett and Jennifer Steele (Harvard Education Press, 2007), and *Data Wise: A Step-by-Step Guide to Using Assessment Results to Improve Teaching and Learning*, edited by Kathryn Parker Boudett, Elizabeth A. City, and Richard J. Murnane (Harvard Education Press, 2005). She received her EdD from Harvard Graduate School of Education in Administration, Planning, and Social Policy.

# Index

# EL
# AMOR
## POR LA
# ORACIÓN

*Un manual devocional para profundizar
su vida de oración en 40 días*

## Alvin VanderGriend

PRAYERSHOP
PUBLISHING

PrayerShop es el brazo publicador de Harvest Prayer Ministries y de la Church Prayer Leaders Network. Harvest Prayer Ministries existe para hacer de cada iglesia una casa de oración. Su tienda de oración en línea: www.prayershop.org, ofrece a la venta más de 400 recursos para la oración.

Diseño: Robert Mason
Editor: Paul Faber

ISBN–13: 978-1-935012-24-5

Publicado en cooperación con:
Alvin J. VanderGriend
606 Woodcreek Drive
Lynden, WA 98264

# PRÓLOGO

Este libro es producto de mi viaje de oración personal. Un viaje que me llevó a una mejor comprensión de la oración, a una mayor intimidad con Dios, a llegar a amar el acto de orar, y a practicarlo casi todo el tiempo.

Aprendí a orar desde mi niñez. La primera oración que recuerdo, la repetía a la hora de las comidas: "Señor, bendice esta comida, por amor de Jesús. Amén". Mis padres me alentaban a orar cuando me levantaba cada mañana, y al acostarme cada noche. Nos dirigían en una oración antes y después de cada comida.

Pero había mucho acerca de la oración que yo no sabía. No sabía que la oración tiene que ver con una relación, una relación de amor con el Padre. No sabía que tenía que pedir bendiciones espirituales para recibirlas. No sabía de la importancia de la intercesión. Mis oraciones se componían de frases aprendidas. Comenzaba con la expresión: "Amado Padre celestial", la cual expresaba mi alabanza. Mi confesión se sintetizaba en la frase: "Perdónanos nuestras deudas". Luego seguía la declaración "en el nombre de Jesús" y terminaba con el "amén".

Esta oración era mi forma de mantenerme en contacto con Dios, algo que uno hace al levantarse, antes de comer, y al acostarse. Se podía orar brevemente usando frases fijas y rutinarias cada día.

Estoy profundamente agradecido por lo que aprendí respecto a la oración en mi niñez Eso estableció algunos fundamentos importantes. Pero al tratar de crecer en mi vida de oración, me sentía imposibilitado. Cada nuevo esfuerzo—y fueron muchos—terminaba en fracaso. Ni siquiera me gustaba orar. Descubrí que el principal problema era que no entendía lo que es la oración, lo que realmente significa orar.

Mi comprensión de la oración ocurrió poco a poco. Primero aprendí que si pedía "de acuerdo con la voluntad de Dios", él me daría lo que yo pidiera. Llegué a entender que la oración era una forma de experimentar intimidad con Dios. Después vinieron otras percepciones. Aprendí que la intercesión es una forma de asociarse con Dios, que una confesión sincera restaura una relación de amor, y que los largos períodos de oración rebosan de gozo. Llegué a comprender que la oración es la clave de la verdadera espiritualidad.

Este libro fue escrito para personas que desean aprender a amar el acto de orar. Quiero asegurarles que es posible aprender a amar la oración, pues amar la oración es amar a Aquel a quien oramos. Y nosotros que conocemos y amamos al Señor podemos hacerlo.

Que Dios les bendiga abundantemente al embarcarse en esta aventura de aprender a amar la oración.

# Seis maneras de usar *El amor por la oración*

1. **Devociones personales**

   Las personas que usan *El amor por la oración* para sus devociones personales profundizan y fortalecen sus vidas de oración, especialmente cuando reflexionan, oran y actúan como se sugiere.

2. **Devociones familiares**

   Familias completas están obteniendo fuerza y profundidad en la oración al usar una lectura de este libro devocional cada día, generalmente a la hora de las comidas. Los miembros de la familia se turnan para leer el texto en voz alta. Discuten las preguntas para reflexionar. Las sugerencias de temas para orar enriquecen el tiempo de oración familiar. La familia se pone de acuerdo respecto a actividades que realizarán según lo recomienda la sección de "acción".

3. **Células de oración**

   Las células de oración usan *El amor por la oración* para fortalecerse en la oración. Los miembros de la célula deciden anticipadamente las lecturas devocionales que han de usar cada semana, después actúan de acuerdo con lo aprendido, y lo conversan cuando se reúnen.

4. **Grupos pequeños**

   Los grupos pequeños usan este material devocional para estudio y discusión. Con anticipación, los miembros leen cinco lecturas devocionales en una sección. Cuando se reúnen, los miembros del grupo comentan sobre el texto, discuten las preguntas para reflexionar, y narran sus experiencias al aplicar las ideas de la sección de "acción". Los participantes se turnan para dirigir al grupo en la sección de oración.

5. **Clases de educación**

   Los miembros de las clases leen con anticipación los cinco devocionales de una sección. Cuando la clase se reúne, el líder destaca los puntos principales de los estudios semanales. Los miembros de la clase añaden sus comentarios o hacen preguntas. El líder pide reacciones a algunas de las preguntas para reflexionar. La clase elige una o más de las sugerencias para la acción en la semana siguiente. En la clase siguiente, los miembros informan de sus experiencias.

6. **Toda la iglesia**

   Las iglesias pueden usar *El amor por la oración* para un programa de 40 días con énfasis en la oración. Los miembros o las familias utilizan los devocionales, y un pastor predica sobre el tema semanal de las devociones. Los grupos pequeños, las células familiares o las clases de educación en la iglesia discuten los temas semanales.

La iniciativa "40 Días de Oración" fue diseñada para ayudar a las iglesias a convertirse en casas de oración. La oración debe ser el centro y el alma de cada congregación. Las Escrituras hacen de la oración una prioridad de la iglesia. El Señor dijo: "Mi casa será llamada casa de oración para todos los pueblos" (Isaías 56:7; ver Mateo 21:13). La Biblia establece una norma elevada para la oración: "Oren en el Espíritu en todo momento, con peticiones y ruegos. Manténganse alerta, perseveren en oración por todos los santos" (Efesios 6:18).

La oración constante y ferviente hace una gran diferencia en la vida de una iglesia. Las iglesias que oran tienden a ser iglesias saludables.

# Contenido

# ¿DE QUÉ SIRVE LA ORACIÓN?

# Día 1

# Amistad con Dios

*"Me has dado a conocer la senda de la vida; me llenarás de alegría en tu presencia,*
*y de dicha eterna a tu derecha".*—Salmo 16:11

L os seres humanos fuimos creados para vivir en comunión con Dios, cuyo propósito es que tengamos vida y la disfrutemos en una relación con él. Sin esta relación, somos como ramas cortadas de un árbol, como un artefacto eléctrico desconectado de su fuente de energía.

La oración es la forma en que entramos en contacto con Dios, y nos mantenemos en sintonía con él. Yo solía pensar que la oración era un ejercicio espiritual, una disciplina que uno debía cumplir. Al paso de los años, sin embargo, Dios me enseñó a ver la oración como el tomar parte en una amistad. Uno de los primeros padres de la iglesia la llamó "permanecer en compañía de Dios". ¡Me gusta esa idea!

Hace varios años, cuando estaba tratando de definir lo que es la oración, Dios me guió a través de una serie de pasos. Primero pensé que la oración era simplemente *hablar con Dios.*

Después me vino la idea de una relación, y comencé a ver que la oración es la *parte conversada de una relación con Dios.* Meses después, mi definición volvió a cambiar y comencé a comprender que la oración es *la parte conversada de una relación de amor con Dios.* Pensé que por fin lo había captado, pero Dios agregó un elemento más. Me di cuenta de que *la oración es la parte conversada de la relación de amor más importante de mi vida.*

A veces las personas preguntan cuánto tiempo deben dedicar a la oración cada día. Yo solía sugerir que unos 20 minutos de oración formal por día era suficiente. Respaldaba eso recordándoles las muchas cosas que necesitan ser incluidas en una oración, y agregaba que

20 minutos por día es sólo alrededor del 2% de las horas que pasamos despiertos cada día. Ahora, cuando las personas preguntan cuánto tiempo deben dedicar a la oración, les digo que deben dedicar suficiente tiempo para construir una buena relación. Y, considerando que la relación de la que estamos hablando es la relación de amor más importante de la vida, eso significa bastante tiempo.

¿Qué hace Dios en bien de los que se relacionan con él en amor? El salmista lo explica bien cuando dice "me llenarás de alegría en tu presencia, y de dicha eterna a tu derecha".

¿De qué sirve orar? Nos ayuda a crecer en Cristo, y vivir diariamente en la más importante de todas las relaciones de amor. Pero, por supuesto, esto sólo sucede si ponemos todo de nuestra parte. Así que, ¿qué beneficio está usted obteniendo al orar?

### PARA REFLEXIONAR

+ ¿Qué puede su vida de oración decir respecto a su relación de amor con Dios?
+ ¿Qué más podría hacer para profundizar su amistad con Dios?

### ORAR

+ Alabe a Dios por su amor y por su disposición a tener una relación de amor con usted.
+ Pídale a Dios que haga más fuerte su vida de oración y profundice su relación con él.
+ Pídale a Dios que lo llene con la alegría de su presencia, y le dé dicha eterna a su lado.
+ Agradézcale a Dios por su generosidad al poner estos dones a su alcance.

### ACCIÓN

Intencionalmente, aparte cierto tiempo para pasarlo con Dios. Haga algunas cosas que le ayuden a construir su relación con él durante ese tiempo. Anote las tres cosas más importantes que usted ha obtenido gracias al tiempo que ha pasado con Dios.

# Día 2

# La oración comienza con Dios

*"En nuestra debilidad, el Espíritu acude a ayudarnos. No sabemos qué pedir, pero el Espíritu mismo intercede por nosotros con gemidos que no pueden expresarse con palabras. Y Dios, que examina los corazones, sabe cuál es la intención del Espíritu, porque el Espíritu intercede por los creyentes conforme a la voluntad de Dios".*—ROMANOS 8:26, 27

Deseo compartir un pensamiento radical. Este pensamiento ha transformado mi manea de orar y mi manera de pensar respecto a la oración.

Durante años creí que mis oraciones comenzaban conmigo. Tenía que inventarlas. Tenía que captar la atención de Dios. Como es fácil de entender, con esta forma de pensar, la oración muchas veces era una tarea tediosa.

Aprendí que estaba equivocado. La oración no comienza con nosotros. *La oración comienza con Dios.* Esa es la idea radical que cambió mi vida de oración. Dios es el iniciador. Él nos mueve a orar. Él nos da ideas sobre qué orar. Él nos ha hecho las promesas que reclamamos cuando oramos. Cuando oramos, somos instrumentos de Dios.

Dios está obrando en todo nuestro orar. Él nos da a conocer su voluntad, de manera que pidamos las cosas que él anhela darnos. Por amor, él nos insta a orar por otros de manera que, en respuesta a nuestra intercesión, él pueda derramar bendiciones sobre ellos.

Y es el Espíritu, dice Pablo, el que hace posible nuestra oración. A veces no sabremos por qué orar, pero no necesitamos saberlo. El Espíritu está ahí, revelándonos la voluntad de Dios en las Escrituras y haciendo nacer en nosotros las preocupaciones de oración. Él nos está acicateando por medio de las circunstancias, y abriendo nuestros ojos a las necesidades que nos rodean. Él escudriña nuestro corazón y ve nuestra manera de actuar para llevarnos a un verdadero arrepentimiento. Él nos revela la gloria y la bondad de Dios, de manera que nuestras oraciones pueden estar llenas de alabanza y gratitud. Podemos tener la seguridad de que Dios nos oirá cuando acudamos a él. Dios contesta toda oración que nace en el cielo, cada oración que nace en nuestros corazones por medio del Espíritu Santo, cada oración que está basada en una promesa fiel de su Palabra.

Si la oración comienza con Dios, entonces el primer paso del asunto de aprender a orar es aprender a escuchar los murmullos de Dios, a poner nuestros corazones a tono con él, a responder a sus insinuaciones. Tal vez nuestra primera oración cada día debería ser: "Señor, enséñame a orar. Ayúdame a entender tus propósitos, a sentir tus cargas, a ver lo que tú ves, a oír los gemidos que tú oyes, para que mis oraciones puedan ser placenteras para ti y puedan cumplir tus propósitos".

¿Qué tal si empezamos ahora mismo, rogando: "Señor, enséñame a orar hoy"?

### PARA REFLEXIONAR

+ ¿Es la oración una tarea pesada o una fuente de alegría para usted?
+ ¿Qué más podría usted hacer para estar seguro de que verdaderamente conoce la voluntad de Dios cuando ora?

### ORAR

+ *Alabe* al Señor como el Dios que inicia y escucha las oraciones.
+ *Pídale* a Dios que haga que la oración sea una fuente de alegría en su vida.
+ *Agradezca* a Dios por el privilegio de conocer sus pensamientos y poder presentárselos a él.
+ *Interceda* por sus seres amados que son débiles en la práctica de la oración.

### ACCIÓN

La próxima vez que aparte tiempo para orar, comience diciendo: "Señor, ayúdame en este momento a saber por qué quieres que ore". Manténgase dispuesto a alabar, a agradecer, a confesar, a suplicar. Espere recibir impresiones o sugerencias del Espíritu. Y cuando le lleguen, ore al respecto.

# Día 3

# Celebrando a Dios por medio de la oración

*"Bendeciré al Señor en todo tiempo; mis labios siempre lo alabarán. Mi alma se gloría en el Señor; lo oirán los humildes y se alegrarán. Engrandezcan al Señor conmigo; exaltemos a una su nombre".*—SALMO 34:1–3

A todos nos gusta celebrar, y la vida nos da bastantes oportunidades para hacerlo. Celebramos la Navidad, el Año Nuevo, los cumpleaños, los aniversarios, las graduaciones, las victorias, y mucho más. Pero no hay mejor motivo para celebrar que Dios.

Celebrar significa "honrar o alabar públicamente". Dios merece honor y alabanza más que nadie ni nada. El gran predicador escocés Alexander White, solía aconsejar a sus oyentes que "pensaran magníficamente de Dios". Las personas que piensan magníficamente de Dios, recordando su grandeza y bondad, no pueden menos que celebrar a Dios y expresar su alabanza.

Vivimos en una sociedad a la que le agrada celebrar lo que tiene valor. Exaltamos a héroes deportivos, admiramos a nuestras estrellas cinematográficas favoritas, y nos gloriamos en las "victorias" de nuestra nación. Eso no es malo. Pero en el proceso de exaltar y glorificar, no olvidemos a Aquel que es la fuente de todo lo bueno.

Celebrar a Dios significa por lo menos tres cosas:

En primer lugar, significa *reconocer a Dios por lo que él es*. La gloria de Dios es el esplendor que emite y que puede ser visto y conocido. Cuando glorificamos a Dios, no le damos nada. No agregamos lustre a su ser. Es tan imposible hacerlo como agregar esplendor a una puesta de sol con sólo mirarla. Pero podemos admirar asombrados una

14

puesta de sol y, al mismo tiempo, podemos ver en ella la hermosura y la gloria del Señor. En segundo lugar, significa *amar a Dios por lo que él es*. Esto significa dejar de lado nuestras preocupaciones, nuestras exigencias y nuestras listas de peticiones para enfocarnos en Dios y disfrutar de él. Nada disminuye más nuestro orgullo, nuestro ego, y nuestros deseos egoístas que enfocarnos solamente en Dios.

En tercer lugar, celebrar a Dios significa *darle a Dios lo único que podemos ofrecerle:* nuestros corazones llenos de amor y alabanza. Todo lo demás, él ya lo tiene. Él es totalmente autosuficiente y no necesita nada de nuestra parte. Pero Dios sí pide nuestros corazones, nuestro amor y nuestra adoración. Cuando lo hacemos, él se siente agradecido y feliz.

Comencemos hoy a pensar "magníficamente de Dios". Lo demás vendrá por añadidura.

### PARA REFLEXIONAR

- ¿Cuánto disfruta usted a Dios? ¿Dedica alguna vez un tiempo personal para pensar acerca de Dios y su bondad y para adorarle?
- Piense en algunas formas específicas en las que hoy puede celebrar a Dios.

### ORAR

- *Alabe* a Dios diciéndole cinco cosas que usted aprecia especialmente de él.
- *Pídale* a Dios que le ayude a ver su majestuoso esplendor y pueda realmente disfrutarle y amarle.
- *Agradezca* a Dios por revelarle su gloria y por darle motivos para alabarlo.
- *Confiese*, si ha habido poca alabanza sincera a Dios en su vida, y pídale su perdón.

### ACCIÓN

Aparte un tiempo hoy para meditar en Dios. Esto puede significar fijar su mente en varios de los atributos de Dios: su amor, su sabiduría, su poder, su gracia. Exprésele a Dios sus pensamientos y sus sentimientos.

# Día 4

# Dios necesita nuestras oraciones

*"Entonces Moisés le ordenó a Josué: Escoge algunos de nuestros hombres y sal a combatir a los amalecitas [ ...] yo estaré en la cima de la colina con la vara de Dios en la mano. Mientras Moisés mantenía los brazos en alto, la batalla se inclinaba a favor de los israelitas; pero cuando los bajaba, se inclinaba en favor de los amalecitas".*—ÉXODO 17:9, 11*

Dios a veces nos enseña de maneras sorprendentes. Cuando Israel enfrentó una grave amenaza militar, Josué y el ejército salieron a pelear, pero Moisés subió a una colina a orar. Mientras los brazos de Moisés permanecían levantados en oración, Israel ganaba, pero cuando bajaba los brazos, el enemigo prevalecía.

¿Por qué, nos preguntaremos, permitía Dios que su pueblo sufriera cuando no había oración? La respuesta es que Dios estaba enseñando al pueblo que él elige moverse en respuesta a la oración y que no se moverá si no hay oración.

Aun cuando Dios es todopoderoso, sabio, y capaz de obrar sin nosotros, elige obrar a través de nuestras oraciones. Nos llama a participar de una estrategia de asociación. Sin nosotros, él no obrará.

Cuando Dios me enseñó este importante principio de la oración, lo hizo mediante una simple pero directa aplicación a mi vida. Era como si Dios dijera: "Alvin, cuando tus hijos van a la escuela cada mañana, van a una batalla. Si tú, como padre, mantienes tus manos elevadas, vencerán. Pero si tus manos de oración bajan, perderán". Jamás he olvidado esa lección.

Desde entonces he llegado a entender que si como fieles líderes y feligreses "[levantamos] las manos al cielo con pureza de corazón" (1 Timoteo 2:8), la iglesia se hará más fuerte y podrá resistir los embates del averno. Cuando en sus vecindarios y lugares de trabajo, los creyentes levantan las manos en oración por los que los rodean, los poderes de las tinieblas son forzados a retroceder.

El testimonio más común de los miembros del grupo *Faro* es que a medida que oran por los vecindarios, se produce una transformación. Hablan de garitos que se cierran, de baja en los niveles de criminalidad, de matrimonios restaurados, de familias reunidas de nuevo, y de gente que se convierte. Lo que sucede cuando el pueblo de Dios ora por sus vecinos, es lo mismo que sucedió cuando Moisés oró durante la batalla. Las fuerzas del mal retroceden.

Lo que más necesitamos para solucionar los problemas de nuestra sociedad no es más dinero ni más educación, tampoco necesitamos más ideas, libros o estrategias. Nuestra principal necesidad es la de manos alzadas en oración. "Podemos hacer mucho más con nuestras oraciones que con nuestro trabajo. La oración puede lograr cualquier cosa. Cuando oramos, Dios obra".** En su caso, ¿dónde están sus manos en este momento?

## PARA REFLEXIONAR

♦ ¿En qué sector del reino de Dios están los cristianos venciendo los poderes de las tinieblas gracias a la oración? ¿Hay lugares donde parecen estar perdiendo la batalla porque hay poca oración?

♦ ¿Qué clase de cosas cree que Dios quisiera hacer en su vecindario o en su lugar de trabajo en respuesta a sus oraciones?

## ORAR

♦ *Alabe* a Dios por lo sabio de su plan para gobernar el mundo por medio de las oraciones de su pueblo.

♦ *Pídale* a Dios que le ayude a comprender por qué sus oraciones son tan importantes para él.

♦ *Agradezca* a Dios por honrarle al elegir actuar en respuesta a sus oraciones.

♦ *Comprométase* a orar fielmente por los miembros de su familia, vecinos y colegas, para que Dios pueda obrar en respuesta a sus oraciones.

## ACCIÓN

Párese frente a su casa. Mire a su alrededor. ¿Qué está tratando de hacer el maligno en las vidas de los que viven a su alrededor? Levante sus manos en oración por este vecindario (por lo menos hágalo en su imaginación). Imagínese a Dios, en respuesta a sus oraciones, moviéndose para frustrar lo que el diablo está tratando de hacer.

---

*Para conocer la historia completa, leer Éxodo 17:8–16.
**El cristiano arrodillado.*

# Día 5

# Bienvenido al trono

*"Acerquémonos confiadamente al trono de la gracia para recibir misericordia y hallar la gracia que nos ayude en el momento que más la necesitemos".*—HEBREOS 4:16

El acceso al trono de Dios es la base de toda oración. Todos los que oran deben acercarse al trono. Cada verdadero creyente es bienvenido en ese lugar.

El acceso al trono de Dios es un privilegio asombroso. Aquel a quien nos acercamos es el soberano, el todopoderoso, el santo gobernante del universo. ¡Qué privilegio el sentirnos bienvenidos en su presencia!

El trono de Dios, se nos recuerda, es un trono de gracia, no un trono de juicio. Esto significa que si hemos ido a su presencia mediante la sangre de Cristo, somos aceptables para él. Dios no hace un escrutinio para determinar si somos merecedores o no. Extiende una mano de bienvenida.

Somos invitados a acercarnos con confianza. No nos hallaremos frente a una puerta cerrada. No tendremos que rogar ni arrastrarnos para entrar. Dios nos está esperando. Está contento de que nos hayamos acercado.

A veces cuando oro, me gusta imaginar que estoy ahí en el salón del trono, en el cielo. En mi imaginación, veo al Omnipotente sobre el alto trono. Su gloria llena el lugar. Veo ángeles a su alrededor. Es suficiente para llenarme de terror, excepto por una razón: Dios me reconoce. Él sabe mi nombre. Me mira, sonríe, y extiende una mano de bienvenida. "Dime por qué has venido", me dice.

Esta maravillosa bienvenida no se nos extiende porque seamos buenos o lo merezcamos. Lo que merecemos, debido a nuestros pecados, es que se nos impida el acceso a la presencia de Dios. Pero Cristo ha quitado nuestros pecados y nos ha hecho aceptables ante Dios. Hemos sido adoptados como hijos e hijas. Tenemos un lugar en la familia real.

Podemos acercarnos al trono con nuestras propias preocupaciones. Podemos acudir, también, como intercesores, presentando las necesidades de nuestros familiares, amigos y vecinos.

Los intercesores que son miembros del movimiento *Faro* hablan en forma regular en favor de sus vecinos. Uno de ellos informó que después de que ella y otros habían orado por sus vecinos durante un año, esas personas se hicieron más amigables, dejaron de usar drogas, dos que estaban cesantes consiguieron trabajo, un padre dejó de beber, una mujer fue milagrosamente sanada, una persona fue liberada de un espíritu maligno, varios llegaron a conocer a Cristo, y se inició una serie de estudios bíblicos. ¡Lo que estaba sucediendo ante el trono tuvo un efecto transformador!

Esto es algo de lo que Dios tiene en mente cuando nos extiende una bienvenida. Él quiere cambiarnos, y quiere cambiar nuestro mundo.

### PARA REFLEXIONAR

- ¿Cuánta confianza tiene usted cuando ora?
- Trate de pensar en por lo menos tres razones por las que es posible que los creyentes se acerquen al trono de Dios con confianza.
- Piense en las maneras en que usted puede aumentar su confianza en Dios.

### ORAR

- *Alabe* a Dios porque su gracia y su misericordia están disponibles para usted.
- *Agradezca* a Dios porque le da la bienvenida a su sala del trono.
- *Pídale* a Dios la misericordia y la gracia que generosamente le ofrece, y la confianza que usted necesita para poder orar con más efectividad por sí mismo y por otros.

### ACCIÓN

Realice un "paseo de oración" por su vecindario. Un "paseo de oración" consiste en orar por lo que uno va viendo a medida que pasea. Que lo que usted vea, vaya inspirándole a orar.

# LOS REQUISITOS DE LA ORACIÓN

# Día 1

# La necesidad de un corazón limpio

*"Si en mi corazón hubiera yo abrigado maldad, el Señor no me habría escuchado. Pero Dios me ha escuchado, ha atendido a la voz de mi plegaria".*—SALMO 66:18, 19

E l pecado dificulta la oración. Una persona puede orar y orar sin recibir respuesta, y llegar a la conclusión de que el problema radica en Dios. En realidad, el problema puede estar en el corazón de la persona. David comprendió que si guardaba el pecado en su corazón, el Señor no lo iba a oír.

Una de las peores cosas respecto al pecado, es que obstruye la oración. Cuando guardamos un pecado escondido, estamos desconectados de Dios, porque Dios es santo y no puede tolerar el pecado en su presencia.

Cuando el pecado obstruye la oración, el verdadero problema no es que hayamos pecado, sino que, habiendo pecado, no nos hayamos arrepentido. Es solamente el pecado no confesado, y guardado en el corazón, el que obstruye nuestras oraciones. Los pecados perdonados no obstruyen las oraciones. Los pecadores perdonados son bienvenidos en la presencia de Dios.

Siempre anhelante de que acudamos a él, Dios ha provisto una forma para que el pecado sea removido por la sangre de Jesús, a fin de que podamos venir a él sin obstáculos. El apóstol Juan dice: "Si confesamos nuestros pecados, Dios, que es fiel y justo, nos los perdonará y nos limpiará de toda maldad" (1 Juan 1:9). Cuando han sido perdonados, nuestros pecados desaparecen, y ya no son un obstáculo.

El primer requisito de la oración, entonces, es confesar cualquier cosa que tengamos en nuestro corazón que no es de Dios. Cuando su pecado es perdonado, usted puede tener la seguridad de que Dios le oirá y responderá sus oraciones.

No tema hacer un inventario y arreglar lo que encuentre. Recientemente fui confrontado con una lista de veinte textos bíblicos que identifican el pecado. Al principio pensé: *Mi corazón está limpio ante Dios. No tengo nada que confesar,* pero al revisar la lista, para mi sorpresa, encontré cinco áreas de pecado que necesitaban ser arregladas. Con gran claridad, comprendí lo que era ofensivo para Dios, confesé esas faltas, y pedí la gracia perdonadora de Dios. Sólo así, sentí de nuevo una completa libertad al orar. No podemos disfrutar del privilegio de la oración sin pureza de corazón.

El pecado no sólo obstruye la oración, sino que la oración obstruye el pecado. Los dos están siempre opuestos. Mientras más descuido manifestemos ante el pecado, menos oraremos. Mientras más oremos, menos descuido manifestaremos ante el pecado. Tanto el pecado como la oración son fuerzas poderosas. ¿Cuál de las dos lo controla a usted?

#### PARA REFLEXIONAR

♦ ¿Hay alguna área de su vida sobre la cual tiene dudas ante Dios? Arriésguese a observarla con más detenimiento. Tal vez encuentre ahí un pecado "guardado".

♦ ¿Puede usted decir con confianza lo mismo que David: "[Dios] ha atendido a la voz de mi plegaria" (Salmo 66:19)?

#### ORAR

♦ *Alabe* a Dios porque él "es fiel y justo y perdonará nuestros pecados" (1 Juan 1:9).

♦ *Pídale* a Dios que examine su corazón y su vida, y le revele cualquier pecado que debe desechar.

♦ *Confiese* cualquier pecado al cual el Espíritu Santo llame su atención.

♦ *Agradezca* a Dios por perdonar sus pecados y purificarle de toda maldad, para que usted pueda acudir confiado hasta su presencia.

#### ACCIÓN

Lea en Romanos 12:9–21 la lista de cosas que debe o no debe hacer. Tome nota de cualquiera de estos mandatos que no está cumpliendo. Haga una oración de confesión por áreas específicas de pecado que pueda descubrir en sí mismo. Pídale al Señor que limpie su historia y su corazón. Haga un compromiso nuevo con el Señor.

# Día 2

# La fe que recibe

*"Tengan fe en Dios, respondió Jesús; les aseguro que [...] todo lo que estén pidiendo en oración [...] lo obtendrán".*—MARCOS 11:22–24

La fe es el segundo requisito de la oración verdadera. Las oraciones sin fe son incompletas. Millones de oraciones han sido hechas sin fe y, por lo tanto, han fracasado en su intento. No han sido oraciones verdaderas.

La asombrosa promesa que Jesús hace en Marcos 11:24 parece ofrecer demasiado. ¿Cómo puede Dios ofrecer hacer "todo lo que pedimos en oración"? ¿Y por qué tantos creyentes han pedido, con fe en Dios, y no han recibido respuesta?

La dificultad que nos presenta este pasaje en realidad es la dificultad de comprender la fe.

Tendemos a pensar en la fe como una posesión personal que existe totalmente dentro de nosotros. Creemos que si tenemos suficiente fe, recibiremos lo que pedimos y, en caso contrario, no lo recibiremos.

La fe no es simplemente una posesión. Es un aspecto de una relación. No es algo que poseemos, como una idea o un sentimiento. La fe siempre involucra a otra persona. Confía que otra persona pensará o actuará de cierta manera. Por ejemplo, durante los años en que vivieron mis padres, yo sabía que me darían la bienvenida cada vez que los visitara. Confiaba en que ellos me querían y estarían dispuestos a ayudarme en cualquier ocasión. En otras palabras, yo tenía fe en ellos. Esa fe estaba basada en lo que yo sabía de ellos. La fe en Dios es igual. Es una convicción respecto a quién es Dios, cómo es, y cómo actuará siempre.

Orar con fe no es una convicción interna de que Dios actuará de acuerdo con nuestros deseos si solamente creemos con sinceridad. Involucra la creencia de que Dios siempre responderá nuestras oraciones de acuerdo con su naturaleza, sus propósitos y sus promesas. Dios no quiere que simplemente le lancemos pedidos, esperando que algunos serán contestados. Él quiere que pidamos, sabiendo que él está ahí, reclamando lo que él ha prometido, confiando en que actuará de acuerdo con su naturaleza y sus propósitos. Eso es orar con fe.

Cuando uno le pide a alguien algo de buena fe, no le pide algo que esa persona no estaría dispuesta a dar. Por ejemplo, yo nunca les pediría a mis padres que me dieran más de mi parte de la herencia. Los conozco demasiado bien como para hacerles un pedido tan egoísta e injusto. Del mismo modo, si usted realmente conoce a Dios, sólo le pedirá lo que esté de acuerdo con su voluntad y no cualquier cosa en forma egoísta.

Si usted desea ser más fuerte en la oración, debe hacerse más fuerte en la fe. Si desea hacerse más fuerte en la fe, debe llegar a conocer mejor a Dios. Si desea llegar a conocer mejor a Dios, pase más tiempo con él, leyendo su Palabra y escuchando su Espíritu.

### Para reflexionar

- ¿Por qué cree que Dios ha hecho que la fe sea una condición tan indispensable para la oración?
- ¿Qué puede hacer usted para aumentar su fe?

### Orar

- *Alabe* a Dios por ser confiable.
- *Pídale* a Dios que le aumente la fe, para que pueda orar con más poder.
- *Agradezca* a Dios por su disposición de escuchar y responder las oraciones que usted le hace con fe.
- *Confiese* cualquier falta de fe que pueda descubrir en sí mismo.

### Acción

Pruebe este experimento de oración de fe. Lea Santiago 1:5, y note que revela la naturaleza de Dios y una promesa suya. Si usted está *seguro* de la naturaleza de Dios, según lo revelado en este versículo, y *seguro* de que Dios cumplirá su promesa, pídale sabiduría en conexión con algún asunto práctico que está enfrentando en este momento. Crea, sin dudar, que Dios la proveerá. Agradézcale con anticipación por la sabiduría que él proveerá. Siga pidiendo y confiando hasta que reciba la sabiduría que pidió.

❀

# Día 3

# La vida que puede orar

*"Tenemos confianza delante de Dios, y recibimos todo lo que le pedimos porque obedecemos sus mandamientos y hacemos lo que le agrada".*—1 Juan 3:21, 22

La obediencia es fundamental para una oración efectiva. Sólo las personas que obedecen a Dios tienen el derecho de llegar a su presencia con peticiones.

Dios se deleita en las oraciones de sus hijos obedientes. Cuando queremos lo que Dios quiere y vivimos en la forma en que a él le agrada, tendemos a decir oraciones que Dios contesta como lo esperamos. Y Dios, al contestar nuestras oraciones, apoya lo que él aprueba. Si Dios contestara las oraciones de los desobedientes, estaría avalando o respaldando lo que no aprueba. Eso no coincidiría con el carácter de Dios.

Para decirlo de otra manera, si esperamos que Dios haga por nosotros lo que le pedimos, debemos estar dispuestos a hacer por Dios lo que él pide. Si escuchamos sus mandatos, Dios escuchará nuestras peticiones.

Este principio también explica mucha de la debilidad de la oración. La falta de poder, la falta de perseverancia y la falta de confianza, todas nacen de alguna falla en la vida cristiana. A menudo, cuando la oración fracasa y no recibimos respuestas, pensamos que el problema está en Dios, cuando, en realidad, el problema está en nosotros.

La obediencia que Dios espera de nosotros no está fuera de nuestra posibilidad o de nuestro alcance. Dios, quien se ha comprometido a escuchar las oraciones de sus hijos obedientes, también concede gracia para poder vivir en obediencia. Al ser tocados por su gracia y al tener su Espíritu morando en nosotros, tenemos tanto el deseo como la fuerza para hacer la voluntad de Dios.

Si usted quiere ser poderoso en la oración, pase tiempo con el Señor y pase tiempo estudiando su Palabra. Es ahí donde descubrirá la voluntad de Dios. "Que habite en ustedes la palabra de Cristo" (Colosenses 3:16), y controle lo que ustedes dicen y hacen.

Jesús nos recuerda que si permanecemos en él, y sus palabras permanecen en nosotros, podremos pedir lo que deseamos y nos será dado (Juan 15:7).

Para ser directo, permítame preguntarle: ¿Quiere usted tener confianza cuando ora y recibir de Dios lo que le pide? Entonces, comience a vivir una vida de obediencia. Eso es lo principal.

#### Para reflexionar

+ ¿Qué diferencia cree usted que hace la confianza en su vida de oración?
+ ¿Qué clase de cosas pedirán los que oran confiados en Dios?
+ ¿Qué clase de cosas cree que es más probable que Dios quiera darles a los que obedecen sus mandatos?

#### Orar

+ *Alabe* a Dios por su naturaleza generosa, dispuesta a dar.
+ *Confiese* cualquier falla en cumplir los mandatos de Dios o en hacer lo que a él le agrada, es decir, los pecados que pueden estar obstruyendo una oración efectiva.
+ *Pídale* a Dios los deseos de su corazón obediente. Espere que él le conceda lo que le pide.
+ *Agradezca* a Dios por esta asombrosa promesa respecto a sus oraciones.

#### Acción

Ore por sí mismo la oración de Pablo en Colosenses 1:9–12, una oración que él hizo por los cristianos de Colosas. A medida que Dios le conteste, usted estará creciendo espiritualmente en una forma que proveerá avenidas de obediencia en su vida de oración.

# Día 4

# Orando en el nombre de Jesús

*"Hasta ahora no han pedido nada en mi nombre.*
*Pidan y recibirán, para que su alegría sea completa".*—JUAN 16:24

Al ofrecernos la posibilidad de orar en su nombre, Jesús nos está ofreciendo un privilegio sorprendente. Es como si nos estuviese dando cheques en blanco para que retiremos activos de su cuenta bancaria, seguro de que los usaremos para su honra y para el bien.

Jesús manifiesta una gran confianza en nosotros. Él confía en que su honor y sus intereses están seguros en nuestras manos. Considere lo que significaría poner sus bienes en las manos de otra persona: sus tarjetas de crédito, su hogar, sus inversiones, sus automóviles, sus responsabilidades, todo. Usted elegiría con mucho cuidado a esa persona, ¿verdad?, porque, en realidad, le estaría dando a esa persona el control de su vida y su futuro.

Eso fue exactamente lo que Jesús hizo cuando nos autorizó a usar su nombre en oración. Nos dio autoridad sobre sus cuentas. Nos pidió ejercer control sobre sus bienes: el reino de Dios.

Ejercemos nuestra autoridad por medio de la oración. Cuando oramos, le pedimos al Padre todo lo que necesitamos a fin de hacer la obra que nos encomendó. Cuando oramos, le pedimos a Dios encargarse de las fuerzas demoníacas opuestas a su voluntad. Cuando oramos, dirigimos la gracia y el poder de Dios hacia puntos estratégicos donde son necesarias.

Hay tres frases que nos ayudan a comprender lo que significa orar en el nombre de Jesús.

**1. Hemos sido autorizados a ser los representantes de Cristo.** Cuando acudimos al Padre en el nombre de Jesús, acudimos como personas autorizadas para actuar en su lugar.

Nosotros lo representamos. Cuando acudimos ante el trono, el Padre nos reconoce como personas que están ahí en lugar de su Hijo. Eso nos hace aceptables.

**2. Acudimos a Dios sobre la base de los méritos de Cristo.** Usted y yo no tenemos derechos ante Dios, pero Cristo sí. Por su vida perfecta y su sacrificio, él merece el favor del Padre. Cuando acudimos a Dios en el nombre de Jesús, nos identificamos con él. Venimos a él basados en el mérito de Jesús ante el Padre. Nuestro acceso depende solamente de lo que Jesús hizo.

Trate de imaginarse viniendo ante el Padre por cuenta propia, sin el respaldo de Cristo. Usted no está autorizado a hacer eso, porque no tiene derecho al favor del Padre. Más bien, a causa de sus pecados, usted tiene una enorme deuda con Dios, y no puede esperar nada sino la ira de Dios. Eso es lo opuesto de venir al Padre en el nombre de Jesús.

**3. Acudimos ante el Padre a pedir de acuerdo con la voluntad de Cristo.** Tenemos en nosotros la mente de Cristo, de manera que lo que pedimos es lo que Cristo pediría. Él nos autoriza a pedir en su nombre. Podemos pedir lo que él pediría porque nuestra voluntad está sincronizada con su voluntad.

El Padre ama de tal manera al Hijo, que cuando usamos el nombre de Jesús en oración, captamos de inmediato su atención, captamos de inmediato su disposición, porque hemos tocado su corazón.

#### Para reflexionar

- Piense en la responsabilidad que usted tiene de edificar alguna parte del reino de Cristo. ¿Qué ayuda necesita usted del Señor Jesús para hacerlo bien?
- ¿Qué puede hacer para aprender a estar más consciente de la voluntad de Jesús al orar en su nombre?
- ¿Alguna vez ha agregado las palabras "en el nombre de Cristo" a una oración que, en realidad, no representaba la voluntad de Cristo?

#### Orar

- *Alabe* a Dios por la provisión de su Hijo, Cristo Jesús, como Aquel por cuyo medio usted puede acercarse al trono y conseguir audiencia con Dios.
- *Confiese* cualquier oración egoísta que no representa la mente de Cristo, y que no es conforme a su voluntad.
- *Pida* cualquier cosa que necesita con el fin de cumplir la voluntad de Dios en su vida y en su mundo.

#### Acción

En vez de terminar sus oraciones "en el nombre de Jesús", trate de usar una versión más amplia de la frase, por ejemplo: "Señor, te pido esto porque tu Hijo me autorizó a hacerlo, y porque estoy seguro de que es lo que él quiere que yo pida. Concédemelo, no por algún mérito mío, sino por los méritos de tu Hijo".

# Día 5

# Orando con Perseverancia

*"Jesús les contó a sus discípulos una parábola*
*para mostrarles que debían orar siempre".*—LUCAS 18:1\*

No siempre es fácil orar. Ante las grandes dificultades o la demora en las respuestas, se requiere de gran persistencia. Dios quiere que venzamos la debilidad, y que seamos fuertes en la oración. La parábola de la viuda persistente que hallamos en Lucas 18 ilustra este principio.

Orar con persistencia es insistir con nuestras peticiones ante Dios con urgencia y perseverancia. Significa orar osadamente y con determinación, hasta que llegue la respuesta.

Cuando Dios demora sus respuestas a la oración, siempre hay una buena razón. A veces lo hace para profundizar nuestra fe y desarrollar nuestro carácter. A veces lo hace para probar nuestra fe y ponerla al descubierto. A veces, simplemente, obra de acuerdo a un plan divino que a nosotros nos parece lento. Cuando las respuestas parecen demorar, es importante seguir confiando y seguir orando.

Dios nos ha llamado a ser persistentes en la oración, para que su voluntad pueda ser hecha en la tierra y su nombre pueda ser glorificado. No debemos usar la oración con motivos egoístas. La oración es el medio por el que Dios cumple sus propósitos y derrota a Satanás. Por medio de la oración participamos en el gran plan de Dios. Y no siempre resulta fácil lo que se nos pide hacer.

George Müller es un buen caso de persistencia en la oración. Oró diariamente a favor de cinco amigos inconversos. El primero vino a Cristo después de cinco años; dos más se convirtieron después de quince años. El cuarto fue salvado después de 30 años, y el quinto llegó a ser hijo de Dios después de la muerte de Müller.

La pasión por orar muchas veces se liga a la perseverancia en la oración. La pasión no surge simplemente por emoción humana o aflicción del alma. Es una urgencia derivada de Dios, quien, por medio de su Espíritu que mora en nosotros, le da tanto el contenido como la pasión a nuestras oraciones.

Las oraciones débiles y sin poder no ayudan a vencer las dificultades ni a obtener la victoria sobre la tentación o los problemas. E. M. Bounds afirmó: "El cielo no toma muy en cuenta las peticiones casuales. Dios no se conmueve por los deseos débiles, las oraciones poco sinceras o la flojera espiritual".

Hay, actualmente, una gran necesidad de oraciones poderosas, persistentes. Mucho se logra por medio de oraciones persistentes, mas no por las oraciones débiles y dudosas. Dios tiene mucho que hacer por medio de usted, en su mundo, en su iglesia, en su familia y en su vecindario. Le insto asociarse con Dios por medio de la oración apasionada, persistente.

### PARA REFLEXIONAR

◆ ¿Cómo se describiría mejor su oración de intercesión: osada, apasionada, perseverante, casual, débil, poco sincera?

◆ ¿Sobre qué cosas en su vida cree usted que Dios desea que ore en forma persistente?

### ORAR

◆ *Alabe* a Dios, quien escucha la oración y hace "justicia a sus escogidos, que claman a él día y noche".

◆ *Confiese* cualquier debilidad, duda, superficialidad, flojera o impaciencia que pueda descubrir al examinar su vida de oración.

◆ *Pida* al Espíritu Santo que le imparta osadía, poder, devoción, persistencia y un sentido de urgencia a su vida de oración.

◆ *Agradezca* a Dios por el privilegio de asociarse con él por medio de la oración para cumplir su voluntad en la tierra.

### ACCIÓN

¿Hay alguna cosa por la que usted solía orar, algo que usted sabe que Dios desea que suceda (por ejemplo, la conversión de un ser querido), por la que ha dejado de orar? Si es así, comience a orar de nuevo, con persistencia. Trate de imaginar que cada oración hace que la respuesta se acerque un poco más.

---

*Leer Lucas 18:1–8 para la ambientación de la parábola de Jesús.

TERCERA SEMANA

# RECLAMANDO LAS RIQUEZAS DE DIOS

# Día 1

# Pedir por nosotros mismos

*"Acerquémonos confiadamente al trono de la gracia para recibir misericordia y hallar la gracia que nos ayude en el momento que más la necesitamos".*—HEBREOS 4:16

Nos guste o no—dijo Charles H. Spurgeon—el pedir es la regla del reino. Dios se agrada de que le pidamos, porque somos sus hijos. Su corazón de padre salta de gozo cuando nos acercamos pidiendo. Esta clase de oración nos sigue ubicando en la dependencia de una relación padre-hijo.

Orar es pedir a Dios por nuestras necesidades personales. Deseo enfatizar que está bien pedir la bendición de Dios para nosotros mismos. Algunos creen que pedir por nosotros mismos es una forma de oración más primitiva, que refleja una espiritualidad un tanto egoísta, mientras que las oraciones de alabanza, de gratitud y de intercesión reflejan una espiritualidad más elevada.

Esa manera de pensar no es bíblica. Somos dependientes para siempre de Dios, de modo que constantemente necesitamos estar pidiendo su bendición. Dios tiene mucho para dar, y nuestra necesidad es mucha. Orar por nosotros mismos conecta nuestras necesidades con la generosidad de Dios. La Biblia está llena de casos como éstos.

Jesús recomendó este tipo de oración. Al alentar a sus discípulos a orar, les dijo: "Así que yo les digo: Pidan, y se les dará; busquen, y encontrarán; llamen, y se les abrirá la puerta. Porque todo el que pide, recibe; el que busca, encuentra; y al que llama, se le abre" (Lucas 11:9, 10). A Dios le agrada que sus hijos acudan a él con los detalles pequeños de su vida.

En Hebreos 4:16 se nos invita a acercarnos al trono de la gracia de Dios con confianza para recibir lo que necesitamos de él. Dios nos invita a venir confiados, sabiendo que Jesús ha abierto para nosotros el camino al corazón del Padre, y que Dios ha prometido cubrir nuestras necesidades. Podemos venir con la confianza de que Jesús va a comprendernos, porque "él ha sido tentado en todo de la misma manera que nosotros, aunque sin pecado" (Hebreos 4:15).

El Señor nos invita a venir conscientes de nuestro pecado, pidiendo misericordia, para no recibir el castigo que merecemos. Nos invita a ir a él conscientes de nuestras necesidades, implorando su gracia—gracia por la que recibiremos lo que no merecemos. Jesús está listo para representarnos, y el Padre está listo para recibirnos, no importa cuál sea nuestra necesidad.

Es un insulto a Dios no pedirle su ayuda. Santa Teresa de Ávila declaró: "Uno le hace un cumplido a Dios al pedirle grandes cosas". ¿Qué va a pedir usted?

### Para reflexionar

- ¿Alguna vez ha sentido como un cumplido que le pidan ayuda? ¿Por qué pedir puede ser una manera de hacerle un cumplido a Dios? ¿Por qué Dios puede sentirse insultado si nunca le pedimos?
- ¿Por qué piensa usted que Dios, quien nos conoce mejor de lo que nos conocemos a nosotros mismos, nos ha invitado a acercarnos para pedir?

### Orar

- *Alabe* a Jesucristo, nuestro Sumo Sacerdote, quien nos ha abierto la sala del trono celestial, y que siempre nos comprende totalmente. Si no se ha acercado en forma regular al trono de Dios, para pedir misericordia y gracia, *confiese* eso como un insulto a Dios y un fracaso en reconocer la verdadera naturaleza de su dependencia de él.
- *Agradezca* a Dios por su disposición de perdonarlo y ayudarle en su necesidad.
- *Acérquese* a Dios con confianza, y *pídale* la misericordia que él ha prometido, y la gracia para ayudarle ante cualquier necesidad específica.

### Acción

Haga una lista de por lo menos tres cosas buenas que usted sabe que su Padre celestial desea que tenga (gozo, autocontrol, bondad) y, con persistencia, pídale estas cosas con absoluta confianza. Dios se complacerá en que usted se lo pida, porque está más que deseoso de ayudarle.

# Día 2

# Pedir cosas buenas

*"¿Quién de ustedes, si su hijo le pide pan, le da una piedra? ¿O si le pide un pescado, le da una serpiente? Pues si ustedes, aun siendo malos, saben dar cosas buenas a sus hijos, ¡cuánto más su Padre que está en el cielo dará cosas buenas a los que le piden?"*—Mateo 7: 9–11

Soy padre de cuatro hijos, y siempre he querido cosas buenas para ellos. He deseado profundamente que ellos tuvieran una fe firme, una moral íntegra, excelentes oportunidades de educación, buenos amigos, buenos trabajos, buenos matrimonios, lindos hijos, y vidas estables. He esperado y orado para que sus vidas estén llenas de amor, gozo y paz. He deseado todo esto a pesar de que, como padre terrenal, no puedo hacer todo lo que puede hacer el Padre celestial.

Jesús deja bien en claro que nuestro Padre celestial, quien es perfecto en su amor e ilimitado en su poder, desea cosas buenas para nosotros, sus hijos, y nos asegura que ese amoroso Padre está dispuesto a dar cosas buenas a sus hijos, mucho más que cualquier padre o madre humanos.

Hay un sólo problema. Para recibir las cosas buenas que el Padre quiere darnos, nosotros sus hijos tenemos que pedírselas. No pedirlas es no recibirlas. Eso es lo que algunos creyentes espiritualmente débiles descubrieron. Santiago les dijo: "No tienen, porque no piden" (Santiago 4:2).

Las "cosas buenas" que Jesús tiene en mente son las bendiciones espirituales de gracia, sabiduría, gozo, paz, poder, santidad, etc. Estas cosas están de acuerdo con la voluntad de Dios. Podemos pedírselas al Padre con toda confianza, porque nos ha dado la seguridad de que nos las dará. Él lo ha prometido.

¡Qué promesa tan maravillosa! La obtención de esta promesa revolucionó mi vida espiritual. Escudriñé las Escrituras para ver las cosas buenas que Dios quería darme. Se las pedí y, fiel a su promesa, Dios empezó a dármelas—no en cantidades enormes de una vez, sino poco a poco. Cada vez que yo comenzaba a pedir alguna cosa buena, si tenía paciencia, comenzaba a ver a Dios otorgándome esas cosas buenas.

Dios está deseoso de dar. Está esperando que sus hijos crean su Palabra y le pidan con fe. Como dijo un profeta del Antiguo Testamento: "El Señor recorre con su mirada toda la tierra, y está listo para ayudar a quienes le son fieles" (2 Crónicas 16:9).

Dios probablemente lo está mirando a usted ahora mismo, esperando que le pida buenas cosas. Creo que él se va a decepcionar si usted no se acerca y no le pide toda clase de cosas buenas, las cuales él anhela darle ahora mismo.

## PARA REFLEXIONAR

- ¿Qué cosas buenas le daría usted a su familia o a sus amigos si pudiera?
- ¿Qué considera usted de más valor entre los buenos dones de Dios?
- ¿Por qué es tan importante para Dios que le pidamos?

## ORAR

- *Alabe* al Padre, quien en su poder y amor puede y está dispuesto a dar "buenos dones" a aquellos que se lo piden.
- *Confiese* cualquier esfuerzo para llenar su vida con cosas terrenales en vez de las cosas buenas que el Padre quiere darle.
- *Pida* todas las cosas espiritualmente buenas que se le ocurran.
- *Agradezca* a Dios anticipadamente por lo que le dará en respuesta a su oración.

## ACCIÓN

Siga pidiendo las cosas buenas por las cuales oró ayer. Es una buena idea hacer una lista para que pueda recordar todo. Haga esas peticiones de nuevo hoy, tratando de pensar en todas las razones por las cuales su Padre celestial se las quiere dar. ¿Puede pensar en algún motivo por el cual él no querría dárselo?

# Día 3

# Recibiendo lo que uno pide

*"Esta es la confianza que tenemos al acercarnos a Dios: que si pedimos conforme a su voluntad, él nos oye. Y si sabemos que Dios oye todas nuestras oraciones, podemos estar seguros de que ya tenemos lo que le hemos pedido".*—1 JUAN 5:14, 15

Imagínese lo que sería acercarse a Dios en oración y recibir de él todo y cualquier cosa que le pidamos. Estoy seguro de que, si así fuera pediríamos muchas cosas. Una vez que el sistema de pedir y recibir hubiese sido establecido, tendríamos la osadía de volver y pedir más.

Aunque Dios no ha prometido darnos todo y cualquier cosa que le pidamos, sí ha hecho una asombrosa promesa a los solicitantes, que es aun mejor. Promete darnos cualquier cosa que pidamos que sea conforme a su voluntad.

Pedir lo que está de acuerdo con la voluntad de Dios es pedir aquello que Dios desea para nosotros. Son las cosas que él sabe necesitamos, las cosas que en verdad son buenas para nosotros, las riquezas de su gracia que él quiere que recibamos.

¿Cómo podemos saber lo que está de acuerdo con la voluntad de Dios? Lo descubrimos en la Biblia. Ahí Dios nos dice lo que él desea para nosotros.

Cuando comprendí este principio y quise orar de acuerdo con la voluntad de Dios, el Espíritu Santo me llevó a Romanos 8:29, y me recordó que Dios deseaba que yo "fuese predestinado a ser transformado según la imagen de su Hijo". Entonces hice algo muy sencillo, le dije: "Dios, por favor transfórmame a la imagen de tu Hijo". Esa fue la primera oración que en forma consciente hice de acuerdo con la voluntad de Dios. Él me oyó, y comenzó en mí el proceso que contestaba esa oración. Todavía está trabajando en mí con ese objetivo. Lo que pude observar fue un definido pero gradual cambio en la dirección correcta.

Después de eso, encontré muchas cosas, las cuales podía pedir, que eran conforme a la voluntad de Dios para mi vida. Pedí sabiduría, fe, virtud, amor, gozo, santidad, devoción, la plenitud del Espíritu y mucho más. Sé que Dios escuchó esas oraciones, pues comencé a ver la diferencia en mí.

Si quiere crecer espiritualmente y reclamar las riquezas que Dios tiene para usted, pida esas cosas que están de acuerdo con la voluntad de Dios. Él le oirá y usted recibirá lo que le pide.

Si lo que usted pide no se ajusta a la voluntad de Dios, y usted no lo recibe, ¡agradézcale a Dios! Lo que está fuera de la voluntad de Dios no es bueno para usted.

### PARA REFLEXIONAR

- Piense en los patrones que usa para orar. ¿Está acostumbrado a acercarse a Dios con la confianza de que él oirá y responderá, o tal vez ora simplemente esperando que algo suceda?
- ¿Qué cosas suele pedirle a Dios ahora que sabe que están de acuerdo con su voluntad?
- ¿Tiene tanta confianza que sabe de antemano que obtendrá lo que le ha pedido a Dios y que puede esperar una respuesta afirmativa?

### ORAR

- *Alabe* a Dios por que él sabe lo que es mejor para usted, y por el poder que posee para hacer lo que ha prometido.
- *Confiese* si descubre que, por debilidad en su oración, ha dejado de reclamar las riquezas que Dios le ha prometido.
- *Pídale* a Dios las riquezas espirituales que sabe que están de acuerdo con su voluntad para usted.
- *Agradézcale* a Dios por lo que él le dará aun antes de recibirlo. Si puede hacer esto con sinceridad, es una señal de que confía en que Dios cumplirá sus promesas.

### ACCIÓN

Agregue a sus oraciones de petición—si no lo ha hecho todavía—las cosas más importantes que usted cree que Dios quiere darle. Debe estar dispuesto a orar a largo plazo por esas cosas.

# Día 4

# Cura para la ansiedad

*"No se inquieten por nada, más bien, en toda ocasión, con oración y ruego, presenten sus peticiones a Dios y denle gracias. Y la paz de Dios, que sobrepasa todo entendimiento, cuidará sus corazones y sus pensamientos en Cristo Jesús".*—Filipenses 4:6, 7

Sucede a menudo. Una alarma suena en una habitación llena de gente. De inmediato, alguien se pone de pie, sale y hace una llamada telefónica. Algo exigía atención inmediata, y una llamada telefónica fue el comienzo de la solución.

La vida está llena de cosas que exigen atención inmediata. Los problemas, las frustraciones y las preocupaciones nos provocan ansiedad y nos privan de paz. Dios no quiere que esto suceda, y ha provisto una manera en que podamos ponernos en contacto con él al instante que nos asalta la ansiedad.

La ansiedad es el sistema de alerta de Dios para decirnos que es hora de hablar con él sobre algo que nos preocupa. Dios nos invita a venir a él en oración cuando nos asalta la ansiedad, y ha prometido que nos devolverá la paz.

Podemos ir a Dios con cualquier petición, grande o pequeña. Nada es demasiado grande para su poder. Nada es demasiado pequeño que no le interese. Si es una preocupación para usted, es una preocupación para Dios.

Se nos insta a venir "con gratitud". La gratitud surge al recordar quién es Dios y lo que hace por nosotros. Recuerde que Dios es amor, y que nada puede separarnos de su amor (1 Juan 4:16; Romanos 8:38, 39). Recuerde que Dios es poderoso, y que su fuerte y diestro brazo es nuestra defensa (Salmo 60:5). Recuerde que la bondad y la misericordia de Dios nos seguirán todos los días de nuestra vida (Salmo 23:6), y que siempre debemos ser agradecidos (Colosenses 2:7).

El resultado de la oración es la paz, "la paz de Dios, que sobrepasa todo entendimiento", una paz que los seres humanos no pueden producir.

Dios no sólo obra para bien en las situaciones que ponemos en sus manos (Romanos 8:28), también obra para guardar nuestros corazones y nuestras mentes en Cristo Jesús (Filipenses 4:7).

¿Está Dios llamándole a usted debido a alguna preocupación? Póngase en contacto con él inmediatamente. No se tarde. Él estará feliz de recibirle. Él le ha invitado. Él tiene una paz maravillosa que darle.

### PARA REFLEXIONAR

- Piense en la forma en que ha enfrentado las preocupaciones y la ansiedad en el pasado.
- ¿De acuerdo con este pasaje de las Escrituras, hay alguna forma en que usted puede mejorar la forma en que ha manejado estas cosas?
- ¿Qué señales debe ver para confirmar que ha manejado la ansiedad en una forma que le complace a Dios?

### ORAR

- *Alabe* a Dios, el que oye su oración, el que le otorga paz, el que guarda su corazón y su mente en Cristo Jesús.
- *Pídale* a Dios que le perdone por las muchas veces que ha enfrentado la ansiedad en forma incorrecta.
- *Agradezca* a Dios por la paz que le da en medio de situaciones preocupantes.
- *Pídale* a Dios que le comparta de su paz, y que guarde su corazón y su mente.

### ACCIÓN

Identifique una cosa por la que suele preocuparse. Agréguela a su lista de oraciones de petición.

No deje de darle gracias a Dios por todo lo que él ha hecho ya para bendecirle y ayudarle en el manejo de esta preocupación.

# Día 5

# Cuando Dios dice "no"

*"Para evitar que me volviera presumido por estas sublimes revelaciones, una espina me fue clavada en el cuerpo, es decir, un mensajero de Satanás, para que me atormentara. Tres veces le rogué al Señor que me la quitara; pero él me dijo: 'Te basta con mi gracia, pues mi poder se perfecciona en la debilidad' ".*—2 Corintios 12:7–9

Alguien ha sugerido que Dios contesta las oraciones en estas cinco maneras:

- Sí. Pensé que nunca lo pedirías.
- Sí. Pero no todavía.
- No. Te amo mucho como para darte algo que no te conviene.
- Sí. Pero no como tú piensas.
- Sí. Pero más de lo que puedes imaginar.

*Sí. Pensé que nunca lo pedirías.* Este es un recordatorio de que Dios tiene tantas cosas buenas que darnos, que le resulta difícil esperar hasta que se lo pidamos. Cuando finalmente lo pedimos, él se apresura en contestarnos.

*Sí. Pero todavía no.* Cuando Dios nos hace esperar, puede parecernos un "no", pero en realidad es sólo un "sí" demorado. Cuando Dios demora una respuesta, es siempre por alguna buena razón. Puede estar enseñándonos a depender totalmente de él, preparándonos para recibir la respuesta cuando llegue, o simplemente refinando nuestra oración.

*No. Te amo mucho como para darte lo que no te conviene.* La sabiduría de Dios es muy superior a la nuestra. Cuando lo que pedimos no nos conviene, Dios simplemente dice "no". Nos ama tanto, al grado que no va a satisfacer nuestros deseos si sabe que eso no nos conviene.

*Sí. Pero no como tú piensas.* Esto también puede parecernos un "no", pero es realmente un "sí". Hay que esperar paciente y cuidadosamente la respuesta de Dios.

*Sí. Pero más de lo que puedes imaginar.* Lo que pedimos puede ser bueno y correcto, pero tal vez Dios elija darnos algo mucho mejor. Él ve todo el cuadro, y sabe lo que realmente es bueno para nosotros.

Podemos agregar otra posible respuesta: *No. No hasta que te hayas arrepentido del pecado que lo impide.* Esa también es una respuesta llena de gracia, pues el pecado no confesado ni perdonado hace mucho daño.

Cuando Dios le dijo "no" a la petición de Pablo de que le quitara la espina que lo atormentaba, fue por una buena razón. Al dejarle hincada la espina, Dios le enseñó a Pablo acerca de su gracia y de su poder "perfeccionado en la debilidad". Al fin, Pablo llegó al punto de deleitarse en su debilidad, en los insultos, las persecuciones y las dificultades, al ver que el poder de Dios compensaba sus debilidades (2 Corintios 12:10).

Nuestra confianza no está en la oración, sino en Dios. Cuando parece que la oración no da resultado, no importa demasiado. Dios sigue siendo nuestro Señor, quien nos fortalece con su gracia.

### Para reflexionar

◆ ¿Se ha sentido usted decepcionado porque Dios no ha contestado sus oraciones?

◆ ¿Qué razones puede haber tenido Dios para no darle lo que le ha pedido?

◆ ¿Tiene sentido para usted decir: "Mi confianza no está en la oración, sino en Dios"? ¿Por qué?

### Orar

◆ *Alabe* a Dios por su gracia y su poder, que usa en nuestro beneficio.

◆ *Confiese* cualquier enojo que pueda tener contra Dios, si se siente decepcionado por la forma en que ha contestado o dejado de contestar sus oraciones.

◆ *Pídale* a Dios sabiduría para comprender su mente, y gracia para deleitarse en su bondad, aun cuando él diga que "no" a sus peticiones.

### Acción

Dígale a Dios que está agradecido por las veces que ha dicho "no", pues usted sabe que lo hizo pensando en sus mejores intereses.

# ORAR POR OTROS

# CUARTA SEMANA

## Día 1

# ¿Qué es la intercesión?

*"Supongamos, dijo Jesús, que uno de ustedes tiene un amigo, y a medianoche va y le dice: 'Amigo, préstame tres panes pues se me ha presentado un amigo recién llegado de viaje, y no tengo nada que ofrecerle'. Y el que está adentro le contesta: 'No me molestes. Ya está cerrada la puerta, y mis hijos y yo estamos acostados. No puedo levantarme a darte nada'. Les digo que, aunque no se levante a darle pan por ser amigo suyo, sí se levantará por su impertinencia y le dará cuanto necesite".*—LUCAS 11:5–8

Cuando cambiamos de petición (orar por nosotros mismos) a *intercesión* (orar por otros), cambiamos el enfoque de la oración. Necesitamos orar por nosotros mismos para que podamos recibir todo lo que Dios quiere darnos. Pero también necesitamos orar por otros como un acto de amor generoso.

El *Diccionario de la Real Academia de la Lengua Española* define la palabra intercesión "Hablar en favor de alguien para conseguirle un bien o librarlo de un mal".* Otra definición puede ser: "actuar entre dos partes; suplicar o rogar a favor de otro; mediar". Un intercesor es un mediador que representa a una parte ante la otra. En la intercesión, los que oran acuden a Dios y hacen peticiones en favor de otros.

La historia de Jesús sobre estos amigos muestra el papel del intercesor. Uno de los amigos tiene un amigo en necesidad, el que ha llegado a medianoche, y otro de los amigos tiene pan. Al no poder cubrir la necesidad de la persona que llegó a medianoche, el hombre acude a su otro amigo, y le suplica abiertamente hasta que recibe lo que necesita. Luego, le entrega lo que recibe a su amigo en necesidad. Es un mediador.

La posición del mediador es la posición de un intercesor, que suplica al que tiene mucho en favor del que no tiene nada. En otras palabras, los intercesores operan ante Dios—el Amigo que tiene pan—y ruegan en favor de aquellos que necesitan el pan del cielo.

En la obra de Dios, la oración de intercesión es de primera importancia. La gente necesita desesperadamente nuestras oraciones de intercesión. Muchas personas están sufriendo. Muchas familias están separadas. Muchas iglesias están estancadas. Muchos vecinos viven vidas solitarias, aisladas. La mayoría de la gente en nuestros países no tiene un conocimiento salvador de Jesucristo. Y ellos necesitan mucho más de lo que nosotros podemos darles.

Necesitan lo que sólo Dios puede dar. Y Dios está dispuesto a dar sus buenas dádivas en respuesta a oraciones de intercesión de su pueblo. Es ahí donde nos toca actuar a nosotros. Podemos ser los mediadores para el mundo perdido y sufriente.

### PARA REFLEXIONAR

- ¿Quién en su familia, su iglesia, o su vecindario se encuentra como ese amigo que vino a medianoche? ¿Qué tipo de ayuda necesitan esas personas, que está más allá de sus posibilidades?
- ¿Qué está usted dispuesto a hacer para que reciban lo que necesitan de parte de Dios?

### ORAR

- *Alabe* a Dios porque es el dador de toda buena dádiva.
- *Confiese* cualquier falla de parte suya, en interceder fielmente en favor de las personas necesitadas que le rodean.
- *Comprométase* a interceder ante Dios en favor de su familia, sus amigos, vecinos, compañeros de trabajo, los miembros de la iglesia, y otros.
- *Interceda* ahora mismo en favor de una o más personas necesitadas a quienes Dios le está recordando.

### ACCIÓN

Haga una lista de personas por las que usted cree que Dios está esperando que interceda en forma regular.

Comience con sus familiares y amigos, pero siga más allá, al pedirle a Dios que ponga los intereses de ciertos colegas, de compañeros de estudios, de vecinos o conocidos en su corazón.

---

\* http://buscon.rae.es/drael/SrvltConsulta?TIPO_BUS=3&LEMA=cultura

# Día 2

# Dios busca intercesores

*"Yo he buscado entre ellos a alguien que se interponga entre mi pueblo y yo, saque la cara por él para que yo no lo destruya. ¡Y no lo he hallado! Por eso derramaré mi ira sobre ellos, los consumiré con el fuego de mi ira, y haré recaer sobre ellos todo el mal que han hecho. Lo afirma el Señor omnipotente".*—EZEQUIEL 22:30, 31\*

Hace varios años, estaba haciendo un esfuerzo especial para convertirme en un mejor intercesor. Traté de dedicarle más tiempo a la intercesión, cubrir más necesidades, y orar con mayor fervor. Por un tiempo, las cosas anduvieron bien. Pronto, sin embargo, empecé a saltarme los períodos de oración fijados cuando me resultaba conveniente, pero me preocupaba que pudiera saltarme la oración con tanta facilidad.

Cuando le pedí al Señor que me ayudara con esta irregularidad, me ayudó a entender que mi problema era que yo realmente no creía que la intercesión era capaz de cambiar algo. Me parecía que la vida seguía normalmente a mi alrededor, orara o no.

Entonces, Dios me llevó a Ezequiel 22. Me mostró que los intercesores, quienes por medio de su oración "levantan los muros y cubren la brecha", son vitales para su gobierno del mundo. Cuando le pregunté: "¿Habría sido diferente la historia de Israel si Dios hubiese hallado un intercesor?", la respuesta fue "sí". Cuando le hice otra pregunta: "¿Depende la historia de mi familia, de mi iglesia o de mi vecindario de mi intercesión?", la respuesta nuevamente fue "sí".

Dios busca intercesores, no porque le falte sabiduría o poder para gobernar al mundo sin ellos, sino porque él, en su soberano deseo, ha elegido gobernar el mundo por medio de las oraciones de su pueblo. La intercesión no es opcional. Es una parte necesaria e importante de la forma de trabajar de Dios.

Cuando oramos pasarán cosas que no habrían pasado si no hubiésemos orado. Y no sucederán cosas que habrían sucedido si hubiésemos orado.

En la era del Nuevo Testamento, Dios el Padre siempre encuentra un intercesor para "levantar el muro y cubrir la brecha". El que él encuentra es Jesucristo, quien vive eternamente para interceder. Pero Cristo no ora sólo. Nuestras oraciones de intercesión se unen a las suyas. Y él, por medio de su Espíritu, ora a través de nosotros.

No es sorprendente que el reino esté avanzando y que el evangelio esté esparciéndose a cada nación en el mundo. Esto se debe a la oración. ¿Están las oraciones de usted contribuyendo a este avance mundial de la predicación?

**PARA REFLEXIONAR**

♦ Trate de imaginar a Dios determinando lo que sucederá en su familia, en la cuadra en que vive, en su iglesia, o en su nación, basado en sus oraciones. ¿Cómo se siente al pensar en ello?

♦ ¿Qué le sugiere esto respecto a la importancia de su papel como un intercesor?

**ORAR**

♦ *Alabe* a Dios por la grandeza de su poder y la sabiduría de su elección de gobernar al mundo por medio de las oraciones de su pueblo.

♦ *Confiese* cualquier falla que reconozca en su intercesión.

♦ *Agradezca* a Dios por el enorme privilegio de gobernar el mundo con Dios por medio de sus oraciones de intercesión.

♦ *Pídale* a Dios gracia para ser un fiel intercesor.

**ACCIÓN**

Recuerde cinco maneras importantes de interceder por su familia, amigos, vecinos y compañeros de trabajo: necesidades corporales; asuntos laborales; aspectos emocionales o bendiciones de la vida interior; áreas sociales o de relación en la vida; asuntos espirituales. A muchos que oran les ha sido útil recordar estos puntos. Estas son algunas sugerencias para empezar:

♦ **Corporal** (físico): Orar para que el Padre, que envía "toda buena dádiva y todo don perfecto" (Santiago 1:17), cubra las necesidades físicas de la gente.

♦ **Laboral** (trabajo): Darle apoyo en oración a estas personas en su trabajo y sus estudios, y orar por que cada uno pueda ser diligente en la realización de las tareas encomendadas por Dios.

♦ **Emocional** (vida interior): Orar para que lleven sus preocupaciones, dolores y chascos al Señor, poniendo sobre él todas sus cargas, porque a él le interesa (1 Pedro 5:7).

♦ **Social** (relaciones): Orar porque los miembros de la familia y los amigos sean fuentes de gozo y bendición entre sí, y puedan experimentar juntos la bendición del Señor.

♦ **Espiritual:** Orar para que las personas inconversas que usted lleva al Señor en oración puedan buscar al Señor "mientras se deje encontrar", y llamarlo "mientras esté cercano", y ser totalmente perdonados (Isaías 55:6, 7).

---

*Para conocer el trasfondo de este pasaje, leer Ezequiel 22:23-30.

◗

# Día 3

# El alcance de la intercesión

*"Recomiendo, ante todo, que se hagan plegarias, oraciones, súplicas y acciones de gracias por todos, especialmente por los gobernantes y por todas las autoridades, para que tengamos paz y tranquilidad, y llevemos una vida piadosa y digna. Esto es bueno y agradable a Dios nuestro Salvador, pues él quiere que todos sean salvos y lleguen a conocer la verdad".*—1 TIMOTEO 2:1–4

E. M. Bounds dice, "la oración puede hacer cualquier cosa que Dios puede hacer". E. M. Bounds tiene razón, porque el único poder presente en la oración es el poder de Dios. Más aun, la oración puede llegar a cualquier parte donde Dios puede llegar. Y Dios llega a todas partes, así que su poder puede llegar a cada rincón de la tierra.

Dos frases en los versículos citados más arriba ponen énfasis en el amplio alcance de la oración: "para todos" y "todos los hombres (la gente)". Debido a que Dios quiere que "todos sean salvos y lleguen a conocer la verdad" (1 Timoteo 2:4), él quiere que oremos por todos.

Ole Hallsby, en su libro *Oración,* capta la importancia de la exhortación de Pablo: "Es la voluntad de nuestro Señor que nosotros, que hemos recibido acceso a estos poderes por medio de la oración, vayamos por el mundo trasmitiendo poder celestial a cada rincón de la tierra donde se necesita urgentemente. Nuestras vidas deben ser arroyos de bendición quietos, pero que fluyen constantemente, que a través de nuestras oraciones e intercesiones lleguen a todo nuestro entorno.

"Cuando me siento en mi sillón favorito para mis devociones matinales, imagino que mis oraciones ascienden al trono del cielo, y visualizo a Dios, en respuesta, moviendo sus manos en los lugares adonde mis oraciones van dirigidas. Imagino su poder siendo liberado en la costa oeste al orar por los miembros de mi familia, en la capital de la nación, al interceder por los gobernantes, en países extranjeros al orar por proyectos misioneros, y en las casas y en los corazones de mis vecinos al orar por ellos. Mis oraciones pueden liberar una bendición o motivar un cambio en cualquier lugar del mundo sin que yo me mueva de mi sillón. ¡Qué poder tan maravilloso nos ha dado Dios!"

Aun cuando Dios desearía que hiciésemos oraciones amplias de intercesión, nuestras responsabilidades de oración comienzan cerca del hogar. Nuestra primera responsabilidad es orar por los miembros de nuestra familia, por los parientes y amigos, luego por la familia espiritual en la cual Dios nos ha colocado, y luego por nuestro vecindario, por la comunidad, por la nación y por el mundo.

Si nuestras oraciones se enfocan sólo en los que están cerca, no hemos comprendido el alcance de lo que Dios quiere hacer por medio de la oración. Si se enfocan principalmente en los que están lejos, podremos ser culpables de dejar de pedir por nuestra familia inmediata y de negar la fe (1 Timoteo 5:4, 8).

### PARA REFLEXIONAR

- Imagine que sus oraciones transmiten poder celestial y bendición a las personas en cada rincón del mundo. Piense en algunas de esas personas y lugares.
- Imagine a esas personas experimentando el gozo de ser salvos y llegando al conocimiento de la verdad como resultado de sus oraciones.

### ORAR

- *Alabe* a Dios, quien está presente en todo el universo.
- *Confiésele* a Dios su falla, si sus oraciones han sido demasiado limitadas en comparación con lo aconsejado en 1 Timoteo 2:1–4.
- *Agradezca a* Dios por la profundidad de su preocupación por el mundo.
- *Comprométase* a hacer "peticiones, oraciones, intercesión y acciones de gracias por todos, incluyendo reyes y todos los que están en autoridad".
- *Ore* por que "todos los confines de la tierra; ante él se postrarán" (Salmo 22:27).

### ACCIÓN

Practique los puntos de oración que aprendió en la lectura de ayer, y haga una expansión en cada categoría, según el Espíritu Santo le guíe a orar por las personas en su círculo de influencia.

# Día 4

# Intercediendo por los que no pueden orar por sí mismos

*"Después de haberle dicho todo esto a Job, el Señor se dirigió a Elifaz de Temán y le dijo: 'Estoy muy irritado contigo y con tus dos amigos [...] Vayan con mi siervo Job y ofrezcan un holocausto por ustedes mismos. Mi siervo Job orará por ustedes, y yo atenderé a su oración y no los haré quedar en vergüenza' [...] y el Señor atendió a la oración de Job".*—JOB 42:7–9

Varias encuestas en los Estados Unidos han revelado que cerca del 80% de la población no tiene una relación salvadora con Jesucristo. Eso significa que la gente no tiene un acceso regular al trono de gracia de Dios. Pueden tratar de orar, pero no pueden llegar a Dios, ya que al trono sólo se llega por medio de Jesucristo.

Es una situación horrible—alejados de Aquel que es la fuente de toda gracia y bendición. Esa era la situación en que se encontraban Elifaz y sus amigos, por lo menos temporalmente, cuando Dios les dijo: "Mi siervo Job orará por ustedes y yo atenderé a su oración". Esta fue la forma en que Dios les decía: "No voy a escuchar sus oraciones. Ustedes no tienen acceso a mi trono. Es mejor que consigan que Job ore por ustedes".

La palabra *intercesión* en el lenguaje original del Nuevo Testamento significa: "tener libertad de acceso". Originalmente fue un término técnico que significaba encontrarse con un rey para hacer una petición. En la Biblia, la palabra intercesión significa "hacer una petición a Dios en favor de otros".

El privilegio de acceso se nos da a los creyentes, no sólo para que podamos pedir para nosotros mismos, sino también para que podamos pedir por otros, especialmente por aquellos que no tienen acceso al trono de la gracia. Dios tiene tanto para darles, pero, al haber determinado hace tiempo dar en respuesta a las peticiones, él retiene su gracia de dar hasta que nosotros intercedemos.

Cuando los creyentes comienzan a orar con sinceridad por sus vecinos, las cosas buenas comienzan a suceder. Cuando los miembros de una iglesia en Bakersfield, California, plantaron varias células de oración en un complejo habitacional para orar por los que vivían allí, el administrador se hizo cristiano, los traficantes de drogas se mudaron, la tasa de crímenes disminuyó, muchos comenzaron a asistir a la iglesia, se organizaron estudios bíblicos, y diez personas se entregaron a Cristo. La diferencia fue tan evidente, que la policía, al descubrir la razón de los cambios, pidió a la iglesia que considerara plantar células de oración similares en otros complejos habitacionales.

¿Qué cree usted que Dios quiere que suceda en las vidas de la gente que le rodea? ¿Está dispuesto a ser el que interceda para que Dios pueda cumplir su voluntad en su vecindario gracias a sus oraciones?

#### PARA REFLEXIONAR

◆ Trate de imaginarse como una persona no cristiana y sin nadie que ore por usted.
◆ Considere lo que significaría para usted, si fuera un inconverso, vivir o trabajar cerca de un creyente que orara en forma regular por usted. La oración y la bendición de Dios que viene por medio de la oración, es un don que usted les puede dar a los que no son cristianos y que están a su alrededor. ¡Piénselo!

#### ORAR

◆ *Agradezca* a Dios por el privilegio de tener acceso a su trono, cuyo camino fue abierto para usted por Jesucristo.
◆ Si usted ha fallado y no ha usado su privilegio de acceso a Dios en favor de ciertas personas inconversas, *confiese* este pecado y pida el perdón de Dios.
◆ *Dígale* a Dios que está dispuesto a ser un fiel intercesor, y *pídale* su ayuda para serlo.

#### ACCIÓN

Pídale a Dios que le aclare lo que él quiere lograr en las vidas de las personas no cristianas o familias que él ha puesto en su mente para que ore por ellas. Espere pacientemente la respuesta de Dios. Ore acerca de las cosas que Dios pone en su mente.

○

# Día 5

# La intercesión por los que no son salvos

*"Hermanos, el deseo de mi corazón y mi oración a Dios*
*por los israelitas, es que lleguen a ser salvos".*—ROMANOS 10:1

L a Biblia requiere que oremos por personas que no son salvas. En el segundo capítulo de la *Primera Epístola de San Pablo a Timoteo*, se nos recuerda que Dios quiere que todas las personas sean salvas, y somos instados a orar por todos. Jesús dejó un modelo de una oración para los que no son salvos cuando oró: "No ruego sólo por éstos. Ruego también por los que han de creer en mí por el mensaje de ellos" (Juan 17:20). Y el apóstol Pablo estaba orando por  los inconversos cuando intercedió por los israelitas (Romanos 10:1).

¿Cómo oraremos por los que no son salvos?

Primero, debemos orar que *los que no son salvos sean atraídos por el Padre*. Jesús dijo "Nadie puede venir a mí si no lo atrae el Padre que me envió" (Juan 6:44).

En segundo lugar, debemos orar para *que aquellos que oigan el evangelio lo entiendan*. Jesús advierte que el maligno vendrá y tratará de arrebatar la semilla del evangelio sembrada en el corazón de una persona si no es comprendida (Mateo 13:19). La comprensión espiritual y la iluminación requerida debe provenir de Dios, quien es movido a responder a las oraciones de los creyentes.

En tercer lugar, debemos pedir *que los ojos de los no creyentes sean abiertos para que puedan ver la luz*. Al hacer esta oración, de nuevo estaremos enfrentando al adversario, "el dios de este mundo ha cegado la mente de estos incrédulos, para que no vean la luz del glorioso evangelio de Cristo" (2 Corintios 4:4). Abrir los ojos espirituales es, por supuesto, tarea de Dios. Pero liberar el poder de Dios para abrir los ojos cegados es un asunto de oración, al que Dios nos llama.

Dios honra la oración por los incrédulos. Un grupo de *Faro,* en Grand Rapids, oró por un joven que había huido de su hogar para unirse a una pandilla. El joven retornó a su hogar y se entregó a Cristo. Más tarde, su abuelo entregó su vida a Cristo poco antes de morir, también en respuesta a la oración.

Otro grupo *Faro,* en Michigan, vio a cuatro familias venir al Señor después de ocho meses de reuniones semanales de oración realizadas por sus vecinos.

Esto es evangelización através de la oración, evangelización en la que Dios se mueve en los corazones y las vidas de las personas en respuesta a las fervientes oraciones de los creyentes. ¿Por quiénes de los que deberán creer en Cristo está orando usted?

### PARA REFLEXIONAR

+ ¿Se preocupa lo suficiente por los inconversos para orar fervientemente por su salvación?
+ ¿Se preocuparía más si se tratara de sus propios hijos o familiares que no fueran salvos? Recuerde que todas las personas inconversas son hijos e hijas descarriadas de la familia de Dios. Dios no quiere que "nadie perezca sino que todos se arrepientan" (2 Pedro 3:9).

### ORAR

+ *Alabe* a Dios, pues "tanto amó Dios al mundo, que dio a su Hijo unigénito, para que todo el que cree en él no se pierda, sino que tenga vida eterna" (Juan 3:16).
+ *Agradezca* a Dios por aquellos que oraron por usted y participaron en abrir la puerta de la salvación para usted.
+ Si no tiene una preocupación por los que no son salvos, *pídale* a Dios que ponga esa preocupación en su corazón.
+ *Comprométase,* como socio de Jesucristo, al orar por personas que aún no han sido salvadas.

### ACCIÓN

Coloque la lista de personas que no son salvas, por las que debe orar, en un lugar donde la verá cada día. Pida que el Padre las atraiga a él, y que todos puedan comprender las buenas nuevas de salvación en Jesús, y sus ojos sean abiertos a la luz de la bondad de Dios. Continúe orando por ellos diariamente.

QUINTA SEMANA

# LA ORACIÓN COMO
# FORMA DE VIDA

# Día 1

# La oración como una conversación con Dios

*"Cuando el día comenzó a refrescar, oyeron el hombre y la mujer que Dios andaba recorriendo el jardín; entonces corrieron a esconderse entre los árboles, para que Dios no los viera". —*GÉNESIS 3:8

Queda claro, al leer esta escritura, que Dios se juntaba con Adán y Eva en forma regular al atardecer, para conversar con ellos. Era parte de la rutina normal, probablemente diaria. Así que ese día, cuando oyeron al Señor andando por el jardín, sabían que era tiempo para una conversación con Dios.

Orar es conversar con Dios. Lo que sucedía en forma regular en el jardín—una conversación entre Dios y los seres humanos—era oración. Dicha "oración", por supuesto, no era un monólogo formal, rígido. Creo que más bien era una conversación mutua, relajada, informal, sin inhibiciones. Creo que ese es un buen cuadro bíblico de lo que es la oración.

Lo que sucedía en el jardín nos enseña respecto a la oración. Primero nos muestra que es Dios el que toma la iniciativa en la oración. Era el Señor el que se acercaba a Adán y Eva y los llamaba. Cuando usted siente el deseo de orar, es porque Dios está poniendo ese deseo en usted e invitándole a encontrarse con él. La oración es una relación en la que Dios lleva la iniciativa.

El episodio en el jardín también nos enseña lo que el pecado le hace a la oración. Después de haber pecado, Adán y Eva no querían encontrarse con Dios. En vez de salir al encuentro de su amigo, los vemos escondiéndose entre los árboles, avergonzados y culpables. El temor había reemplazado a la libertad. El pecado había abierto una brecha entre Dios y los primeros seres humanos. La conversación no se podía realizar con Adán y Eva escondidos. El pecado impide la oración.

¿Se ha sentido usted alguna vez poco deseoso de acercarse a Dios? A veces somos como Adán y Eva—le tenemos miedo a Dios, nos escondemos tras las excusas, y somos renuentes a encontrarnos con él. Los pecados no confesados, escondidos en el corazón, nos impiden orar.

Pero la gracia restaura la oración. Notemos que Dios no se aleja ni los deja en su escondite. En vez de ello, les llama y con gracia los ayuda a reconocer el pecado que los ha alejado de él. Dios inicia el proceso que conduce al perdón, a una comunión restaurada, a abrir otra vez los canales de comunicación, a la oración.

Desde el principio, la intención de Dios fue que la oración fuera una conversación con él, tranquila y agradable, como la que solía tener con Adán y Eva en el jardín antes de su caída. Dios vuelve a acercarse a nosotros vez tras vez, con su gracia, pues quiere caminar y hablar con nosotros y disfrutar de nuestra compañía.

Cuando Dios se acerque a conversar con usted hoy, no se esconda. ¡Déle la bienvenida! La gracia ha prevalecido en Cristo. En Cristo sus pecados han sido perdonados. Así que salga a su encuentro sonriente y alegre. Y tenga un diálogo relajado e informal con él, que será un deleite para ambos.

## PARA REFLEXIONAR

- ¿A veces siente reticencia a orar? Si es así, ¿qué es lo que está estorbando su deseo de encontrarse con Dios? Que Dios le ayude a identificar y a solucionar el problema.
- Al orar, ¿está usted consciente de que está hablando con una persona, con un Dios que piensa, siente, actúa, habla y escucha?
- ¿Se siente cómodo al hablar con Dios en un lenguaje claro y en forma relajada, informal y sin inhibiciones?

## ORAR

- *Alabe* a Dios, quien está con nosotros por medio de su Espíritu, y siempre está dispuesto a conversar con nosotros.
- *Confiese* cualquier cosa que lo haya distanciado de Dios.
- *Agradezca* a Dios por una vida de oración construida alrededor de conversaciones diarias, relajadas, agradables, sin inhibiciones, con él.
- *Interceda* por la gente que lo rodea, cuyas vidas de oración están bloqueadas porque se están escondiendo de Dios.

## ACCIÓN

Salga a caminar al final del día, consciente de que Jesús está caminando a su lado. Háblele como le hablaría a un amigo, háblele acerca de las cosas que usted está sintiendo, pensando y haciendo. Trate de imaginar lo que él le diría.

# Día 2

# Vivir conforme a la oración

*"Oren sin cesar, den gracias a Dios en toda situación, porque esta es su voluntad para ustedes en Cristo Jesús".*—1 TESALONICENSES 5:17—19

O rar sin cesar no quiere decir que no debemos hacer otra cosa sino orar. Significa que vivimos todas nuestras horas y días conscientes de la compañía de Dios, de que de una u otra manera, estamos en su presencia.

Significa *caminar y hablar con Dios*. Cuando Enoc, el héroe de la fe del Antiguo Testamento, "andaba con Dios", significaba que Dios era su compañero en todas sus actividades diarias (Génesis 5:22). Cuando uno viaja con un amigo, encuentra mucho de qué hablar; ve muchas cosas, puede compartir muchas experiencias y tomar decisiones. Cuando uno viaja por la vida con Dios, sucede lo mismo. Y aunque usted no pueda verlo ni tocarlo físicamente, Dios está con usted, es un ser que piensa, siente, se comunica y sabe escuchar.

Orar sin cesar quiere decir tener el hábito de hablar con Dios sobre sus experiencias cotidianas. Las actividades repetidas pueden convertirse en detonadoras de una mayor consciencia de Dios. El famoso general norteamericano "Stonewall" Jackson, dijo una vez: "Tengo tan fijado el hábito, que nunca alzo un vaso de agua para beber sin pedir la bendición de Dios, nunca cierro una carta sin poner una palabra de oración bajo el sello, nunca echo una carta al correo sin elevar una plegaria, nunca me olvido de hacer una petición en mis salas de clase por los cadetes que están presentes y por los que van a venir a la siguiente clase".

Usted probablemente tiene algunas cosas que son detonadoras en su vida, al levantarse en la mañana, al sentarse a comer, o al acostarse para dormir. Un amigo mío ora cada vez que se sienta tras el volante de su automóvil. Otros han aprendido a orar por cada persona con la que se encuentran, por cada situación de necesidad que escuchan en las noticias, cada vez que entran en su lugar de trabajo, cada vez que suena el teléfono, cada vez que oyen la sirena de una ambulancia o presencian un accidente, o cada vez que pasan frente a una iglesia.

Orar sin cesar significa compartir nuestros *pensamientos* con Dios. Nuestras mentes nunca duermen. No importa lo que estamos haciendo, desde la mañana a la noche, nuestras mentes siempre están activas. Las noticias de la mañana, el desayuno apresurado, el tráfico en el camino al trabajo, los desafíos del trabajo, el cuidado de los niños, la comunicación con su cónyuge, el momento del descanso mirando la televisión, todas estas cosas ocupan nuestra mente de alguna manera. Y Dios quiere ser parte de todos nuestros pensamientos        .

Orar sin cesar también significa compartir nuestros *sentimientos* con Dios. Los sentimientos son reacciones interiores espontáneas ante cosas que experimentamos en la vida. Dios quiere ser parte de nuestros sentimientos. Es por eso que el Espíritu impulsó a Santiago a escribir: "¿Está afligido alguno entre ustedes? Que ore. ¿Está alguno de buen ánimo? Que cante alabanzas" (Santiago 5:13).

Trate de desarrollar el hábito de llenar su día con breves oraciones. Cada oración tendrá una dulce respuesta del Señor.

## Para reflexionar

+ ¿Qué "detonadores" hay en su vida? ¿Cuáles podría agregar hoy?
+ ¿Cree que Dios realmente quiere tener contacto con usted? ¡Es verdad! ¿Cómo se siente al recordarlo?

## Orar

+ *Alabe* a Dios como el Dios personal que disfruta de su compañía y le imparte gozo.
+ *Confiese* el mal hábito de dejar a Dios fuera de sus pensamientos, sentimientos y experiencias.
+ *Pídale* a Dios su ayuda para orar sin cesar. Esto no es algo que uno pueda hacer en forma natural.
+ *Interceda* por miembros de su familia, por amigos y vecinos, para que ellos puedan tener una mayor conciencia de Dios y un deseo de caminar y hablar con él.

## Acción

Trate de agregar por lo menos un "detonador" nuevo cada día, durante la próxima semana.

# Día 3

# Oyendo al Cielo

*"Mis ovejas oyen mi voz; yo las conozco y ellas me siguen".*—JUAN 10:27

La oración es un diálogo entre el creyente y Dios, un diálogo de amor. Es una forma de comunicación mutua que involucra tanto el hablar como el escuchar. Ese es el tipo de relación que Dios quiere tener con nosotros. La oración no es completa si solamente nosotros hablamos y esperamos que Dios se limite a escuchar. La verdadera oración requiere ambas cosas.

Cuando Jesús dijo: "Mis ovejas oyen mi voz", quería decir que los verdaderos creyentes reconocen y responden a su voz. Están siempre sintonizados con él, listos a responder a su llamado. Ese es el tipo de "escuchar" que la oración requiere.

Una mañana, un turista viajaba por un país oriental, y vio a una cantidad de ovejas en un redil. Los pastores estaban a la entrada y llamaban a sus ovejas una por una, para sacarlas al campo a pastar.

—¿Me permitirían llamar a algunas de sus ovejas?—les preguntó el viajero.

—Por supuesto—dijo uno de los pastores, con una sonrisa. Y le enseñaron lo que debía decir. El hombre llamó a una oveja, usando las palabras que le dijo el pastor, pero ninguna oveja se movió, a pesar de que la llamó varias veces. Entonces el pastor se adelantó, y usando las mismas palabras, llamó a la oveja y ésta reaccionó en respuesta a su llamado. Conocía su voz.

Orar es escuchar la voz de nuestro Pastor. En realidad, cuando oramos, probablemente es más importante escuchar que hablar. Después de todo, Dios tiene más que decir que usted o que yo. Antes de ir corriendo a la presencia de Dios con sus pensamientos y necesidades, esté atento a lo que Dios está tratando de decirle.

Escuchar a Dios también significa una disposición a obedecer. Dios no habla sólo para darle a la gente una oportunidad de decidir si desean obedecer o no. Dios les habla a los que lo toman en serio y están dispuestos a hacer cualquier cosa que él les pida.

Al escuchar, asegúrese de que la voz que usted oye es la voz del Pastor. Hay otras voces que claman por su atención, la voz del maligno, las voces del mundo, y las voces interiores de sus propios deseos egoístas. Cuanto mejor conozca usted al Pastor, mejor conocerá su voz.

Si usted no está seguro de ello, pídale a Jesús que abra sus oídos a su voz, y que los cierre ante las voces malintencionadas del enemigo. Jesús lo hará con mucho agrado.

Si esta forma de "escuchar" es nueva para usted, comience pidiéndole al Pastor que sincronice sus oídos con su voz. Esté consciente de su cercanía. Espere oír su voz. Esté preparado para que su voz llegue a usted en cualquier momento del día y para cualquier propósito. Y esté preparado para responder.

¡El Pastor ansía que usted oiga su voz! ¿Está usted ansioso de escucharle?

**Para reflexionar**

- ¿Quién es el que habla más en su vida de oración? ¿Significa la oración una comunicación mutua entre usted y Dios?
- ¿Puede recordar alguna ocasión en que Dios pareció decirle algo aun cuando usted no estaba conscientemente escuchándole? ¿Qué le estaba diciendo Dios?
- ¿Puede usted decirle con honestidad a Dios: "Haré lo que tú digas"?

**Orar**

- *Alabe* al Pastor, quien nos habla para que podamos oír su voz y seguirle.
- *Agradezca* a Dios por decirnos la verdad acerca de sí mismo, acerca de nosotros, y acerca de nuestro mundo.
- *Confiese* cualquier falta de deseo o cualquier fracaso personal en oír la voz de Dios.
- *Pídale* a Dios que le ayude a abrir su corazón a sus impresiones y a cerrar sus oídos a los malintencionados susurros del maligno.
- *Interceda* por aquellos que no están escuchando la Palabra de Dios o la voz de su Espíritu y, por ello, están alejándose de la verdad.

**Acción**

Pídale a Dios que le indique cómo quiere que usted trate a una persona con la cual tiene una relación difícil. Haga un compromiso, anticipadamente, de hacer lo que Dios le indique. Espere en oración silenciosa la dirección de Dios. Anote lo que usted cree que él le está diciendo. Confírmelo con su Palabra. Cuando esté seguro de lo que Dios le está diciendo, haga lo que él le pide.

# Día 4

# Orando en forma común y corriente

*"Oren en el Espíritu en todo momento, con peticiones y ruegos. Manténganse alerta y perseveren en oración por todos los santos".* —EFESIOS 6:18

¿Advirtió usted los "todos" en este pasaje? "Todo momento", "por todos los santos". ¡Qué manera más sencilla de decir que la oración es tremendamente importante, que *toda* la vida debe ser llevada a Dios en oración!

La oración no comienza con usted, sino con Dios. "Orar en el Espíritu" significa orar con la ayuda del Espíritu, bajo la influencia del Espíritu. Significa orar los pensamientos que el Espíritu pone en nosotros. Lo que es imposible con nuestra propia fuerza, se hace posible con la ayuda del Espíritu.

Orar "en toda ocasión" significa que la oración debe abarcar toda la vida misma. Háblele a Dios de sus problemas, de sus gozos, de sus tentaciones, de sus luchas. Deje que él tome parte en su vida cotidiana: en su trabajo, al pagar sus cuentas, en su tiempo libre, en sus compras, en sus visitas al doctor, y en el tiempo que pasa con sus amigos. Nada hay en nuestra vida sobre lo cual no podamos orar. Déle la bienvenida a Dios en el centro de su vida, a veces mundana, generalmente atareada, ocasionalmente agotadora, y siempre compleja. Ore acerca de las cosas comunes y corrientes.

Ore "todo tipo de oraciones". Que no exista una bendición por la que no diga una palabra de gratitud, ningún pecado sin una confesión, ninguna necesidad sin una oración de súplica, y ningún atisbo de la gloria de Dios sin una oración de alabanza. Si la oración es la parte hablada de una relación de amor con Dios, mantenga esa relación hablando con Dios acerca de todo tipo de cosas.

Ore "siempre". Esto significa que la oración no debe ser limitada a tiempos o días especiales. Nunca debe dejarse de lado. No hay ningún tiempo mejor para orar que cualquier momento. La oración debe ser natural, una parte constante de todos nuestros días y de todas nuestras noches.

Asegúrese también de orar por "todos los santos". Esto no sería posible si significara orar por cada cristiano en el mundo, y por su nombre. Pero usted puede orar por los cristianos que conoce, por sus familiares, por sus amigos, por los miembros de su iglesia, por sus vecinos. Es bueno orar por categorías: por los líderes de la iglesia, por los cristianos que son perseguidos, por los cristianos que están en posiciones de poder, por los cristianos que aparecen en los medios masivos de comunicación, por los creyentes de entornos étnicos distintos, por los cristianos de países específicos con grandes necesidades.

Gracias a la oración el más débil de los creyentes no debe temer "las artimañas del diablo" ni "potestades que dominan este mundo" (Efesios 6:11, 12). Cada verdadero creyente puede vivir en comunión constante con el aliado más poderoso en el mundo: Dios. En él tenemos la fuerza para resistir. La oración es el recurso otorgado por Dios para mantener nuestra relación con él.

### Para reflexionar

◆ Repase las últimas 24 horas de su vida. ¿Puede pensar en algún atisbo de la gloria de Dios que merezca alabanza, una dádiva que merezca una palabra de gratitud, un pecado que deba ser confesado o una necesidad que clama por ayuda de parte de Dios? ¿Le está hablando usted a Dios sobre estas cosas?

◆ ¿Qué "santos" (otros cristianos) necesitan sus oraciones ahora mismo para poder resistir las asechanzas del maligno?

### Orar

◆ *Alabe* al Espíritu de Dios, el único que conoce los pensamientos de Dios y puede revelárnoslos.

◆ *Agradezca* al Espíritu por ayudarnos a orar como debemos, y por poner en nuestros corazones oraciones que agradan a Dios.

◆ *Confiese* cualquier fracaso que haya sufrido al no practicar todos los tipos de oración, en todas las ocasiones, y por no seguir orando por todos los santos.

◆ *Pida* la ayuda del Espíritu para estar consciente de la presencia de Dios y hablar con él durante todo el día y en todas las circunstancias.

◆ *Interceda* en favor de otros cristianos que necesitan sus oraciones para poder resistir las asechanzas del maligno.

### Acción

Cada vez que empiece a orar, ya sea en momentos fijos o a la carrera, deténgase y pida al Espíritu Santo que dirija sus oraciones y le inspire los pensamientos y las palabras adecuadas.

# Día 5

# Un encuentro privado con el Padre

*"Pero tú, cuando te pongas a orar, entra a tu cuarto, cierra la puerta, y ora a tu Padre, que está en lo secreto. Así tu Padre, que ve lo que se hace en secreto, te recompensará".*

—MATEO 6:6

Pocas cosas en la vida son más preciosas que el tiempo que pasamos a solas con Dios. El propósito de ese tiempo es construir una relación personal más profunda con él. Dentro del recogimiento de nuestra vida de oración, al pasar más tiempo con el Señor, nuestro amor por él crece, y somos transformados más y más a la imagen de Cristo.

Cuando Jesús dice, "Entra a tu cuarto, cierra la puerta y ora a tu Padre", nos está diciendo, "Entra en un lugar privado, donde puedas aislarte y comunicarte con Dios en oración". Algunos llaman a este período especial su "devocional personal".

Muchos de los grandes santos de la Biblia practicaban esto. David oraba cada mañana (Salmo 5:3). Daniel oraba tres veces cada día (Daniel 6:10). Ana y Simeón oraban diariamente en el templo (Lucas 2:25, 36, 37). Pablo oraba constantemente por los nuevos creyentes en las iglesias que fundaba. Jesús, quien tenía una comunión perfecta con su Padre, sentía que era importante tener períodos privados para comunicarse con él. Lucas informa que "solía retirarse a lugares solitarios a orar" (Lucas 5:16). Las personas que conozco que tienen una fe vibrante, tal como los personajes citados, construyeron sus vidas espirituales alrededor de un tiempo consistente dedicado a Dios.

Una vida devocional diaria disciplinada no es una opción para un cristiano en crecimiento. Es una obligación. La oración es la parte conversada de una relación de amor con Dios. No se construye una relación de amor manteniéndose alejado de la otra persona. Se construye manteniéndose en estrecho contacto. Dios quiere que tengamos una relación muy cercana con él. Cuando así lo hacemos, salimos ganando. Dios nos llena con el gozo de su presencia (Salmo 16:11).

Pero las devociones personales no son simplemente un asunto de que *nosotros* deseemos y necesitemos pasar tiempo con Dios. *Dios desea* pasar tiempo con nosotros, tanto como sea posible. Dios tuvo mucho agrado en crearnos y salvarnos. Él nos conoce y nos ama. Se goza en expresar su amor cuando pasamos tiempo con él. Somos importantes para él. "El Señor honra al que le es fiel" (Salmo 4:3). Sofonías declara que Dios "se deleita" en nosotros, nos aquieta con su amor y se regocija por nosotros con cantos (Sofonías 3:17). El tiempo que pasamos con Dios cada día es el tiempo adecuado para derramar su amor sobre nosotros. Esto es un deleite para Dios. Y nos puede deleitar a nosotros también. Es parte de la recompensa.

Nunca he conocido a una persona que lamente el tiempo que ha dedicado a pasar con Dios. ¿Es usted uno de ellos?

### Para reflexionar

♦ ¿Cómo está usted obedeciendo la orden de Cristo de "entrar a tu cuarto, cerrar la puerta, y orar al Padre"? ¿Está usted recibiendo la recompensa prometida?

♦ Trate de imaginar que está mirando la faz de Dios mientras él se deleita en usted. ¿Qué supone usted que hace Dios para deleitarse con nosotros? ¿Qué hace Dios para impartirle quietud por medio de su amor? ¿Puede oír el canto de Dios cuando se regocija por usted?

### Orar

♦ *Alabe* a Dios por su gran amor, un gran amor para usted, una persona a quien él conoce por nombre.

♦ *Agradezca* a Dios por darle la oportunidad de encontrarse con él en forma privada en cualquier momento que usted elija, y por su disposición de recibirlo.

♦ *Confiese* cualquier renuncia suya en su relación con Dios que lo induce a sentirse retraído.

♦ *Pídale* a Dios ayuda y dirección para mejorar su vida devocional privada.

♦ *Interceda* por familiares y amigos que necesitarían pasar más tiempo con el Señor.

# MODELOS DE ORACIONES DE LA BIBLIA

# Día 1

# El Padrenuestro

*"Ustedes deben orar así: 'Padre nuestro que estás en el cielo, santificado sea tu nombre, venga tu reino, hágase tu voluntad en la tierra como en el cielo. Danos hoy nuestro pan cotidiano. Perdónanos nuestras deudas, como también nosotros hemos perdonado a nuestros deudores. Y no nos dejes caer en tentación, sino líbranos del maligno'". —*Mateo 6: 9–13

Llamamos a esta oración El Padrenuestro y La Oración de nuestro Señor. Pero en realidad es la oración de los discípulos. Lo sabemos porque Jesús nunca necesitó orar pidiendo perdón por sus pecados, como él nos enseña que debemos hacer en este pasaje.

Se trata de un *modelo* de oración. Jesús no dijo: "Esto es lo que ustedes deben orar", dijo: "Esto es como deben orar". No era su intención que la oración se repitiera en forma mecánica. Por supuesto que no es malo usar esas palabras como una oración, siempre que salgan del corazón.

Las palabras de apertura: "Padre nuestro que estás en el cielo", aclaran desde el principio nuestra relación con Dios. Aquel a quien oramos está ciertamente "en el cielo"—el majestuoso, soberano Dios del universo—. Pero para sus hijos que se acercan a él en oración, Dios es un Padre amoroso.

Este modelo de oración contiene seis peticiones. Las primeras tres se refieren a temas que tienen que ver con Dios; las otras tres se refieren a los seres humanos. Este ordenamiento de las peticiones, nos recuerda que Dios debe tener el primer lugar en nuestra vida de oración.

Lo que podría ser más sorprendente de las primeras tres peticiones es que Dios quiere que oremos sobre cosas que le conciernen a él. Dios es perfectamente capaz de santificar su nombre, de hacer crecer su reino, y de imponer su voluntad, sin que nosotros se lo pidamos. Pero Dios ha elegido actuar en respuesta a nuestras peticiones. Y es por eso que nos pide orar por estos asuntos, para que él pueda glorificar su nombre, acercar a nosotros su reino, y hacer su voluntad, todo en respuesta a nuestras oraciones. Eso es lo que hace que nuestras oraciones sean tan importantes.

Cuando le pedimos a Dios que santifique su nombre, le estamos pidiendo que se mueva en el mundo en las maneras que le den gloria y honor. "Venga tu reino", es una petición de que Dios establezca su reino en el corazón y la mente de la gente. "Hágase tu voluntad en la tierra como en el cielo", es un ruego porque Dios ayude a la gente a someterse a su voluntad con tanta disposición y tan completamente, como lo hacen los ángeles en el cielo.

Las peticiones cuatro, cinco y seis se refieren a necesidades humanas. El hecho de que Jesús nos enseñó a orar por "nuestro pan cotidiano", nos recuerda que él se preocupa de nuestro cuerpo, y quiere proveer para nuestras necesidades físicas según se lo pidamos. "Perdónanos nuestras deudas" es la oración de cristianos quienes, habiendo entrado en una maravillosa relación con Dios, quieren estar libres de cualquier pecado que podría impedir dicha relación.

"No nos dejes caer en tentación", es una oración para que Dios nos sostenga frente a las tentaciones de las fuerzas del mal que habitan este mundo y que tratan de alejarnos de Dios.

Jesús dijo a sus discípulos: "Ustedes deben orar así". ¿Es usted un discípulo de Jesús? Entonces, es así como usted debe orar.

### Para reflexionar

+ ¿Refleja el orden de su vida de oración el orden del Padrenuestro? ¿Qué porcentaje del tiempo que usted dedica a la oración lo dedica a asuntos que se enfocan en Dios?

+ ¿Le interesa a usted lo suficiente la gloria de Dios, su reino y su voluntad para hacer estas peticiones de corazón?

+ ¿Puede usted creer que Dios quizá *no* santifique su nombre, ni haga venir su reino, ni imponga su voluntad en ciertas ocasiones sólo porque usted no oró para que eso suceda?

### Orar

La mejor forma de usar un modelo de oración es recordar la idea central de cada petición y ampliarla. Trate de hacerlo ahora en una oración, dedicando un par de minutos a cada petición.

### Acción

Repita una versión ampliada del Padrenuestro diariamente durante la próxima semana e imagine algunas maneras en que Dios está respondiendo sus peticiones. Imagine a Dios, por ejemplo, haciendo sentir su presencia en un servicio de adoración (santificando), bendiciendo las cosechas con lluvia y sol (dando pan), y dándoles a los cristianos la fuerza para resistir las tentaciones.

# Día 2

# Una escalera de oración

*"Por esta razón me arrodillo delante del Padre, de quien recibe nombre toda familia en el cielo y en la tierra. Le pido que, por medio del Espíritu y con el poder que procede de sus gloriosas riquezas, los fortalezca a ustedes en lo íntimo de su ser, para que por fe Cristo habite en sus corazones. Y pido que, arraigados y cimentados en amor, puedan comprender, junto con todos los santos, cuán ancho y largo, alto y profundo es el amor de Cristo; en fin, que conozcan ese amor que sobrepasa nuestro conocimiento, para que sean llenos de la plenitud de Dios".*—EFESIOS 3:14–19

L a ferviente oración de Pablo por la familia de Dios nos da un bosquejo de cómo orar por otros: una escalera de oración que debemos ascender, la cual consta de seis pasos:

**1. Orar por fuerza interior en el poder del Espíritu Santo.** Proverbios 4:23 dice que del corazón "mana la vida". Y Jesús enseñó que "el que es bueno, de la bondad que atesora en el corazón produce el bien; pero el que es malo, de su maldad produce el mal, porque de lo que abunda en el corazón habla la boca" (Lucas 6:45). Lo que sucede en el interior de la persona es de vital importancia. Nuestras oraciones son capaces de afectar lo que sucede en otros creyentes.

**2. Orar para que Cristo pueda vivir en el corazón de los creyentes por la fe.** Cristo desea vivir y actuar en la tierra hoy en los creyentes y por medio de ellos. Lo hace a medida que ellos se someten a sus exhortaciones y tienen su mentalidad, su voluntad, su visión, su valentía, su amor y su poder. Cuando oramos de esta manera por otros, pedimos que Cristo pueda vivir más y más en nosotros y cumplir su voluntad por medio de nosotros.

**3. Orar para que los creyentes estén cimentados en el amor de Dios.** Las personas por quienes oramos necesitan estar arraigadas en el amor, y nutridas por el amor de Dios, tal como una planta es nutrida a través de sus raíces. Necesitan estar establecidos en amor, tener el amor de Dios como un fundamento sólido en sus vidas.

**4. Orar para que los creyentes capten la amplitud del amor de Cristo.** Esto quiere decir, que conozcan cuán *ancho y largo, alto y profundo* es ese amor. Un escritor desconocido captó el significado de esta frase cuando escribió:

*Podríamos llenar de tinta los océanos,*
*y si los cielos fueran un pergamino,*
*si cada brizna de pasto fuera una pluma*
*y cada hombre un escritor por profesión,*
*describir el amor del Dios de lo alto*
*dejaría secos los océanos,*
*y el pergamino no alcanzaría a contenerlo*
*aunque se extendiera de cielo a cielo.*

**5. Orar para que los creyentes puedan experimentar el amor de Cristo.** Es maravilloso si las personas por quienes oramos pueden llegar a captar el alcance del amor de Cristo. Es aun más importante que ellos lo experimenten. Eso es lo que pedimos para ellos cuando oramos por ellos, que "conozcan ese amor que sobrepasa nuestro conocimiento".

**6. Orar para que los creyentes puedan ser llenados con la naturaleza misma de Dios.** En estas palabras la escalera de la oración de Pablo alcanza el peldaño más alto. Orar para que *sean llenos de la plenitud de Dios* es pedirle a Dios derramarse en nosotros, los hijos de su familia terrenal, con una plenitud espiritual como la que Dios mismo posee.

¿Qué más podríamos pedir por otros? ¿Ha pedido usted estas cosas a Dios para otros y para sí mismo?

**Para reflexionar**

◆ ¿Cuánto esfuerzo invierte usted al orar por el bienestar espiritual de otros? ¿Qué debe hacer para parecerse más a Pablo en sus oraciones de intercesión? ¿Qué diferencia espera ver al orar de esta manera por otros?

◆ Tome nota de que Pablo ora por "toda la familia" de Dios. ¿Es un modelo que usted imita?

**Orar**

◆ *Alabe* a Dios por su poder y amor, lo único que hace posible orar de esta manera.

◆ *Confiese* cualquier falla en la oración que este pasaje le haga recordar.

◆ *Pida* a Dios mayor comprensión de su poder y amor para que le resulte natural orar por otros de esta manera.

◆ *Agradezca* a Dios porque le ama y está dispuesto y es capaz de derramar en usted su plenitud.

◆ *Interceda,* usando la escalera de oración, por las personas que Dios ha puesto sobre su corazón.

**Acción**

Anote los nombres de las personas por quienes desea orar la "escalera de oración". Coloque la lista en un lugar donde podrá verla cada día.

○

# Día 3

# Una oración por riquezas espirituales

*"Por eso, desde el día en que lo supimos, no hemos dejado de orar por ustedes. Pedimos que Dios les haga conocer plenamente su voluntad con toda sabiduría y comprensión espiritual, para que vivan de manera digna del Señor, agradándole en todo. Esto implica dar fruto en toda buena obra, crecer en el conocimiento de Dios y ser fortalecidos en todo sentido con su glorioso poder. Así perseverarán con paciencia en toda situación, dando gracias con alegría al Padre".*—COLOSENSES 1: 9–12.

Hace algunos años, esta gran oración de Pablo por los cristianos de Colosas me llevó en un viaje espiritual de oración. Comenzó al contemplar la asombrosa profundidad y alcance de la oración de Pablo por los colosenses, y pensé: "Qué bueno sería tener a Pablo como compañero de oración." Después se me ocurrió que si oraba por estas bendiciones para mí mismo, Dios sin duda me concedería lo que yo le pedía, ya que todas están de acuerdo con su voluntad. Comencé a hacerlo de inmediato.

Después pensé: "No puedo esperar que Pablo ore de esta manera por mí, pero *yo puedo ser el que ore así por otros".* Así que comencé a hacer estas peticiones en forma regular por mi esposa y mis hijos, y también por otros familiares y amigos.

Lo que más me impresiona es que estas peticiones de intercesión son todas de naturaleza espiritual. No hay oración por asuntos físicos o materiales de la vida. Por supuesto que debemos orar por cosas físicas como salud, energía y protección. Pero en la oración de Pablo, las bendiciones espirituales claramente sobrepasan lo físico.

Trate de imaginar, por ejemplo, lo que sucedería en la vida espiritual de una persona si todo lo que pidiera en oración le fuera concedido en mayor grado. Esa persona:

Profundizaría día tras día en el conocimiento de la voluntad de Dios.

Aplicaría los principios bíblicos al diario vivir por la sabiduría y la percepción del Espíritu Santo.

Viviría una vida cristiana ejemplar que le daría crédito a Jesucristo y gozo al corazón de Dios.

Se dedicaría a toda clase de actividades fructíferas del ministerio.

Continuaría creciendo en el conocimiento de Dios.

Soportaría con gozo y paciencia las experiencias más duras de la vida gracias al poder de Dios que obra en su interior.

Gozoso, daría gracias a Dios el Padre, al mismo tiempo mirando con confianza hacia adelante, a la vida en el nuevo y glorioso reino de luz.

¡Me gustaría ser esa persona! ¿A usted también? Lo mismo sentirían muchos creyentes que viven y trabajan cerca de usted, y sus oraciones pueden ayudar a que esto sea una realidad para ellos.

Estoy seguro de que las oraciones de Pablo hicieron una gran diferencia en la congregación de Colosas por la cual él oraba. Dios, como ustedes saben, está ansioso de contestar esta clase de oraciones, porque lo que se está pidiendo es exactamente lo que Dios quiere que suceda en nuestras vidas y en la iglesia.

¿Habrá algunas personas a las que usted desearía bendecir de esta manera?

### PARA REFLEXIONAR

◆ ¿Son las cosas que Pablo pidió para los colosenses (1:9–12) las mismas que usted *realmente* desea en su vida? Si es así, pídalas, y no sólo de vez en cuando, sino cada día.

◆ Imagine lo que sucedería en su familia o en su congregación si se orara cada día por una persona con una oración como ésta. ¿Hay alguna manera de hacerlo?

### ORAR

◆ *Alabe* la bondad de Dios, quien está dispuesto y es capaz de bendecirnos con toda bendición espiritual en los lugares celestiales.

◆ *Agradezca* a Dios por darnos la oración como el medio para llevar sus bendiciones a otros y a nosotros mismos.

◆ ¿Ha pecado usted al dejar de orar por personas que conoce (1 Samuel 12:23)? Si es así, *confiéselo* a Dios y comience de nuevo de inmediato.

◆ *Pídale* a Dios que haga por usted lo mismo que Pablo pidió para los colosenses.

◆ *Interceda* por sus hijos, sus nietos, sus padres, sus amigos y otros seres queridos, usando este método.

### ACCIÓN

Memorice 2 Corintios 1:9–12 para que pueda orar estos versículos diariamente sin tener que mirar el texto. Al orar por estos temas, trate de ampliarlos y adecuarlos a personas y situaciones específicas.

# Día 4

# Una oración para conocer mejor a Dios

*"Pido que el Dios de nuestro Señor Jesucristo, el Padre glorioso, les dé el Espíritu de sabiduría y de revelación, para que lo conozcan mejor. Pido también que les sean iluminados los ojos del corazón para que sepan a qué esperanza él los ha llamado, cuál es la riqueza de su gloriosa herencia entre los santos, y cuán incomparable es la grandeza de su poder a favor de los que creemos".*—EFESIOS 1:17–19

P ablo creía que la mayor necesidad de los cristianos en Éfeso era conocer mejor a Dios. Esa quizá también sea hoy la mayor necesidad en la iglesia. Una forma importante en que Pablo trabajaba para que esto sucediera era orando.

Pablo comienza confirmando a quién le ora: "el Dios de nuestro Señor Jesucristo, el Padre glorioso". Nuestra confianza al orar no es la oración misma sino Aquel a quien oramos, nuestro Padre celestial. Los padres buenos, por su misma naturaleza, desean amar, proteger, proveer, guiar y abrazar a sus hijos e hijas. Es la naturaleza de nuestro Padre celestial hacer todas estas cosas, y las hace a la perfección. Es por ello que podemos acercarnos a Dios con absoluta confianza.

Toda la oración de Pablo en este caso se refiere a ayudar a personas que conocemos y amamos a conocer *mejor* a Dios. No se sienta satisfecho si sus seres queridos simplemente conocen la Biblia, o acerca de Dios, o si conocen a Dios un poco. Ore siguiendo este modelo de oración para ellos, pidiéndole al Padre que los ayude a que ellos "le conozcan mejor". Conocer algo acerca de Dios, y conocer a Dios, es muy diferente de conocer bien a Dios.

Conocer *bien* a Dios significa conocer lo que Dios realmente es: cómo piensa, cuál es su voluntad, cómo obra, y cómo se siente respecto a usted. Significa saber lo que le agrada a Dios y lo que le disgusta. Significa desear lo que Dios desea. Significa compartir los gozos y las tristezas de Dios.

Lo que Pablo pidió para que esto sucediera fue "el Espíritu de sabiduría y de revelación". El Espíritu conoce a Dios perfectamente y él nos puede ayudar a conocer a Dios cada vez mejor, pues el Espíritu mora en nuestros corazones.

Las personas que conoce bien a Dios tienen "iluminados los ojos del corazón" para conocer las siguientes cosas:

**1. La esperanza a que él los ha llamado.** Cuando la Biblia utiliza la palabra "esperanza", ésta no significa un fuerte deseo como en el lenguaje común. Significa estar absolutamente seguro, porque Dios lo ha prometido. El conocer a Dios nos da una certeza respecto adonde vamos. Nos da "esperanza".

**2. La riqueza de su gloriosa herencia.** Conocer bien a Dios no sólo es estar seguros de donde pasaremos la eternidad, sino también saber cuán buena será, una gloriosa herencia.

**3. La grandeza incomparable de su poder a favor de los que creemos.** Conocer bien a Dios es conocer por experiencia su gran poder, depender de ese poder, sentirlo, y sentir que corre a través de nuestras venas, al vivir para Dios en medio de una cultura mundana torcida y perversa.

¿Es esto lo que usted desea para sí mismo y para las personas por quienes intercede? Entonces pídale al Padre estas cosas. ¡Él lo escuchará!

### PARA REFLEXIONAR

+ ¿Cuán bien conoce usted a Dios? Como punto de partida, piense en una persona que usted conoce realmente bien, y compare su "conocimiento" de Dios con la forma en que conoce a dicha persona.

+ ¿Cómo puede lograr conocer mejor a Dios? ¿Qué lugar ocupa la oración en ese proceso?

+ Piense acerca de la *esperanza* respecto a su futuro, las *riquezas* que heredará, y el *gran poder* de Dios que está obrando en usted.

### ORAR

+ *Alabe* "al Espíritu de sabiduría y de revelación" por lo que sabe y por su disposición de revelárselo a usted y a las personas por quienes ora.

+ *Agradezca* a Dios por su disposición de usar su "incomparable gran poder" para asegurar su salvación ahora y por la eternidad.

+ Si no ha hecho mucho esfuerzo para conocerle mejor, *confiéselo* a Dios y *pida* su perdón. Aproveche el perdón que Dios le ofrece libremente.

+ *Pida* al glorioso Padre que le ayude a usted y a aquellos por los que usted ama a "conocerlo mejor".

### ACCIÓN

Decida que usted personalmente se esforzará para conocer a Dios mejor. Eso podría incluir leer y estudiar la Palabra de Dios, formar parte de un grupo de estudio bíblico, participar en un retiro espiritual personal, asistir más a la iglesia, leer literatura cristiana apropiada.

○
# *Día 5*

# La oración de Jabes

*"Jabes le rogó al Dios de Israel: bendíceme y ensancha mi territorio; ayúdame y líbrame del mal, para que no padezca aflicción. Y Dios le concedió su petición".*—1 CRÓNICAS 4:10

L a oración de Jabes es un osado modelo de una oración que podemos hacer para nosotros mismos, y también para otros.

El libro de Bruce Wilkinson *La Oración de Jabes,* ha hecho mucho para popularizar esta oración en el mundo evangélico. Desde su publicación, me he encontrado con varios cristianos quienes, después de leer el libro, han aprendido a orar de esta manera por sí mismos y han experimentado respuestas sorprendentes.

Cuando pedimos con sinceridad las cosas que Dios desea para nosotros, él siempre está listo para responder. El hecho de que Dios le concedió su petición confirma que la oración de Jabes fue sincera y estaba de acuerdo con la voluntad de Dios.

Jabes creía en la oración. Su vida fue cambiada gracias a la oración. Pidió cuatro cosas. Su primera oración fue: "Bendíceme". Dios desea bendecirnos, pero quiere hacerlo en respuesta a nuestra petición. Esa es la forma en que Dios ha elegido obrar. De manera que cuando Jabes hizo esta petición, Dios se sintió complacido y envió su bendición.

Luego Jabes oró: "ensancha mi territorio". A primera vista podría parecer un deseo egoísta de prosperidad material. Pero si Jabes hubiese tenido una motivación incorrecta, no creo que Dios se lo hubiera concedido. Los que oran por motivos incorrectos no reciben respuesta a su oración (Santiago 4:3). En el caso de Jabes, esa era una petición para la restauración de una heredad perdida. "Ensancha mi territorio", probablemente significa orar por la oportunidad de librarse de cualquier cosa que le estaba impidiendo vivir plenamente dentro de la promesa de Dios para nosotros.

En tercer lugar, Jabes rogó: "Ayúdame". Dios ha prometido fortalecernos y ha manifestado su disposición de actuar en favor de los que él ama. Jabes estaba diciendo:

"Señor, ensancha mi territorio y dame la oportunidad de servirte. No lo puedo hacer con mis propias fuerzas, así que ayúdame". Esta es la oración de una persona humilde que sabe que su fuerza radica en el Señor.

En cuarto lugar, Jabes oró: "Líbrame del mal". La mayor fuente de maldad en este mundo es Satanás. Esta parte de la oración de Jabes es similar a la última petición del Padrenuestro: "No nos dejes caer en tentación, mas líbranos del mal" (Mateo 6: 13).

El pasaje termina con una declaración muy importante. "Y Dios le concedió su petición". Dios lo hizo porque estaba complacido con la oración de Jabes. También estará complacido si usted hace una oración por sí mismo, no sólo una vez, sino día tras día. Dios quiere bendecirlo. Dios desea ensanchar sus oportunidades de servicio. Dios desea fortalecerlo. Dios desea protegerlo del mal. Él desea hacer todas estas cosas en respuesta a su petición. Esta oración puede ser, como dice Bruce Wilkinson, "la clave para una vida de extraordinario favor de Dios".

### Para reflexionar

- ¿Desea usted las cuatro cosas por las que oró Jabes con tanta ansiedad que está dispuesto a pedirlas vez tras vez?
- ¿Qué diferencia haría para usted recibir en respuesta una medida aun mayor de estas bendiciones de Dios?
- ¿Hay una manera egoísta de hacer esta oración? ¿Qué impediría que fuera una oración egoísta?

### Orar

- *Alabe* a Dios, quien oye y responde las oraciones que están de acuerdo con su voluntad.
- *Agradezca* a Dios por las bendiciones, oportunidades de servicio, fortaleza y protección que le ha dado en el pasado.
- *Confiese* cualquier letargo espiritual o flojera que le ha impedido alcanzar su total potencial en el reino de Dios.
- *Pídale* a Dios cada bendición espiritual, y oportunidades para el ministerio tan grandes como las que usted pueda acometer, más la fortaleza para el servicio, y su protección contra el maligno.

### Acción

Dígale a Dios que usted está listo para servirle en cualquier momento, en cualquier lugar, haciendo cualquier cosa que él le pida, siempre que usted tenga la seguridad de que es una tarea que él le asigna.

# HÉROES DE ORACIÓN

# Día 1

# Jesús: Hombre de oración

*"Muy de madrugada, cuando todavía estaba oscuro, Jesús se levantó,
salió de la casa, y se fue a un lugar solitario".*—MARCOS 1:35

*"Él, por su parte, solía retirarse a lugares solitarios".*—LUCAS 5:16

*"Por aquel tiempo se fue Jesús a la montaña a orar,
y pasó toda la noche en oración a Dios".*—LUCAS 6:12

Nadie ha orado como Jesús oraba. La oración era vital en la vida de Jesús. E. M. Bounds ha escrito de Jesús: "La oración era el secreto de su poder, la ley de su vida, la inspiración de su trabajo, y la fuente de sus riqueza, su gozo, su comunión, y su fuerza". Los evangelios contienen no menos de 18 referencias a la vida de oración de Jesús, 14 temas de oración distintos sobre los cuales enseñó y 8 oraciones.

De alguna manera, es sorprendente pensar que la oración era necesaria para Jesús. Después de todo, es el Hijo de Dios, el que hoy oye y contesta nuestras oraciones. Pero la oración era necesaria para Jesús durante los días de su ministerio en la tierra, porque él era verdaderamente humano y compartía totalmente nuestra humanidad, excepto que sin pecado. Al tomar nuestras limitaciones sobre sí, aceptó incluso la limitación de depender del Padre y tener que comunicarse con él en oración.

A Jesús le gustaba orar. La oración era para él un estilo de vida. Oró en cada ocasión importante en su vida: durante su bautismo en el río Jordán, antes de llamar a sus discípulos, antes de la transfiguración, antes de la última cena, antes de la cruz, en la cruz, al morir, y antes de ascender al cielo. Jesús oró en momentos de gozo (Lucas 10:21), y cuando su corazón estaba afligido (Juan 12: 27, 28). Ganó victorias anticipadamente por medio de la oración (Juan 11:41, 42) y evitó la tentación después de sus victorias gracias a la oración (Juan 6:15). Oraba tanto que adquirió la reputación de ser un hombre de oración (Mateo 19:13).

La vida de oración de Jesús era muy variada. Oraba temprano en la mañana, al final de un largo día, y a menudo durante el día. Oraba en lugares solitarios, en la montaña, en el desierto, en un jardín, y dentro de templos y hogares. Una vez se le describe arrodillado en oración (Lucas 22:41), en otra ocasión postrado (Mateo 26:39), y otra vez de pie, con los ojos fijos en el cielo (Juan 11:41). Oraba en privado (Lucas 9:18), y en público (Juan 11:41, 42).

Jesús también sabía como escuchar en oración. En Juan 7:16 dice: "Mi enseñanza no es mía, sino del que me envió". Y más tarde hizo notar que el Padre le ordenaba "qué decir y cómo decirlo", y que cualquier cosa que él dijera era justo lo que el Padre le había dicho que dijera (Juan 12:49, 50).

La vida de oración de Jesús no terminó con su viaje terrenal. Hoy él "está a la derecha de Dios e intercede por nosotros" (Romanos 8:34). Y "porque él vive para interceder" por nosotros, puede salvarnos completamente (Hebreos 7:25).

¿Quiere usted ser como Jesús? ¡Entonces aprenda a orar como Jesús! No hay una mejor manera de orar.

### PARA REFLEXIONAR

◆ Si alguien escribiera una breve historia de su vida, ¿figuraría la oración en forma prominente? Considere cuáles áreas de su vida necesitan ser mejoradas si usted desea ser más como Jesús.

◆ ¿Qué grado de prioridad cree usted que Jesús quiere que la oración tenga en su vida?

### ORAR

◆ *Alabe* a Jesús por darnos un modelo de oración fuerte.

◆ *Confiese* cualquier falla en la oración que usted reconozca al comparar su vida de oración con la de Jesús.

◆ *Agradezca* al Espíritu Santo por su habilidad y disposición para purificar nuestras oraciones y ayudarnos cuando no sabemos cómo orar bien (Romanos 8:26).

◆ *Pídale* a Cristo la gracia para orar como él oraba.

### ACCIÓN

Lea y medite en los pasajes de las Escrituras mencionados en esta lectura. Al leer cada referencia, pregúntele al Señor qué desea que usted aprenda de ella, e introdúzcalo en su propia vida de oración.

# Día 2

# Pablo, el hombre que oraba constantemente

*"Dios [...] me es testigo de que los recuerdo a ustedes sin cesar".*—Romanos 1:9, 10

*"Siempre que oramos por ustedes, damos gracias a Dios, el Padre de nuestro Señor Jesucristo [...] no hemos dejado de orar por ustedes".*—Colosenses 1: 3, 9

*"Al recordarte de día y de noche en mis oraciones, siempre doy gracias a Dios".*—2 Timoteo 1:3

Para mí, el apóstol Pablo es un gran héroe de oración, el segundo después de Jesucristo. Al estudiar el patrón de su vida de oración, me asombré de encontrar no menos de doce pasajes en las cartas de Pablo en que usa palabras que denotan "tiempo", tales como *constantemente, no hemos dejado, cada vez, y noche y día, para describir sus oraciones en favor de otros.* ¡Qué gran ejemplo de su exhortación de "orar sin cesar"! (1 Tesalonicenses 5:17).

Una razón por la cual Pablo oraba constantemente era para expresar su gratitud a Dios por otros creyentes. Vez tras vez, Pablo comienza sus cartas con palabras como "siempre doy gracias a Dios". Notemos también que Pablo agradecía a Dios por esas personas, en vez de agradecerles a ellos directamente. A mí me gusta que me agradezcan, pero es aún mejor que alguien le dé gracias a Dios por mí. De esa manera, Dios recibe el crédito, y yo recibo la confirmación y el gozo que da servir a Dios.

Pablo también oró constantemente porque le interesaban mucho las personas por quienes oraba. Lo notamos en sus frases "los llevo en el corazón", "los quiero a todos con el entrañable amor de Cristo Jesús" (Filipenses 1:7, 8). Un amor sincero tiende a inspirar oraciones de corazón. Cierta vez un joven me dijo que mis oraciones congregacionales lo aburrían durante los servicios. Le pregunté si se sentía aburrido cuando yo oraba por su abuela.

"No"—me dijo—, "en ese caso estoy sintonizado". Admitió que se aburría con las otras oraciones porque no le interesaban las personas por quienes se estaba orando. El amor hace nacer la oración.

Pablo también sabía que sus oraciones harían una gran diferencia en las vidas de sus "hijos e hijas" en la fe. Oró por que ellos aumentaran y sobreabundaran en amor los unos por los otros (1 Tesalonicenses 3:12), que fueran iluminados los ojos de su corazón para que supieran a qué esperanza él los había llamado (Efesios 1:18; 3:19), para que discernieran lo que es mejor (Filipenses 1:9), y vivieran de una manera digna del Señor, agradándole en todo (Colosenses 1:10).

Finalmente, Pablo sabía que necesitaba el apoyo de otros en oración. "Les ruego, por nuestro Señor Jesucristo y por el amor del Espíritu, que se unan conmigo en esta lucha y que oren a Dios por mí" (Romanos 15:30). "Oren también por mí para que, cuando hable, Dios me dé las palabras para dar a conocer con valor el misterio del evangelio por el cual soy embajador en cadenas" (Efesios 6:19). Y, "Porque sé que, gracias a las oraciones de ustedes y a la ayuda que me da el Espíritu de Jesucristo, todo esto resultará en mi liberación" (Filipenses 1:19).

Pablo, el gran hombre de oración, es también el que dijo, "les ruego que sigan mi ejemplo"; "los elogio porque se acuerdan de mí en todo y retienen las enseñanzas tal como se las transmití" (1 Corintios 11:1; 4:16). Para esto, necesitamos de mucha gracia.

### PARA REFLEXIONAR

◆ ¿Qué es lo que más le impresiona respecto a la vida de oración de Pablo?

◆ Las Escrituras nos llaman a seguir el ejemplo de Pablo. ¿Cuáles elementos de la vida de oración de Pablo debería incorporar usted en su propia vida de oración?

◆ En forma personal, ¿aprecia usted el apoyo de otros en oración por su propio crecimiento espiritual y sus actividades en el ministerio? ¿Comparte con ellos lo que deben saber para orar en forma específica al respecto?

### ORAR

◆ *Agradezca* a Dios por otros en su familia, congregación o círculo de amigos. Dígale a Dios cosas específicas respecto a ellos por las que usted se siente agradecido.

◆ ¿Le aburre orar por otros? ¿Se deberá a que usted no los ama lo suficiente?

◆ *Ore* pidiendo mayor habilidad para ver lo bueno en otros, para que se interese en el bienestar de ellos, y por la seguridad de que sus oraciones harán una diferencia en sus vidas.

### ACCIÓN

Lea los siguientes pasajes que hablan de la fidelidad de Pablo en la oración, su gratitud por las personas, su profundo amor. Romanos 1:9, 10; 10:1; 1 Corintios 1:4; Efesios 1:16; 3:14; Filipenses 1:3–8; Colosenses 1:3, 9; 1 Tesalonicenses 1:2; 3:9, 10; 2 Tesalonicenses 1:3, 11; 2 Timoteo 1:3; Filemón 4. Considere sus implicaciones para usted.

# Día 3

# Elías: un hombre común que oraba con poder

*"Elías era un hombre con debilidades como las nuestras. Con fervor oró que no lloviera, y no llovió sobre la tierra durante tres años y medio. Volvió a orar, y el cielo dio su lluvia y la tierra produjo sus frutos".*—SANTIAGO 5:17, 18*

Cuando nos encontramos con un hombre de oración como Elías, nos sentimos tentados a pensar: *Yo nunca podría orar de esa manera.* Pero Santiago, al citar a Elías como un modelo de oración poderosa, descarta esa forma de pensar al comentar que Elías era un hombre común, tal como nosotros. Santiago nos está diciendo que si Elías, una persona común y corriente podía orar así, nosotros también podemos hacerlo.

Esto es verdad, porque el poder de la oración no está en la persona ni en las palabras de la oración. Todo el poder de la oración es el poder de Dios liberado a través de la oración. Fue Dios el que impidió que lloviera durante tres años y medio, y fue Dios quien permitió que volviera a llover. Pero la oración jugó su papel. Fueron las oraciones de Elías las que movieron a Dios a actuar de ese modo. Este hombre común y corriente oró, ¡y miren lo que sucedió! Dios sigue actuando en respuesta a las oraciones de personas comunes y corrientes.

A veces las oraciones de las personas comunes son oraciones de fe simple, expresadas tranquila y confiadamente. Ese fue el caso al enfrentar Elías a los profetas de Baal (1 Reyes 18:16–39). Después de que los profetas de Baal habían clamado a sus dioses con gritos, danzas y derramamiento de sangre, sin recibir respuesta, Elías se adelantó y oró simplemente: "Señor, Dios de Abraham de Isaac y de Israel, que sepan todos hoy que tú eres Dios de Israel, y que yo soy tu siervo y he hecho todo esto en obediencia a tu palabra. Respóndeme, Señor, respóndeme, para que esta gente reconozca que tú, Señor, eres Dios, y que estás convirtiendo a ti su corazón". Con esa oración, cayó fuego del cielo y consumió el holocausto de Elías, y la leña y las piedras e incluso el agua en la zanja alrededor del altar.

Esto no quiere decir que cualquier oración débil, superficial, poco sincera, será poderosa y efectiva. Santiago destaca que Elías oró con fervor. La oración con fervor fue lo que obtuvo resultados. Y esa oración llena de fervor ilustra el argumento de Santiago de que, según la traducción de J. B. Phillips, "un enorme poder se hace posible a través de la ferviente oración de un hombre bueno".

Las oraciones de la gente común también deben ser persistentes. Para que la lluvia volviera a caer, Elías subió al Monte Carmelo, y oró con fervor. Vez tras vez envió a su siervo a mirar el horizonte para ver si había alguna señal de una nube que evidenciara la respuesta a la oración. Fue hasta la séptima vez, cuando el siervo vio una pequeña nube, tan pequeña como una mano. Entonces Elías dejó de orar y bajó del monte.

¿Habrá algo que Dios quiere lograr por medio de sus oraciones? ¿Por qué no le pregunta en forma sincera y persistente, y espera los resultados?

## PARA REFLEXIONAR

- ♦ ¿Ha sentido alguna vez que usted no puede orar poderosamente como algunos "supercristianos" que conoce? ¿Qué diría Santiago al respecto?
- ♦ ¿Alguna vez se ha desanimado después de orar media docena de veces por algo? ¿Qué habría pasado si Elías hubiera dejado de orar a la sexta vez?
- ♦ Repase algunas de sus oraciones recientes. ¿Fueron "fervorosas" o sólo superficiales?

## ORAR

- ♦ *Alabe* a Dios por el poder que hace posible una oración poderosa.
- ♦ *Agradezca* a Dios porque escucha y contesta las oraciones de sus hijos e hijas comunes y corrientes, y nos da la posibilidad de orar con poder.
- ♦ *Pídale* a Dios que le revele el asunto sobre el cual él desea que usted ore, y que le ayude a orar con fervor y en forma persistente.
- ♦ *Ore* para que Dios actúe en favor de su iglesia, para que se haga fuerte en la oración y sea efectiva en el ministerio.

## ACCIÓN

Dígale a Dios que usted está listo para orar ferviente y persistentemente acerca de cualquier cosa que él ponga en su corazón, aunque se trate de algo grande y vital. Escuche esperando la dirección de Dios.

---

*Lea la historia completa de la victoria de oración de Elías en 1 Reyes 17–18.

# Día 4

# Josafat: Victoria por medio de la oración

*"Señor, Dios de nuestros antepasados, ¿no eres tú el Dios del cielo, y el que gobierna todas las naciones? ¡Es tal tu fuerza y tu poder que no hay quien pueda resistirte! [...] No sabemos qué hacer".—*2 CRÓNICAS 20:6, 12*

Josafat está bien arriba en mi lista de héroes de oración. Su liderazgo en oración ganó la victoria cuando Israel estaba siendo atacado por una enorme coalición de ejércitos de tres naciones vecinas.

Lo primero que hizo Josafat fue proclamar ayuno—la oración es siempre parte del ayuno—. Luego, se paró frente a la gente que había venido de cada pueblo de Judá, los guió en una asombrosa oración, una oración que reconocía el poder de Dios y lo impotentes que ellos eran como seres humanos. Comenzaba con las palabras "¿No eres tú el Dios del cielo y el que gobierna a todas las naciones?" y terminaba diciendo "No sabemos qué hacer". Ese es siempre un buen principio y un buen final al enfrentar una crisis. Una oración humilde es nuestra arma más potente contra los ardides del enemigo.

Entonces Josafat "oye" una palabra del Señor, quien le habla a él y al pueblo por medio de un profeta: "Escuchen [...] no tengan miedo ni se acobarden cuando vean ese gran ejército, porque la batalla no es de ustedes, sino mía" (2 Crónicas 20:15). Josafat no tenía idea de cómo Dios iba a pelear, pero confiaba en que cumpliría lo prometido. Siempre se puede confiar en la palabra de Dios.

Sabemos que Josafat y el pueblo confiaban en Dios porque desde ese momento dejaron de clamar y comenzaron a alabar. "Se postraron rostro en tierra y adoraron al Señor (20:18). Si usted realmente cree en las promesas del Señor, la alabanza es la única reacción apropiada.

Josafat y su pueblo confiaban tan firmemente en Dios que hicieron lo que era militarmente impensable; pusieron un coro al frente del ejército. El coro dirigió al ejército en la alabanza a Dios, cantando: "Den gracias al Señor, su gran amor perdura para siempre" (20:21). Los que realmente confían en el Señor no siempre hacen las cosas de manera convencional.

Mientras marchaban alabando a Dios, aun antes de llegar a los frentes de batalla, el Señor, fiel a su promesa, confundió al enemigo, y terminaron destruyéndose ellos mismos. Dios, al actuar en respuesta a las oraciones de su pueblo, siempre cumple lo prometido. Esa es la clase de confianza que debemos tener cuando oramos.

Esta asombrosa experiencia de oración de Josafat y el pueblo de Israel, terminó donde había empezado, en el templo, con otro servicio de alabanza.

Hay una sola forma exitosa de enfrentar una crisis y de derrotar al enemigo que quiere vencernos, y es a través de la oración, pero no de cualquier oración. Este tipo de victoria exige una oración que comienza, continúa y termina con alabanza.

### Para reflexionar

◆ ¿Cuánto tiempo dedica usted a la alabanza? ¿Alguna vez ha comenzado, seguido y terminado una oración con alabanza, como lo hizo Josafat?

◆ ¿Alguna vez se ha sentido tan seguro de la intervención de Dios que ha dejado de pedir y, simplemente, ha empezado a alabar a Dios en medio de una crisis? La alabanza tiende a fijar nuestros ojos en Dios y a alentar la confianza.

### Orar

◆ *Alabe* a Dios por el poder y la fuerza que están en su mano, y porque nadie puede oponerse a él.

◆ *Agradezca* a Dios por su disposición de escuchar la oración y librar a los que confían en él.

◆ Si hay poca alabanza en sus oraciones, tal vez sea tiempo de *confesarle* a Dios que usted ha sido negligente en la alabanza, lo que es muy importante para él.

◆ *Pídale* a Dios un corazón listo para alabarlo.

◆ *Ore* para que la iglesia de Jesucristo, al enfrentar las fuerzas del maligno, pueda ser librada. *Ore* para que Dios confunda al enemigo y lo haga destruirse a sí mismo.

### Acción

Lea 2 Crónicas 20:1–30. Tome nota de que fue el conocimiento que tenía Josafat de Dios, y de sus victorias y de sus promesas cumplidas en el pasado, lo que motivó su osadía al orar. ¿Qué sabe usted acerca de la naturaleza, las actividades y las promesas de Dios que puede servirle para reforzar sus oraciones?

---

*Lea la historia completa de esta victoria a través de la oración en 2 Crónicas 20:1–30.

# Día 5

# David: Renovación mediante la confesión

*"Purifícame con hisopo, y quedaré limpio; lávame, y quedaré más blanco que la nieve. Anúnciame gozo y alegría; infunde gozo en estos huesos que has quebrantado. Aparta tu rostro de mis pecados y borra toda mi maldad. Crea en mí, oh Dios, un corazón limpio, y renueva la firmeza de mi espíritu".*—Salmo 51:7–10

Quizás usted se sorprenda al enterarse que Dios se complace si nos estamos sintiendo agobiados e infelices y estamos llenos de vergüenza y desesperación, *siempre que esa situación se deba a un pecado nuestro.* Él sabe que la culpa que un creyente siente lo impulsará a volver a Jesucristo y a su gracia.

David era un héroe de oración, y no porque hubiera pecado, sino porque, habiendo pecado, halló el camino de regreso a Dios.

Esta es la historia de David y Betsabé. El ejército de David sale a la batalla mientras él se queda atrás. Mientras mata el tiempo en la terraza de su palacio, ve a la hermosa Betsabé bañándose en una terraza vecina. Lleno de lujuria, la manda buscar, se acuesta con ella, y la embaraza. Meses después, para cubrir su adulterio, hace arreglos para que su esposo sea asesinado por el enemigo en una emboscada.

Viviendo una mentira, y habiendo cometido tanto adulterio como asesinato, David no siente ni remordimiento ni vergüenza. Aunque debía haberlo sentido. Así que Dios le manda un profeta, a Natán, quien atrapa a David en una simple historia de un hombre rico que roba y mata el cordero favorito de un hombre pobre para alimentar a sus invitados. Cuando David, indignado, declara que el hombre rico de la historia de Natán debe morir, el profeta se vuelve y le dice "Tú eres ese hombre" (2 Samuel 12:7).

Entonces David siente remordimiento. Remordimiento y vergüenza. Al ir perdiendo la fuerza y al caer sobre él la mano de Dios, exclama: "Mis huesos se fueron consumiendo por mi gemir de todo el día" (Salmo 32:3). Ese es el momento que Dios está esperando. David ha llegado al punto de necesitar la gracia. Entonces surge la gran oración de confesión que llena el Salmo 51.

La verdadera confesión lleva al perdón, a la liberación de la culpa y de la vergüenza, y a la restauración del gozo y de la alegría. Cuando exclamamos con sincero dolor: "He pecado", ese no es simplemente un reconocimiento de que no somos personas buenas. Es el tipo de confesión que está llena de esperanza y lleva a obtener un corazón limpio, a la eliminación de la culpa, y a la eliminación de la vergüenza.

Yo solía pensar que la confesión era el más penoso y desagradable de todos los elementos de la oración. Pero por medio del caso de David, quien halló perdón mediante la oración, he llegado a comprender que la confesión es la oración que más satisface, que más nos da esperanza, y que es la más liberadora.

Que no lo abrume el tener que confesar sus pecados. La verdad es que la verdadera confesión lo levantará, como ninguna otra cosa podría hacerlo.

### PARA REFLEXIONAR

◆ ¿Ha sentido o siente usted culpa o vergüenza debido al pecado? Si es así, como hizo David, vuelva a Dios y a la purificación que él provee.

◆ ¿Ha considerado que confesar es penoso o desagradable, o cree que puede ser liberador y esperanzador? ¿Qué le sugiere el Salmo 51?

### ORAR

◆ *Alabe* a Dios por su misericordia. La misericordia significa que Dios no nos trata como merecemos.

◆ *Agradezca* a Dios por el sentimiento de "culpa" que nos impulsa a volver a los brazos del amor perdonador de Dios.

◆ *Confiese* cualquier pecado del que esté consciente, y no haya confesado.

◆ *Pídale* a Dios un corazón limpio, una vida renovada y un espíritu recto.

◆ *Ore* para que Dios le dé a su iglesia sensibilidad ante el pecado y una disposición de confesar cuando sea necesario.

### ACCIÓN

Lea el Salmo 51 lentamente. Use y expanda las palabras de David, donde y cuando sean aplicables, como una base para su propia oración.

---

*Para el trasfondo de esta confesión, lea 2 Samuel 11–12 y el Salmo 51.

# LA ORACIÓN HACE LA DIFERENCIA

# Día 1

# La oración libera
# el poder de Dios

*"La oración del justo es poderosa y eficaz".*—SANTIAGO 5:16

"La oración, en sí misma, no posee ningún poder", escribió C. Samuel Storms. Me sorprendió esa declaración, y no la comprendí hasta que leí lo que él escribió a continuación: "La oración es poderosa porque Dios es poderoso, y la oración es el medio por el cual ese divino poder es liberado y canalizado hacia nuestras vidas". En otras palabras, todo el poder en la oración es activado cuando oramos.

Cuando usted ora por otra persona, no hay nada que fluya de usted a ella, ninguna vibración, ninguna fuerza o energía. Pero los poderes suyos van hacia el cielo, y el poder de Dios se mueve de él a la persona por la cual usted ora.

Cuando la Biblia dice que "la oración es poderosa y efectiva", quiere decir que Dios actúa poderosamente y con efectividad por medio de las oraciones de su pueblo. La oración es el instrumento por el cual Dios ha elegido dirigir su poder en el universo. Ole Hallesby nos da un cuadro mental de cómo sucede esto. "Este poder es tan rico y tan móvil que todo lo que tenemos que hacer cuando oramos es señalar a una persona o a las cosas a las que deseamos que se aplique el poder, y él, el Señor dueño de este poder, dirigirá el poder necesario hacia el lugar deseado". ¡Qué arreglo más maravilloso—Dios asociado con seres humanos para realizar sus propósitos!

R. A. Torrey, entusiasmado por la enormidad de este poder, declara: "La oración es la llave que abre todas las bodegas de la infinita gracia y poder de Dios. Todo lo que Dios es, y [...] tiene, está a disposición de la oración. La oración puede hacer cualquier cosa que Dios puede hacer, y como Dios puede hacer todo, la oración es omnipotente".

La oración puede lograr lo que la acción política no puede lograr, lo que no puede lograr la educación ni las fuerzas militares o los comités de planificación. En comparación, todo eso es impotente.

La oración puede mover montañas. Puede cambiar los corazones humanos, las familias, los vecindarios, las ciudades y las naciones. Es la única fuente de poder, porque es el poder del Dios Todopoderoso.

Este poder está a disposición del cristiano más humilde. Fue "un hombre como nosotros" el que oró para que no lloviera, y Dios detuvo la lluvia en Israel durante tres años y medio. ¿Dónde se sentirá hoy el poder de la oración de usted?

### Para reflexionar

- ¿A dónde le gustaría a Dios que se dirigiera hoy su poder de oración?
- ¿Qué cree usted que desearía Dios que usted hiciera en su vecindario o en su lugar de trabajo en respuesta a la oración?

### Orar

- *Alabe* a Dios por el gran poder con el que él se mueve en nuestro mundo y que rige los asuntos de los hombres.
- *Agradezca* a Dios por su disposición de escuchar nuestras oraciones y dirigir su poder a los lugares y a las personas, gracias a tales oraciones.
- *Confiese* si usted ha dejado de usar este gran privilegio para hacer avanzar la causa de Dios en el mundo por medio de la oración.
- *Pídale* a Dios que usted pueda ser poderoso y efectivo como orador en el futuro.
- *Interceda* por aquellos que viven o trabajan cerca de usted, para que el poder y la gracia de Dios llenen sus vidas.

### Acción

Al interceder hoy por otros, imagine un cuadro mental de sus oraciones subiendo al cielo al trono de Dios, y a Dios dirigiendo su gracia y su poder a la tierra hacia la persona por quien usted está orando.

# Día 2

# La clave de las grandes obras

*"Les aseguro que el que cree en mí las obras que yo hago también él las hará, y aun las hará mayores, porque yo vuelvo al Padre. Cualquier cosa que ustedes pidan en mi nombre, yo la haré; así será glorificado el Padre en el Hijo".*—JUAN 14:12, 13

Jesús pronunció estas palabras poco antes de ser arrestado y crucificado. Acababa de decirles a sus discípulos que iba a dejarlos. La noticia los dejó perplejos y confundidos—confundidos respecto al futuro de su obra por el Señor, y temerosos de no poder hacerlo.

Las palabras de Jesús tenían el objetivo de disminuir los temores de los discípulos. Les aseguró que ellos *iban a poder* hacer el trabajo. En realidad, iban a poder seguir haciendo lo que estaban haciendo—y podrían hacer cosas aun mayores.

A primera vista, eso parece algo raro. Después de todo, él había predicado grandes sermones, había atraído grandes multitudes, había hablado palabras de gran sabiduría, había caminado sobre el agua, había calmado una tempestad, había sanado a los enfermos y aun había resucitado muertos. ¿Cómo podrían los discípulos hacer estas cosas?

Jesús les explicó que eso sería posible porque él iba a volver al Padre, y ellos podrían pedir en su nombre cualquier cosa que necesitaran para hacer la obra de ensanchar el reino de Dios.

El hecho de que Jesús iba a volver al Padre significaba que tendría todo poder en el cielo y en la tierra. Con ese poder, él continuaría su misión en la tierra de una manera diferente—por medio de ellos.

El hecho de *pedir en su nombre* los ligaría con él. Por medio de la oración, su poder estaría a su disposición al cumplir ellos el ministerio "hasta los confines de la tierra" (Hechos 1:8). La oración sería la "parte hablada" de esta asociación en el ministerio, en la que él proveería el poder y ellos harían el trabajo.

Estas palabras de Jesús, aunque debían confortar y alentar a los primeros discípulos, también estaban dirigidas a nosotros. Jesús dirigió estas palabras a *"el que cree en mí"*. Eso nos incluye a usted—si usted es cristiano—, y a mí.

¡Qué combinación más poderosa: Cristo en el trono del universo, dándonos poder a nosotros, sus discípulos, aquí en la tierra para construir su reino. Nosotros pedimos, él actúa, y la obra se realiza: grandes victorias para la gloria de Dios el Padre.

¿Qué está haciendo Jesús hoy por medio de usted?

## Para reflexionar

* ¿Han sido la mayoría de sus oraciones peticiones por cosas que construyen el reino de Dios, o han sido peticiones más egoístas?
* ¿Qué cosas desearía el Cristo ascendido realizar por medio de usted?
* ¿Hay algún lugar en que usted ve grandes cosas que están sucediendo en el cuerpo de Cristo hoy?

## Orar

* *Alabe* a Dios por las grandes obras que él hizo mientras estuvo en la tierra, y por las grandes obras que él ha realizado por medio de sus discípulos desde entonces.
* *Confiese* si usted reconoce que sus oraciones han sido motivadas por el egoísmo, y no fueron orientadas hacia el ministerio.
* *Agradezca* a Dios porque está dispuesto a escuchar y contestar las oraciones que usted hace en el nombre de Jesús.
* *Interceda* por sus vecinos y colegas usando el modelo del Padrenuestro.

## Acción

Haga una breve lista de los ministerios que el Cristo ascendido podría desear que usted realizara para glorificar al Padre. Dígale al Señor que usted está dispuesto a hacer cualquier cosa que él le pida. Haga lo que él le pida, confiando en el poder de la oración.

# Día 3

# La fuerza para mantenerse en pie

*"Oren en el Espíritu en todo momento, con peticiones y ruegos.*
*Manténganse alerta y perseveren en oración por todos los santos".*—Efesios 6:18*

D ios nos ha dado la oración para que podamos ayudarnos unos a otros a mantenernos firmes. El diablo es un ser astuto que siempre busca cómo hacernos caer. Pero Dios provee maneras para ayudarnos a mantenernos victoriosos sobre los poderes del mal.

Pablo nos advierte en Efesios 6 contra las artimañas del diablo y "las potestades que dominan este mundo de tinieblas", que siempre nos enfrentan. Cuatro veces Pablo usa la palabra "pónganse" para alentarnos a resistir las "fuerzas espirituales del mal" (Efesios 6:11–14).

Para mantenernos firmes se requiere que primero nos pongamos la armadura de Dios. Somos protegidos contra el diablo al conocer la verdad, al ser justos, al conocer el evangelio de la paz, al confiar en Dios, al ser salvos, y al usar la Palabra de Dios como es debido. Pero el consejo de Pablo no termina al decir que debemos "ponernos toda la armadura de Dios", sino que sigue diciendo: "Oren en el Espíritu en todo momento, con peticiones y ruegos. Manténganse alerta y perseveren en oración por todos los santos". En otras palabras, el apoyo en oración que nos damos unos a otros es una parte importante de nuestra defensa contra el diablo.

El apoyo en oración abarca todo. Es "en todo momento", "siempre" y "para todos los santos". Si estamos en medio de una fraternidad de cristianos que oran unos por otros, la posibilidad de caer disminuye mucho.

Hace varios años, un grupo de cuatro amigos formamos un grupo de apoyo en oración, y nos reuníamos durante hora y media cada semana. Nos comprometimos a compartir nuestras vidas lo más fielmente posible, estudiábamos la Palabra de Dios, juntos tratábamos de alcanzar metas espirituales y apoyarnos unos a otros diariamente en oración. Lo que sucedió en los meses siguientes nos sorprendió a todos. La primera sorpresa fue que cada semana uno de nosotros necesitaba un apoyo en oración especial para enfrentar una situación difícil. En segundo lugar, todos crecimos espiritualmente, y, en tercer lugar, cada miembro del grupo comenzó a participar en una posición clave en el ministerio en una iglesia o denominación dentro de los dos años siguientes.

Al mantenernos unidos y al apoyarnos mutuamente con nuestras oraciones, Dios nos dio la fuerza para obtener grandes victorias.

La intención de Dios es que *todos* los creyentes sean fortalecidos, que *todos* asuman con responsabilidad su deber de apoyar *siempre* a otros en oración, en *todas* las ocasiones.

Es una orden difícil de cumplir. Va más allá de la oración personal casual que la mayoría de los cristianos está acostumbrado a hacer. Pero "los que oran en el Espíritu" lo pueden hacer.

### Para reflexionar

- ¿Siente usted que está recibiendo el apoyo en oración que necesita para mantenerse firme?
- ¿Está dándoles apoyo en oración a los que lo rodean?
- ¿Hay algo más que usted podría hacer para apoyar a los que lo rodean en oración?

### Orar

- *Agradezca* a Dios por su plan para proveer apoyo en oración para cada miembro de su cuerpo.
- *Agradézcale* por las personas que le han dado a usted apoyo en oración en el pasado: padres, abuelos, pastores, maestros, dirigentes de la iglesia, y muchos otros.
- Si usted está consciente de que no está apoyando a otros en oración, *confiéselo* a Dios.
- *Pídale* a Dios que ayude a la comunidad de creyentes a la que usted pertenece a poner en práctica el consejo de Efesios 6.
- *Comprométase* a apoyar en oración en forma seria a quienes le rodean.

### Acción

Haga una lista mental de los creyentes que usted sabe que necesitan apoyo en oración ahora mismo. Piense en pastores, maestros, evangelistas, misioneros, líderes religiosos, cristianos en otras posiciones de liderazgo, cristianos que trabajan en los medios, como también dentro de su propia iglesia. Proporcióneles el apoyo en oración que necesitan.

---

*Lea Efesios 6:10–20, para conocer el trasfondo.

# Día 4

# La oración derrota a Satanás

*"Simón, Simón, mira que Satanás ha pedido zarandearlos a ustedes como si fueran trigo. Pero yo he orado por ti, para que no falle tu fe. Y tú, cuando te hayas vuelto a mí, fortalece a tus hermanos".*—Lucas 22:31, 32

Hay dos fuerzas poderosas activas en el mundo: el poder de Dios y el poder de Satanás. El poder de Dios es infinitamente más grande, pero nosotros somos afectados por ambos.

Satanás, decidido a destruirnos, anda a nuestro alrededor "como león rugiente buscando a quien devorar" (1 Pedro 5:8). Dios, preocupado de nuestra salvación, provee "todas las cosas que necesitamos para vivir como Dios manda" (2 Pedro 1:3).

En vista de que el poder de Satanás es superior al nuestro, estamos constantemente en peligro. Pablo nos recuerda que luchamos "contra poderes, contra autoridades, contra potestades que dominan este mundo de tinieblas, contra fuerzas espirituales malignas" (Efesios 6:12). Pero ya que el poder de Dios es superior al de Satanás, estamos seguros en las manos de Dios. Él es nuestra constante fuente de protección.

La oración es el medio otorgado por Dios por el cual su poder actúa en defensa de nosotros, para que podamos resistir los embates del diablo. Cuando Pedro estaba siendo probado severamente por Satanás, Jesús vino en su defensa con la oración. Él dijo: "Yo he orado por ti, para que no falle tu fe".

Estamos inmersos en una batalla que debemos pelear sobre nuestras rodillas. La oración es el poder con el cual somos equipados para vencer al diablo. Enfrentarlo con nuestra propia fuerza es necedad, y un camino seguro a la derrota.

El diablo teme a nuestras oraciones más que a cualquier otra cosa. Un poderoso guerrero de oración dijo una vez: "¿Saben que nada hay que el diablo tema más que la oración? Su gran empeño es evitar que oremos. A él le encanta vernos metidos hasta las orejas en el trabajo, siempre que no oremos. A él no le preocupa si somos estudiosos de la Palabra, siempre que seamos débiles respecto a la oración. Alguien ha dicho: "Satanás se ríe de nuestros afanes, se burla de nuestra sabiduría, pero tiembla cuando oramos".

No es raro que Satanás tiemble. Por medio de la oración, el poder del Dios omnipotente se levanta contra él. Y él pierde toda posibilidad de ganar.

El reino de Dios se construye con oración, y con oración se destruye el reino del maligno. Cuando no hay oración, no hay grandes obras, y el reino no crece. Debemos orar tanto que Dios sea glorificado y su reino pueda venir en toda su plenitud.

## PARA REFLEXIONAR

◆ ¿Hasta qué punto está usted consciente de que sus oraciones pueden derrotar los empeños del maligno?

◆ ¿Hay alguien entre las personas que usted conoce que está siendo probado por Satanás y que necesita de sus oraciones?

## ORAR

◆ *Alabe* al Dios omnipotente, quien puede destruir las obras del diablo y proteger a sus hijos.

◆ *Pídale* a Cristo que le enseñe cómo usar la oración como un arma para derrotar a Satanás y para ayudar a extender el reino de Dios.

◆ *Comprométase* a apoyar en oración a las personas que le rodean, sobre todo, a los que usted supone que están bajo el ataque del maligno.

◆ *Ore* por aquellos que viven o trabajan cerca de usted, pidiéndole a Dios que los defienda de los poderes del maligno.

## ACCIÓN

Lea el periódico o escuche las noticias en la radio, y pregúntese: "¿Está el diablo metido en este problema?" Si la respuesta es afirmativa, entonces enfrente al diablo con oración.

# Día 5

# La oración le da forma a la historia

*"Se acercó otro ángel y se puso de pie frente al altar. Tenía un incensario de oro,*
*y se le entregó mucho incienso para ofrecerlo, junto con las oraciones de todo el pueblo de*
*Dios, sobre el altar de oro que está delante del trono. Y junto con esas oraciones, subió el*
*humo del incienso desde la mano del ángel hasta la presencia de Dios. Luego el ángel tomó*
*el incensario y lo llenó con brasas del altar, las cuales arrojó sobre la tierra; y se produjeron*
*truenos, estruendos, relámpagos y un terremoto".*—APOCALIPSIS 8:3–5

¿Puede ver el cuadro? Las oraciones de los santos, acumuladas a través de las edades en el altar de la oración, esperan el día cuando Dios actúe de acuerdo con ellas. Llegará finalmente el día cuando sean contestadas y, lanzadas sobre la tierra, provocarán cambios decisivos que marcarán el principio del fin de la historia.

¿Se ve usted en ese cuadro? Podrá incluirse si alguna vez ha orado por la venida de Cristo, o si alguna vez ha orado para que todo lo malo algún día sea corregido. Sus oraciones, junto con las de miles de millones de otros creyentes, un día serán contestadas, cuando Dios le ponga fin al mundo de pecado y establezca su glorioso reino.

La memoria de Dios es perfecta. Nunca olvida una oración. ¿Se ha dado cuenta de que Dios a veces responde una oración mucho tiempo después de que usted la hizo? Dios toma con mucha seriedad cada oración, formulada en nombre de su Hijo, aun aquellas que fueron hechas miles de años atrás.

Actualmente, de acuerdo con David Barret, experto en estadísticas, hay aproximadamente 170 millones de creyentes que están orando por un avivamiento de la iglesia y por la evangelización mundial. Hay diez millones de grupos pequeños orando por un despertar espiritual, y para que se consume la Gran Comisión. Dios ha oído cada una de esas oraciones y las responderá de acuerdo con su promesa y su propósito. ¡Ese va a ser un gran día!

Las oraciones de los santos le dan forma a la historia. La historia cambió de forma cuando Moisés, desde el monte, levantó sus manos intercediendo ante un campo de batalla (Éxodo 17: 8–13). La historia cambió cuando Elías oró "para que no lloviera" y no llovió durante tres años y medio en Israel (Santiago 5:16). La historia cambió cuando los primeros cristianos oraron sin cesar hasta el amanecer, y Pedro milagrosamente escapó de la prisión (Hechos 12:1–17).

En un sentido muy real, el futuro del mundo está en las manos de los cristianos que oran. También lo está el futuro de su vecindario y el de su iglesia, si usted es un cristiano que ora. Yo espero que sus oraciones contribuirán a un glorioso futuro para el reino de Dios en el lugar donde usted vive, y en un futuro aun más glorioso en los días por venir.

### Para reflexionar

- ¿Cree usted que las vidas de los seres queridos por los que usted ora son cambiadas gracias a sus oraciones?
- ¿Cree usted que está influyendo en la historia de su iglesia, de su vecindario o de su país? ¿Cuánto están contribuyendo sus oraciones a la obra de Dios en ellos?

### Orar

- *Alabe* a Dios por ser el Gobernante de las naciones, el que puede cambiar la historia.
- *Agradezca* a Dios por escuchar sus oraciones y responderlas en el tiempo oportuno.
- *Pida* el perdón de Dios si sus oraciones han sido tan débiles que en nada han contribuido al cambio de la historia.
- *Comprométase* a orar fiel y ferventemente.
- *Ore* para que, al llegar la historia a su fin, "el Señor omnipotente enjugará las lágrimas de todo rostro y quitará de toda la tierra el oprobio de su pueblo" (Isaías 25:8).

### Acción

En los días y las semanas venideras, coloque sobre el altar del cielo muchas oraciones por paz y justicia en el mundo, y por el pronto retorno de Cristo.

APÉNDICE A

# La oración de bendición

**CORPORAL O FÍSICO**: Orar por salud, protección, fortaleza y buen estado físico. *"Busquen primeramente el reino de Dios y su justicia, y todas estas cosas les serán añadidas"* (Mateo 6:33).

Señor, que _____ puedan buscar primero tu reino, y que descubran que también les has suplido el alimento, la ropa, la salud, y la protección.

**LABORAL:** Orar por un buen empleo, el ingreso y la seguridad financiera. *"Hagan lo que hagan, trabajen de buena gana, como para el Señor y no como para nadie en este mundo, conscientes de que el Señor los recompensará con la herencia. Ustedes sirven a Cristo el Señor"* (Colosenses 3:23, 24).

Señor, te ruego que bendigas a _____ para que sean diligentes en el trabajo, consciente que te están sirviendo a ti en todo lo que hacen, conscientes de que su herencia de una vida abundante para siempre, proviene de ti.

**EMOCIONAL** (vida interior): Orar por el gozo, la paz, la paciencia y el autodominio. *"Al de carácter firme lo guardarás en perfecta paz, porque en ti confía"* (Isaías 26:3).

Señor, dales a _____ la capacidad de concentrarse en ti, y de saber siempre que estás listo para suplir todas sus necesidades y para impartirles de tu paz.

**SOCIAL** (relaciones): Orar por los matrimonios, la familia, los amigos, por el perdón y el amor. *"Sean bondadosos y compasivos unos con otros, y perdónense mutuamente, así como Dios los perdonó a ustedes en Cristo"* (Efesios 4:32).

Señor, ayuda a a ser _____ bondadosos, compasivos, y que perdonen a los demás como tú lo haces con ellos. Dales una cadena de amistades que les apoyen y que puedan tener buenas relaciones con los demás.

**ESPIRITUAL:** Orar por salvación, crecimiento espiritual, gracia y esperanza. *"Prueben y vean que el Señor es bueno; dichosos los que en él se refugian"* (Salmo 34:8).

Señor, te ruego que _____ entiendan cuán bueno eres. Llámalos para que se refugien en ti. Que puedan crecer en la gracia y en el conocimiento del Señor Jesucristo.

**Nota:** Utilice este método para orar por miembros de la familia, amigos, vecinos y colegas.

# Orando "con todo tipo de oraciones"

**ALABANZA:** *"¡Qué profundas son las riquezas de la sabiduría y del conocimiento de Dios! ¡Qué indescifrables sus juicios e impenetrables sus caminos!"* (Romanos 11:33).

Señor, te alabo por las riquezas de tu sabiduría y conocimiento, y me regocijo en tus *indescifrables caminos*. Exalto tu nombre y...

**GRATITUD:** *"Así que mi Dios les proveerá de todo lo que necesiten, conforme a las gloriosas riquezas que tiene en Cristo Jesús"* (Filipenses 4:19).

*Gracias*, Señor, por suplir todas mis necesidades: temporales, corporales, emocionales, espirituales y eternas. Estoy agradecido especialmente por...

**CONFESIÓN:** *"No se preocupen por su vida, qué comerán o beberán; ni por su cuerpo, cómo se vestirán"* (Mateo 6:25).

*Perdóname*, Señor, por estar ansioso por aquellas cosas que me han estado sucediendo de las cuales tú tienes total control. Confieso que...

**PETICIÓN:** *"Permanezcan en mí, y yo permaneceré en ustedes. Así como ninguna rama puede dar fruto por sí misma, sino que tiene que permanecer en la vid, así tampoco ustedes pueden dar fruto si no permanecen en mí"* (Juan 15:4).

*Ayúdame*, Señor, a vivir unido a ti. Gracias por tu disposición de vivir en comunión conmigo, para que yo pueda dar mucho fruto siendo tu discípulo. Te pido que...

**INTERCESIÓN:** *"Por causa de mi nombre todo el mundo los odiará, pero el que se mantenga firme hasta el fin será salvo"* (Mateo 10:22).

Te ruego, Señor, por los cristianos que están siendo perseguidos en cualquier parte del mundo, para que puedan permanecer firmes. Además te ruego que...

**SUMISIÓN:** *"Ámense los unos a los otros con amor fraternal, respetándose y honrándose mutuamente [...] Vivan en armonía los unos con los otros. No sean arrogantes"* (Romanos 12:10, 16).

Señor, estoy decidido amar a mis hermanos en Cristo y a honrarlos más que a mí mismo. Estoy dispuesto a...

**Nota:** Medite en cada uno de los versículo anteriores, consciente de que Dios le está diciendo a usted lo que él *piensa*. Responda a Dios diciéndole lo que usted *piensa*. Esta es una de las formas de orar con las Escrituras. Trate de tomar la misma cantidad de tiempo para cada elemento.

APÉNDICE C

# Oraciones de alabanza

### Alabe a Dios porque él es…

**AMOROSO:** *"¡Fíjense qué gran amor nos ha dado el Padre, que se nos llame hijos de Dios! ¡Y lo somos!"* (1 Juan 3:1).

Padre, te alabo por tu abundante amor, y me regocijo de que me hayas hecho tu hijo. Cuando pienso en ese amor, yo…

**REY SOBERANO:** *"De ti proceden la riqueza y el honor; Tú lo gobiernas todo. En tus manos están la fuerza y el poder, y eres tú quien engrandece y fortalece a todos"* (1 Crónicas 29:12).

Te exalto, mi Dios y Rey. Con tu poder y fortaleza tocas mi vida y…

**PODEROSO:** *"Al que puede hacer muchísimo más que todo lo que podamos imaginarnos o pedir, por el poder que obra eficazmente en nosotros, ¡a él sea la gloria en la iglesia y en Cristo Jesús por todas las generaciones, por los siglos de los siglos! Amén"* (Efesios 3:20, 21).

Te glorifico, oh Dios, por tu gran poder. Usa tu poder en mí para…

**GENEROSO:** *"Dios puede hacer que toda gracia abunde para ustedes, de manera que siempre, en toda circunstancia, tengan todo lo necesario, y toda buena obra abunde en ustedes"* (2 Corintios 9:8).

Señor, te honro por tu maravillosa gracia que actúa en mi corazón y en mi vida. Por tu gracia yo sé que…

**BUENO:** *"Prueben y vean que el Señor es bueno; dichosos los que en él se refugian"* (Salmo 34:8).

Señor, te alabo por tus bondades, y deseo probarlas tanto como sea posible. Porque por tus bondades yo…

**SANTO:** *"[Los serafines se llamaban] y se decían el uno al otro: 'Santo, santo, santo es el Señor Todopoderoso; toda la tierra está llena de su gloria' "* (Isaías 6:3).

En armonía con los ángeles reunidos ante el trono, yo te alabo diciendo: "Santo, santo, santo es el Señor Todopoderoso". Veo tu santidad en…

**MISERICORDIOSO:** *"¿Qué Dios hay como tú, que perdone la maldad y pase por alto el delito del remanente de su pueblo? No siempre estarás airado, porque tu mayor placer es amar"* (Miqueas 7:18).

Yo te alabo, Señor, como un Dios misericordioso, lento para la ira y abundante en amor bondadoso. Estoy tan feliz de que…

106

APÉNDICE D

# Oraciones de gratitud

## Gracias a Dios por...

**LAS NECESIDADES SUPLIDAS:** *"Así que mi Dios les proveerá de todo lo que necesiten, conforme a las gloriosas riquezas que tiene en Cristo Jesús"* (Filipenses 4:19).

Gracias, Señor, por suplir mis necesidades físicas, emocionales y espirituales. Eres tan generoso con tus riquezas que yo...

**EL ESPÍRITU SANTO:** *"Pues si ustedes, aun siendo malos, saben dar cosas buenas a sus hijos, ¡cuánto más el Padre celestial dará el Espíritu Santo a quienes se lo pidan!"* (Lucas 11:13).

Padre, tener tu Espíritu es para mí tener toda bendición espiritual que tú das: vida, sabiduría, poder, conducción y el fruto del Espíritu. Muchas gracias por...

**LA FORTALEZA:** *"El Señor recorre con su mirada toda la tierra, y está listo para ayudar a quienes le son fieles"* (2 Crónicas 16:9).

Gracias, Dios, por la fortaleza que das para servirte. Tú siempre sabes cómo ayudar. Estoy tan agradecido de que...

**ESCUCHAR LAS ORACIONES:** *"Sepan que el Señor honra al que le es fiel; el Señor me escucha cuando lo llamo"* (Salmo 4:3).

Dios, estoy tan agradecido de que estés siempre dispuesto a escuchar cuando oro. No puedo creer que yo sea tan especial para ti que...

**LA PAZ:** *"La paz les dejo; mi paz les doy. Yo no se la doy a ustedes como la da el mundo. No se angustien ni se acobarden"* (Juan 14:27).

Gracias, Señor, por darme tu paz. Es lo que realmente necesito en medio de un mundo agitado, lleno de ansiedad y desconcierto. Con ella yo puedo...

**VIDA ETERNA:** *"Dios nos ha dado vida eterna, y esa vida está en su Hijo. El que tiene al Hijo, tiene la vida; el que no tiene al Hijo de Dios, no tiene la vida"* (1 Juan 5:11, 12).

Gracias, Padre, por darme el don de la vida eterna, la vida que está en tu Hijo, Jesucristo. Nunca he tenido un regalo mejor. Teniendo esto, yo...

**LAS ESCRITURAS:** *"Toda la Escritura es inspirada por Dios y útil para enseñar, para reprender, para corregir y para instruir en la justicia, a fin de que el siervo de Dios esté enteramente capacitado para toda buena obra"* (2 Timoteo 3:16, 17).

Gracias, Señor, por darme tu Palabra para que yo pueda conocer la verdad sobre ti y aprender a vivir realmente. Yo estaré...

APÉNDICE E

# Oraciones de confesión

**Confiéselo a Dios si...** *su respuesta a alguna de las siguientes preguntas es (sí).*

**PREOCUPACIÓN:** *"No se preocupen por su vida, qué comerán o beberán; ni por su cuerpo, cómo se vestirán. ¿No tiene la vida más valor que la comida, y el cuerpo más que la ropa?"* (Mateo 6:25).

¿Estoy preocupado por las cosas materiales? ¿Estoy excesivamente ansioso por el dinero? ¿Me preocupa exageradamente mi apariencia?

**AVARICIA:** *"No acumulen para sí tesoros en la tierra, donde la polilla y el óxido destruyen, y donde los ladrones se meten a robar. Más bien, acumulen para sí tesoros en el cielo [....] Porque donde esté tu tesoro, allí estará también tu corazón"* (Mateo 6:19–21).

¿Atesoro más las posesiones materiales que las riquezas espirituales? ¿Está mi corazón inclinado principalmente hacia las cosas? ¿Poseo muchas cosas innecesarias?

**LASCIVIA:** *"Pero yo les digo que cualquiera que mira a una mujer y la codicia ya ha cometido adulterio con ella en el corazón"* (Mateo 5:28).

¿He mirado de forma lasciva a alguna persona, revista, programa de televisión, o la pornografía de la Internet? ¿Tengo pensamientos lascivos y/o me involucro en actos lascivos?

**ARROGANCIA:** *"Nadie tenga un concepto de sí más alto que el que debe tener, sino más bien piense de sí mismo con moderación, según la medida de fe que Dios le haya dado"* (Romanos 12:3).

¿Me siento orgulloso de mis habilidades, mis logros, mi apariencia personal, o mi cuenta bancaria? ¿Veo a los demás, de varias maneras, como menos importantes que yo?

**RENCOR:** *"Que se toleren unos a otros y se perdonen si alguno tiene queja contra otro. Así como el Señor los perdonó, perdonen también ustedes"* (Colosenses 3:13).

¿Hay alguien a quien yo no he perdonado? ¿Hay alguien a quien estoy evitando deliberadamente? ¿Guardo rencor? ¿Estoy hablando con otros sobre las ofensas de los demás?

**DESHONESTIDAD:** *"Dejen de mentirse unos a otros, ahora que se han quitado el ropaje de la vieja naturaleza con sus vicios, y se han puesto el de la nueva naturaleza, que se va renovando en conocimiento a imagen de su Creador"* (Colosenses 3:9, 10).

¿Exagero, minimizo, cubro mis faltas con medias verdades, o engaño a los demás? ¿Digo "mentiras blancas" pensando que está bien?

**OBSCENIDAD:** *"Eviten toda conversación obscena. Por el contrario, que sus palabras contribuyan a la necesaria edificación y sean de bendición para quienes escuchan* (Efesios 4:29).

¿Uso un lenguaje indecoroso o digo chistes de doble sentido? ¿Rebajo a los demás con lo que les hablo o con lo que hablo a otros acerca de ellos?

APÉNDICE F

# Oraciones de petición

Usted puede **pedir a Dios…**

…cualesquiera de las siguientes bendiciones espirituales para usted, con la confianza de que le será concedido lo que pide, porque éstas están de acuerdo con la voluntad de Dios (1 Juan 5:14, 15). Se entiende que usted está pidiendo con fe y con un corazón puro.

A — *permaneciendo* en Cristo (Juan 15:4, 5)

B — *bendecido* con todo tipo de bendición espiritual en Cristo (Efesios 1:3)

C — *transformados* a la imagen de Cristo (Romanos 8:29)

D — *liberado* del maligno (Mateo 6:13)

E — *capacitados* para las obras de servicio (Efesios 4:11–13)

F — *perdonado* de mis pecados (Mateo 6:12)

G — *gracia sobre gracia* de su plenitud (Juan 1:16)

H — *santidad* en todo lo que hago (1 Pedro 1:16)

I — *integridad* y rectitud (Salmo 25:21)

J — *alegría en el Señor*, alegría completada en el Señor (Juan 15:11)

K — *conocimiento* y buen juicio (Filipenses 1:9)

L — *amor* a Dios y al prójimo (Mateo 22:37–39)

M — *meditar* en la Palabra de Dios (Salmo 1:2)

N — *mente renovada*, nueva criatura (Efesios 4:23, 24)

O — *obediencia* hacia todo lo que Cristo manda (Mateo 28:20)

P — *oración* en el Espíritu Santo (Efesios 6:18)

Q — *serenidad* y confianza son tu fortaleza (Isaías 30:15)

R — *justicia,* paz y alegría en el Espíritu (Romanos 14:17)

S — *fortaleza,* en el gran poder del Señor (Efesios 6:10)

T — *pensando* de tal forma que honre a Dios (Filipenses 4:8)

U — *útil* para el Señor (2 Timoteo 2:21; 1 Pedro 4:10)

V — *virtudes,* cubiertas con amor (Colosenses 3:14)

W — *adoración* en espíritu y en verdad (Juan 4:24)

X — *escudriñado por* el Espíritu (Salmo 139:23, 24)

Y — *anheloso* por Dios (Salmo 84:2; Isaías 26:9)

Z — *celo* en el servicio al Señor (Romanos 12:11)

## APÉNDICE G

# Oraciones de sumisión

**Sométase a Dios…**

Trate de decir un sincero "sí" a cada uno de estos mandamientos de Dios y a las preguntas críticas que siguen a cada versículo. Planee formas prácticas de vivir según esa respuesta afirmativa.

**AMOR:** *"El amor debe ser sincero. Aborrezcan el mal; aférrense al bien. Ámense los unos a los otros con amor fraternal, respetándose y honrándose mutuamente"* (Romanos 12:9, 10).

¿Odio en realidad la maldad? ¿Me dedico con amor a los demás? ¿Están las personas que me conocen impresionadas por la forma en que honro a los demás?

**ORACIÓN:** *"Oren en el Espíritu en todo momento, con peticiones y ruegos. Manténganse alerta y perseveren en oración por todos los santos"* (Efesios 6:18).

¿Oro en todo momento "con peticiones y ruegos"? ¿Estoy cubriendo fielmente con mis oraciones a todos los cristianos en mi derredor?

**DONES ESPIRITUALES:** *"Cada uno ponga al servicio de los demás el don que haya recibido […] Así Dios será en todo alabado por medio de Jesucristo"* (1 Pedro 4:10, 11).

¿Conozco mis dones espirituales? ¿Los estoy usando para servir a los demás?

**EL REINO DE DIOS:** *"Más bien, busquen primeramente el reino de Dios y su justicia, y todas estas cosas les serán añadidas"* (Mateo 6:33).

¿Estoy invirtiendo mi vida en actividades espirituales? ¿Reflejan mis decisiones los deseos de Dios en vez de los míos?

**CONTROL DEL PENSAMIENTO:** *"Hermanos, consideren bien todo lo verdadero, todo lo respetable, todo lo justo, todo lo puro, todo lo amable, todo lo digno de admiración, en fin, todo lo que sea excelente o merezca elogio. En esto pensad"* (Filipenses 4:8).

¿Pienso normalmente dentro de estos parámetros?

**MI CUERPO:** *"¿Acaso no saben que su cuerpo es templo del Espíritu Santo, quien está en ustedes? […] Por tanto, honren con su cuerpo a Dios."* (1 Corintios 6:19, 20).

¿Me cuido y evito prácticas que degeneren o pongan en peligro mi cuerpo?

**USO DEL TIEMPO:** *"Sean […] sabios, aprovechando al máximo cada momento oportuno, porque los días son malos"* (Efesios 5:15, 16).

¿Estoy usando mi tiempo de tal manera que cuente y glorifique al Señor?

# Intercediendo por los que no son salvos

**Interceda por las personas que no son salvas por…**

**SALVACIÓN**: *"El deseo de mi corazón, y mi oración a Dios por los israelitas, es que lleguen a ser salvos"* (Romanos 10:1).

Únase a Pablo en oración por la salvación de los judíos. Pregúntele a Dios si hay una nación en especial por la que usted debe orar.

**QUE DIOS LOS ATRAIGA:** *"Nadie puede venir a mí si no lo atrae el Padre que me envió"* (Juan 6:44).

Pídale a Dios que atraiga a las personas específicas que usted menciona. Ore para que ellas respondan al llamado de Dios.

**COMPRENSIÓN:** *"Cuando alguien oye la palabra acerca del reino y no la entiende, viene el maligno y arrebata lo que se sembró en su corazón"* (Mateo 13:19).

Ore para que los que oigan el evangelio lo entiendan.

**QUE LES ABRA LOS OJOS:** *"El dios de este mundo ha cegado la mente de estos incrédulos, para que no vean la luz del glorioso evangelio de Cristo"* (2 Corintios 4:4).

Ore para que los ojos de los no creyentes sean abiertos, para que puedan ver la luz de la verdad.

**ARREPENTIMIENTO:** *"El Señor [...] no quiere que nadie perezca sino que todos se arrepientan"* (2 Pedro 3:9).

Ore por los miembros de su familia, amigos, vecinos y compañeros de trabajo que no son salvos para que se arrepientan y no se pierdan.

**FE:** *"Porque tanto amó Dios al mundo, que dio a su Hijo unigénito, para que todo el que cree en él no se pierda, sino que tenga vida eterna"* (Juan 3:16).

Ore para que muchos crean y tengan vida eterna.

**NUEVOS CREYENTES:** *"No ruego sólo por éstos. Ruego también por los que han de creer en mí por el mensaje de ellos"* (Juan 17:20).

Únase a Jesús en oración por el vasto número de personas (se estima que son 160,000 por día) que están ingresando en el Reino de Dios. Ore por los que aún están por venir.